UNDERGROUND

AN ONI PRESS PUBLICATION

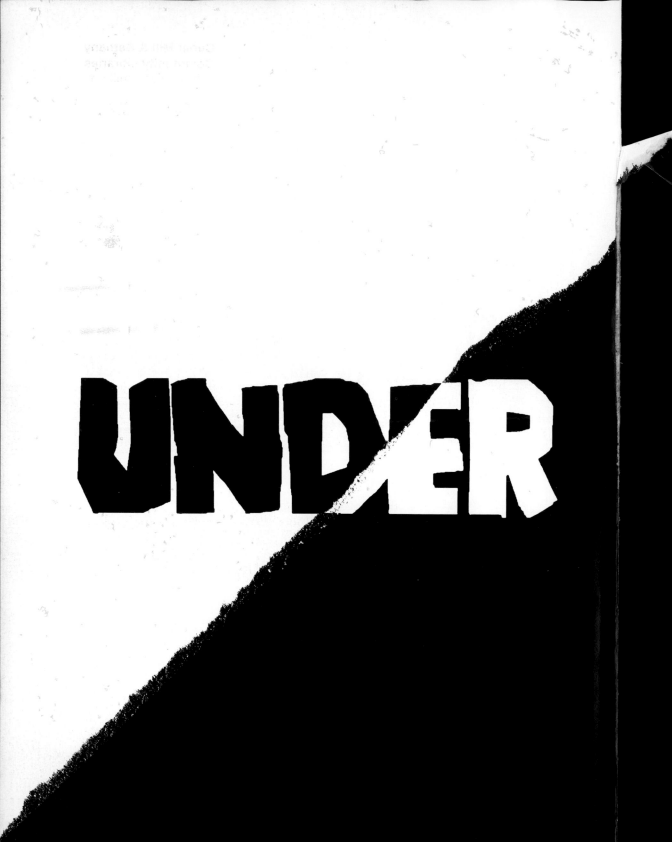

UNDER

GROUND

Created by
JEFF PARKER and **STEVE LIEBER**

Written by **JEFF PARKER**
Illustrated by **STEVE LIEBER**
Colored by **RON CHAN**
Lettered by **STEVE LIEBER**

Cover by **STEVE LIEBER**

Collection Edited by **JASMINE AMIRI**
Designed by **ANGIE KNOWLES**

PUBLISHED BY ONI-LION FORGE PUBLISHING GROUP, LLC

James Lucas Jones, president & publisher
Sarah Gaydos, editor in chief
Charlie Chu, e.v.p. of creative & business development
Brad Rooks, director of operations
Amber O'Neill, special projects manager
Margot Wood, director of marketing & sales
Katie Sainz, marketing manager
Tara Lehmann, publicist
Holly Aitchison, consumer marketing manager
Troy Look, director of design & production
Kate Z. Stone, senior graphic designer
Hilary Thompson, graphic designer
Sarah Rockwell, graphic designer
Angie Knowles, digital prepress lead
Vincent Kukua, digital prepress technician
Jasmine Amiri, senior editor
Shawna Gore, senior editor
Amanda Meadows, senior editor
Robert Meyers, senior editor, licensing
Desiree Rodriguez, editor
Grace Scheipeter, editor
Zack Soto, editor
Chris Cerasi, editorial coordinator
Steve Ellis, vice president of games
Ben Eisner, game developer
Michelle Nguyen, executive assistant
Jung Lee, logistics coordinator

Joe Nozemack, publisher emeritus

1319 SE MARTIN LUTHER KING, JR. BLVD.
SUITE 240
PORTLAND, OR 97214

ONIPRESS.COM 🅕 🅞 🅘 **LIONFORGE.COM**

First Edition: September 2021
ISBN 978-1-62010-987-8
eISBN 978-1-62010-845-1

Printed in Canada.

Library of Congress Control Number: 2021931944

CHAPTER ONE

...CORRESPONDENT NORA COCHRAN WENT TO MARION YESTERDAY TO HEAR MORE.

A QUIET TOWN HAS BECOME A FOCAL POINT FOR CONSERVATIONISTS AND BUSINESSMEN. MANY OF MARION'S POPULACE WANTS STILLWATER CAVE OPENED AS A SHOW CAVE FOR PUBLIC USE...

CURRENTLY THE CAVE IS UNDER STATE PARK'S JURISDICTION AND IS CLOSED EXCEPT TO CAVERS WITH SPECIAL PERMITS.

MUCH EXCAVATION IS NEEDED TO MAKE THE LARGEST ROOMS ACCESSIBLE TO AVERAGE TOURISTS...

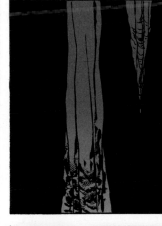

-AND THE TOWN'S BIGGEST ENTREPENEUR, WINSTON BAREFOOT, HAS OFFERED TO FOOT MOST OF THE BILL.

STILLWATER WILL BE THE JEWEL OF THE APPALACHIANS! DON'T WORRY ABOUT ME, HON, MY MOTELS AND OUTDOOR STORE WILL BENEFIT FROM ALL THE TOURISM. SO I'M HAPPY TO HELP.

CAVING ENTHUSIASTS AREN'T HAPPY HOWEVER, AND ONE OF THE MOST VOCAL IS ALSO A PARK RANGER, WESLEY FISCHER.

OPENING STILLWATER TO THE GENERAL PUBLIC WILL DESTROY FRAGILE FORMATIONS THAT TOOK THOUSANDS OF YEARS TO FORM. WE HAVE A LOT TO LEARN ABOUT THE AREA'S HISTORY FROM THIS CAVE.

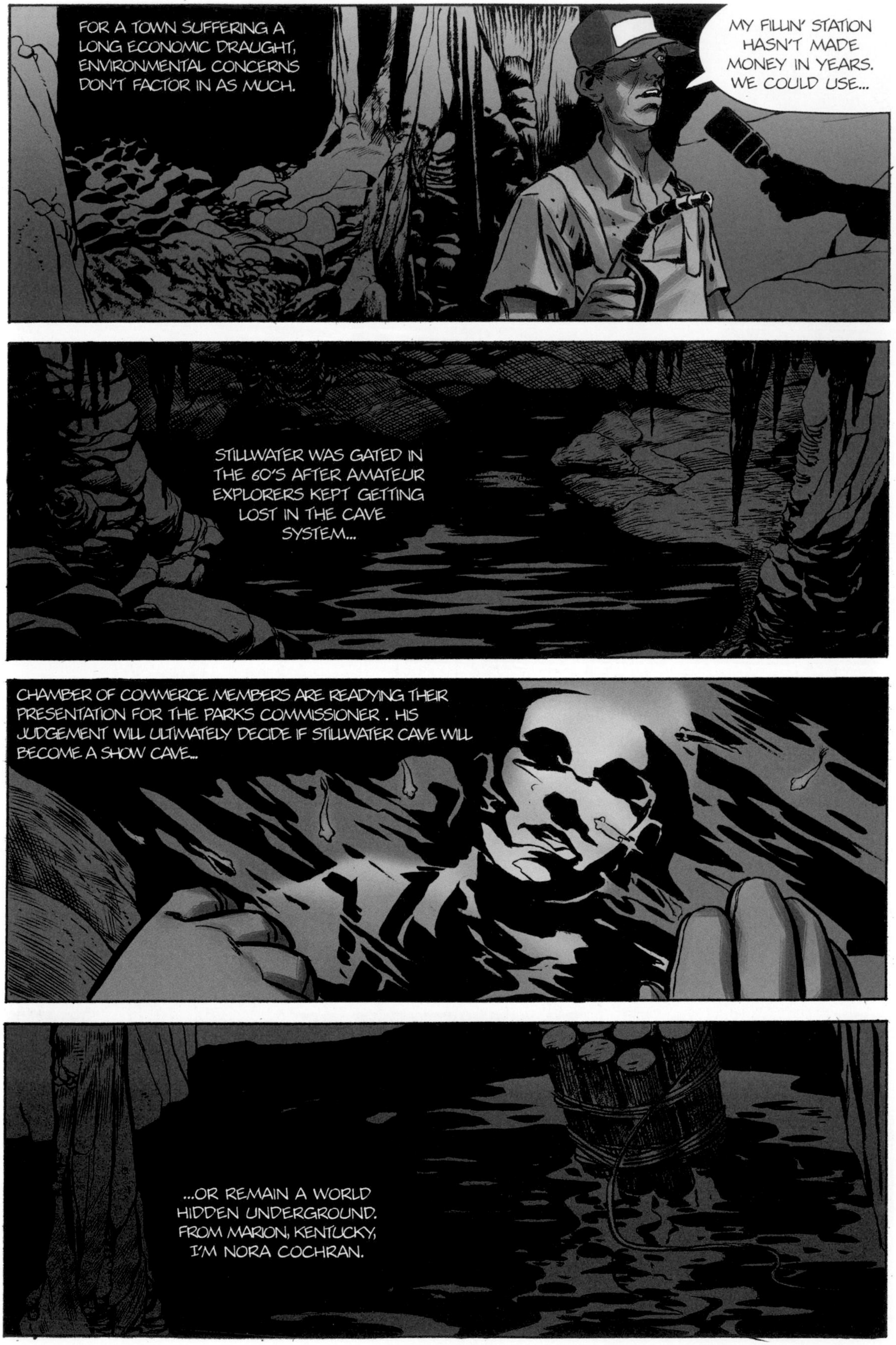
FOR A TOWN SUFFERING A LONG ECONOMIC DRAUGHT, ENVIRONMENTAL CONCERNS DON'T FACTOR IN AS MUCH.
MY FILLIN' STATION HASN'T MADE MONEY IN YEARS. WE COULD USE...
STILLWATER WAS GATED IN THE 60'S AFTER AMATEUR EXPLORERS KEPT GETTING LOST IN THE CAVE SYSTEM...
CHAMBER OF COMMERCE MEMBERS ARE READYING THEIR PRESENTATION FOR THE PARKS COMMISSIONER . HIS JUDGEMENT WILL ULTIMATELY DECIDE IF STILLWATER CAVE WILL BECOME A SHOW CAVE...
...OR REMAIN A WORLD HIDDEN UNDERGROUND. FROM MARION, KENTUCKY, I'M NORA COCHRAN.

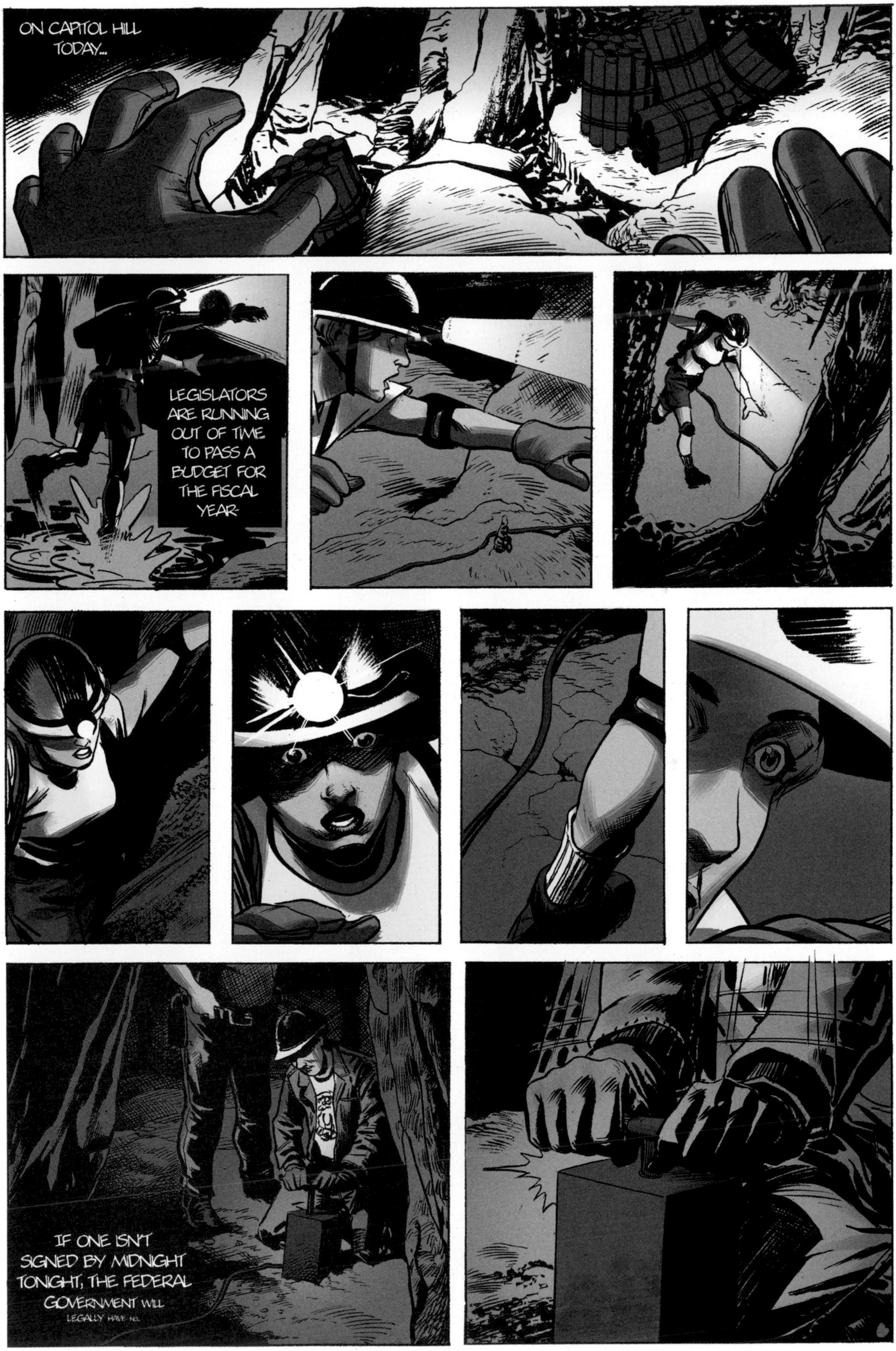
ON CAPITOL HILL TODAY...
LEGISLATORS ARE RUNNING OUT OF TIME TO PASS A BUDGET FOR THE FISCAL YEAR.
IF ONE ISN'T SIGNED BY MIDNIGHT TONIGHT, THE FEDERAL GOVERNMENT WILL
LEGALLY HAVE NO.

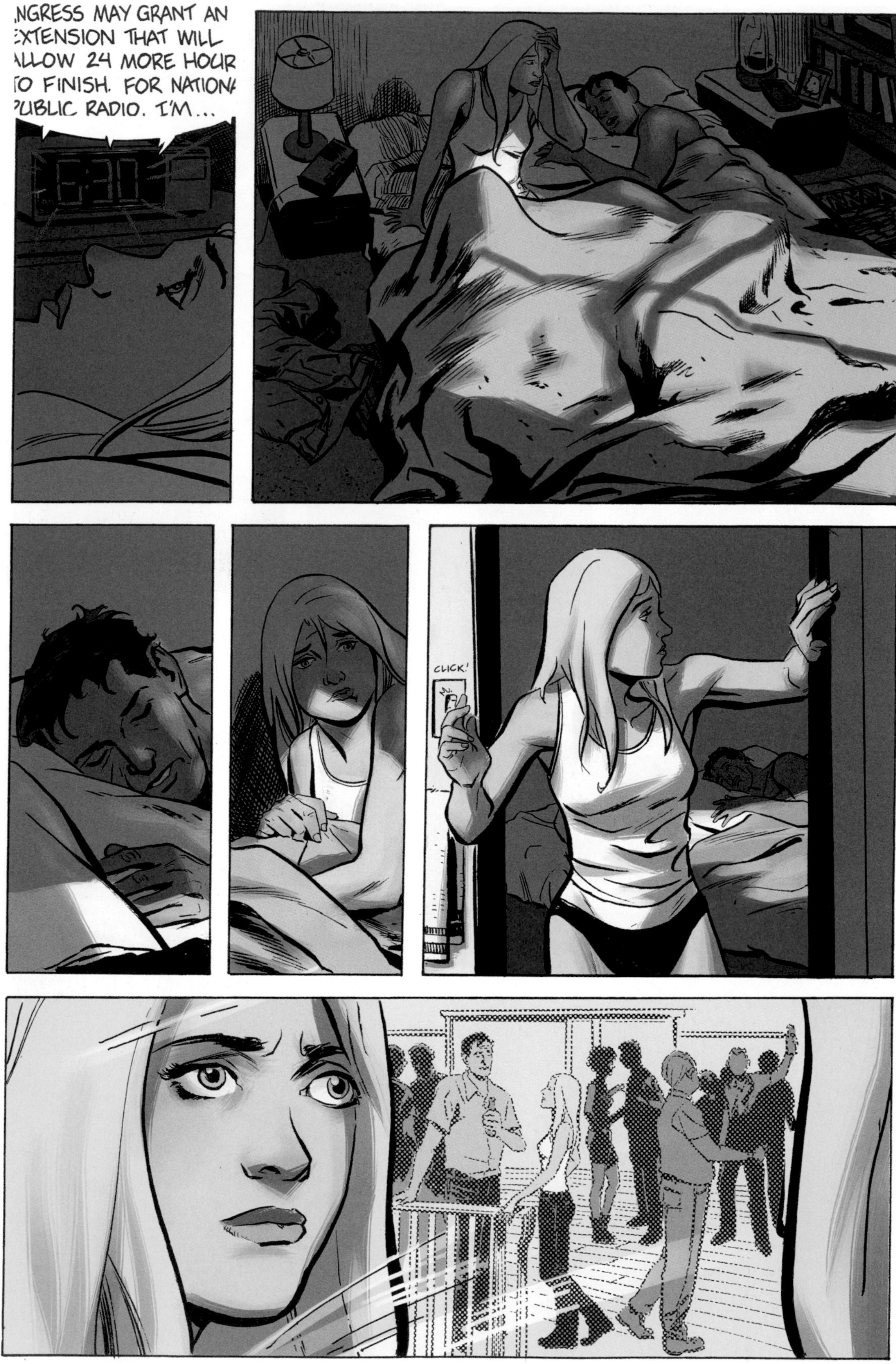

NGRESS MAY GRANT AN EXTENSION THAT WILL ALLOW 24 MORE HOUR TO FINISH. FOR NATIONA PUBLIC RADIO. I'M...
6:30
CLICK!

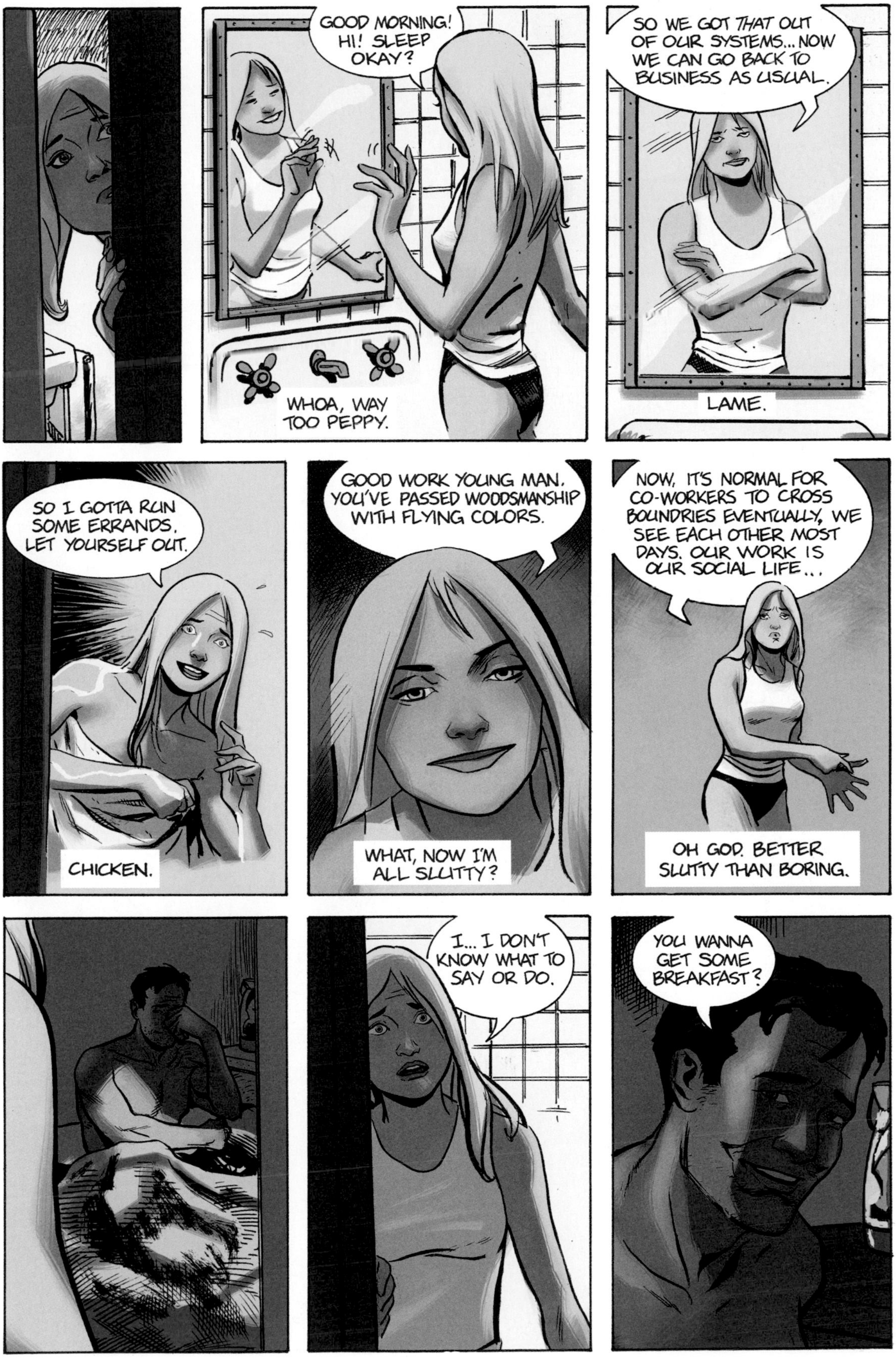
GOOD MORNING! HI! SLEEP OKAY?
WHOA, WAY TOO PEPPY.
SO WE GOT THAT OUT OF OUR SYSTEMS... NOW WE CAN GO BACK TO BUSINESS AS USUAL.
LAME.
SO I GOTTA RUN SOME ERRANDS. LET YOURSELF OUT.
CHICKEN.
GOOD WORK YOUNG MAN. YOU'VE PASSED WOODSMANSHIP WITH FLYING COLORS.
WHAT, NOW I'M ALL SLUTTY?
NOW, IT'S NORMAL FOR CO-WORKERS TO CROSS BOUNDRIES EVENTUALLY, WE SEE EACH OTHER MOST DAYS. OUR WORK IS OUR SOCIAL LIFE...
OH GOD. BETTER SLUTTY THAN BORING.
I... I DON'T KNOW WHAT TO SAY OR DO.
YOU WANNA GET SOME BREAKFAST?

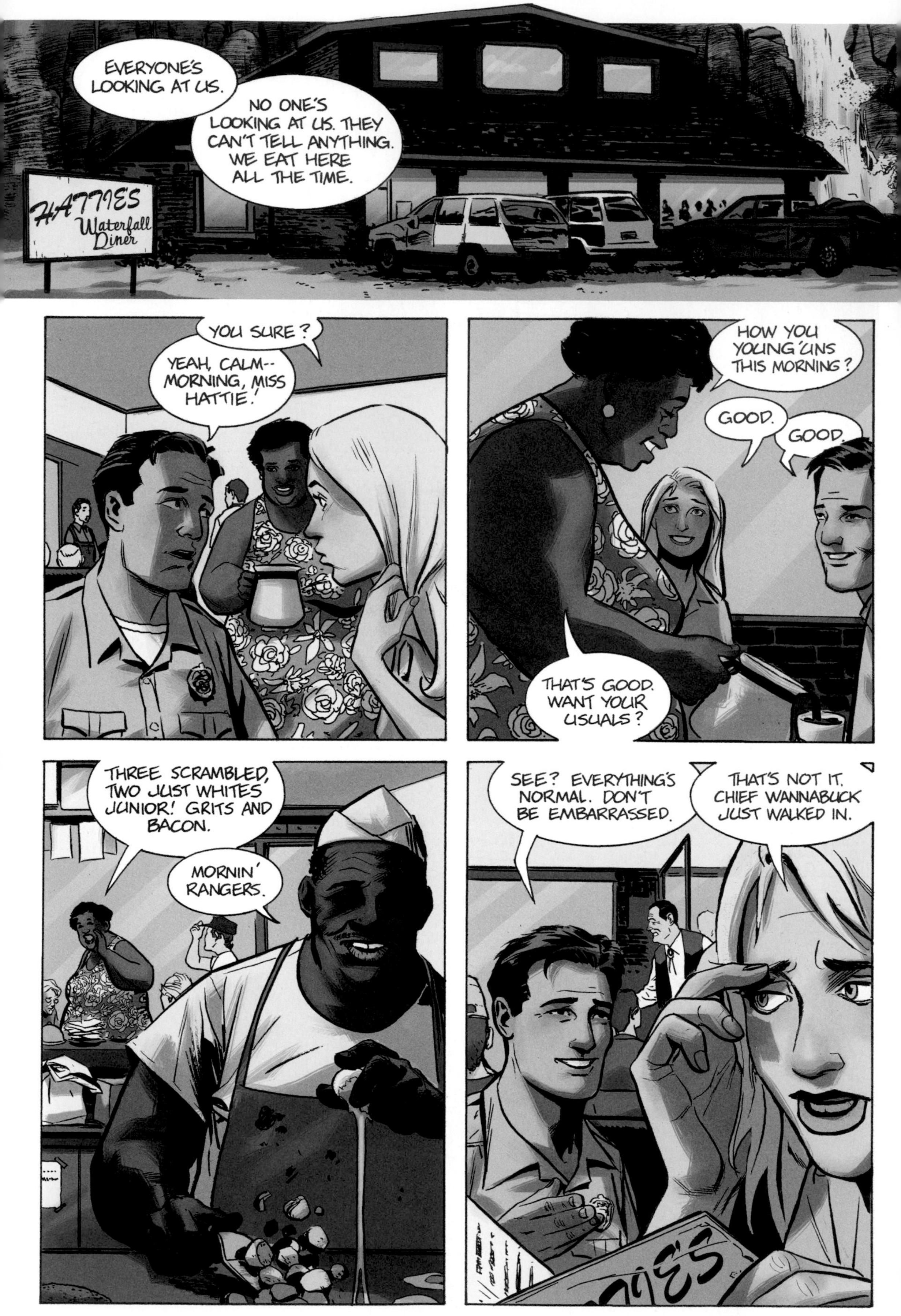
EVERYONE'S LOOKING AT US.
NO ONE'S LOOKING AT US. THEY CAN'T TELL ANYTHING. WE EAT HERE ALL THE TIME.
HATTIE'S Waterfall Diner
YOU SURE?
YEAH, CALM-- MORNING, MISS HATTIE!
HOW YOU YOUNG 'UNS THIS MORNING?
GOOD.
GOOD.
THAT'S GOOD. WANT YOUR USUALS?
THREE SCRAMBLED, TWO JUST WHITES' JUNIOR! GRITS AND BACON.
MORNIN' RANGERS.
SEE? EVERYTHING'S NORMAL. DON'T BE EMBARRASSED.
THAT'S NOT IT. CHIEF WANNABUCK JUST WALKED IN.

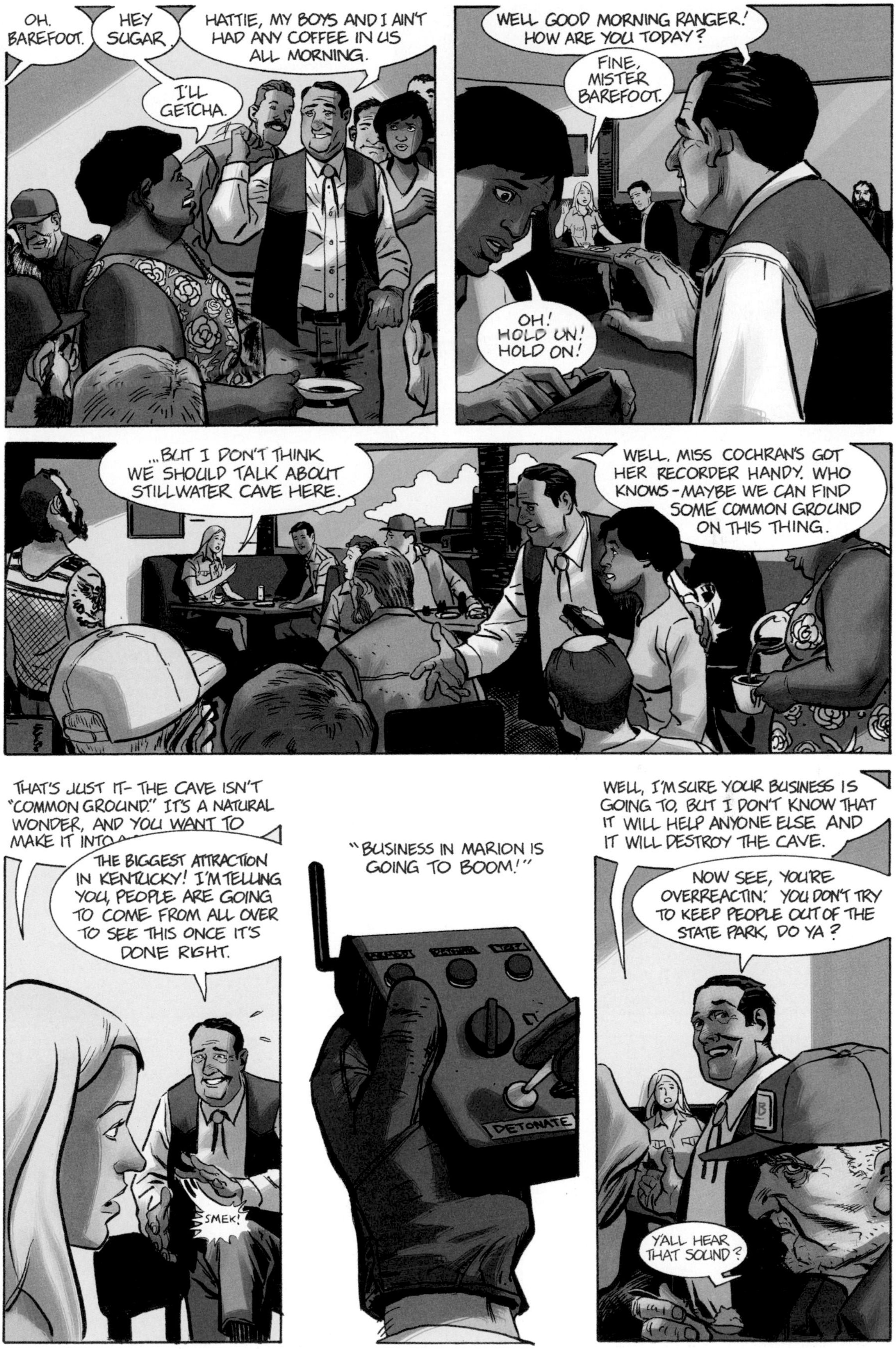
OH. BAREFOOT.
HEY SUGAR.
HATTIE, MY BOYS AND I AIN'T HAD ANY COFFEE IN US ALL MORNING.
I'LL GETCHA.
WELL GOOD MORNING RANGER! HOW ARE YOU TODAY?
FINE, MISTER BAREFOOT.
OH! HOLD ON! HOLD ON!
...BUT I DON'T THINK WE SHOULD TALK ABOUT STILLWATER CAVE HERE.
WELL, MISS COCHRAN'S GOT HER RECORDER HANDY. WHO KNOWS - MAYBE WE CAN FIND SOME COMMON GROUND ON THIS THING.
THAT'S JUST IT- THE CAVE ISN'T "COMMON GROUND." IT'S A NATURAL WONDER, AND YOU WANT TO MAKE IT INTO
THE BIGGEST ATTRACTION IN KENTUCKY! I'M TELLING YOU, PEOPLE ARE GOING TO COME FROM ALL OVER TO SEE THIS ONCE IT'S DONE RIGHT.
SMEK!
"BUSINESS IN MARION IS GOING TO BOOM!"
DETONATE
WELL, I'M SURE YOUR BUSINESS IS GOING TO, BUT I DON'T KNOW THAT IT WILL HELP ANYONE ELSE. AND IT WILL DESTROY THE CAVE.
NOW SEE, YOU'RE OVERREACTIN'. YOU DON'T TRY TO KEEP PEOPLE OUT OF THE STATE PARK, DO YA?
Y'ALL HEAR THAT SOUND?

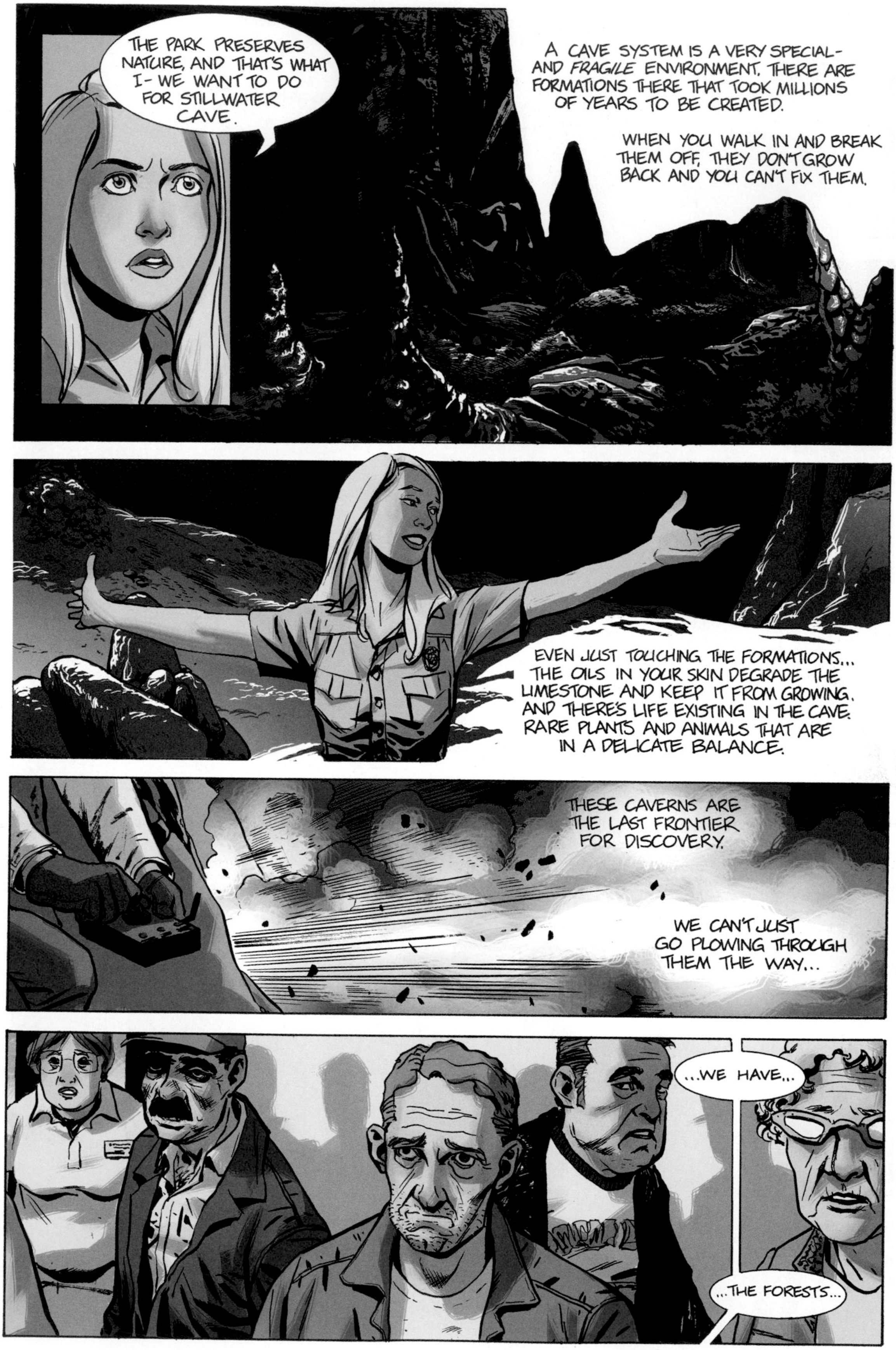
THE PARK PRESERVES NATURE, AND THAT'S WHAT I- WE WANT TO DO FOR STILLWATER CAVE.
A CAVE SYSTEM IS A VERY SPECIAL- AND *FRAGILE* ENVIRONMENT. THERE ARE FORMATIONS THERE THAT TOOK MILLIONS OF YEARS TO BE CREATED.
WHEN YOU WALK IN AND BREAK THEM OFF, THEY DON'T GROW BACK AND YOU CAN'T FIX THEM.
EVEN JUST TOUCHING THE FORMATIONS... THE OILS IN YOUR SKIN DEGRADE THE LIMESTONE AND KEEP IT FROM GROWING. AND THERE'S LIFE EXISTING IN THE CAVE. RARE PLANTS AND ANIMALS THAT ARE IN A DELICATE BALANCE.
THESE CAVERNS ARE THE LAST FRONTIER FOR DISCOVERY.
WE CAN'T JUST GO PLOWING THROUGH THEM THE WAY...
...WE HAVE...
...THE FORESTS...

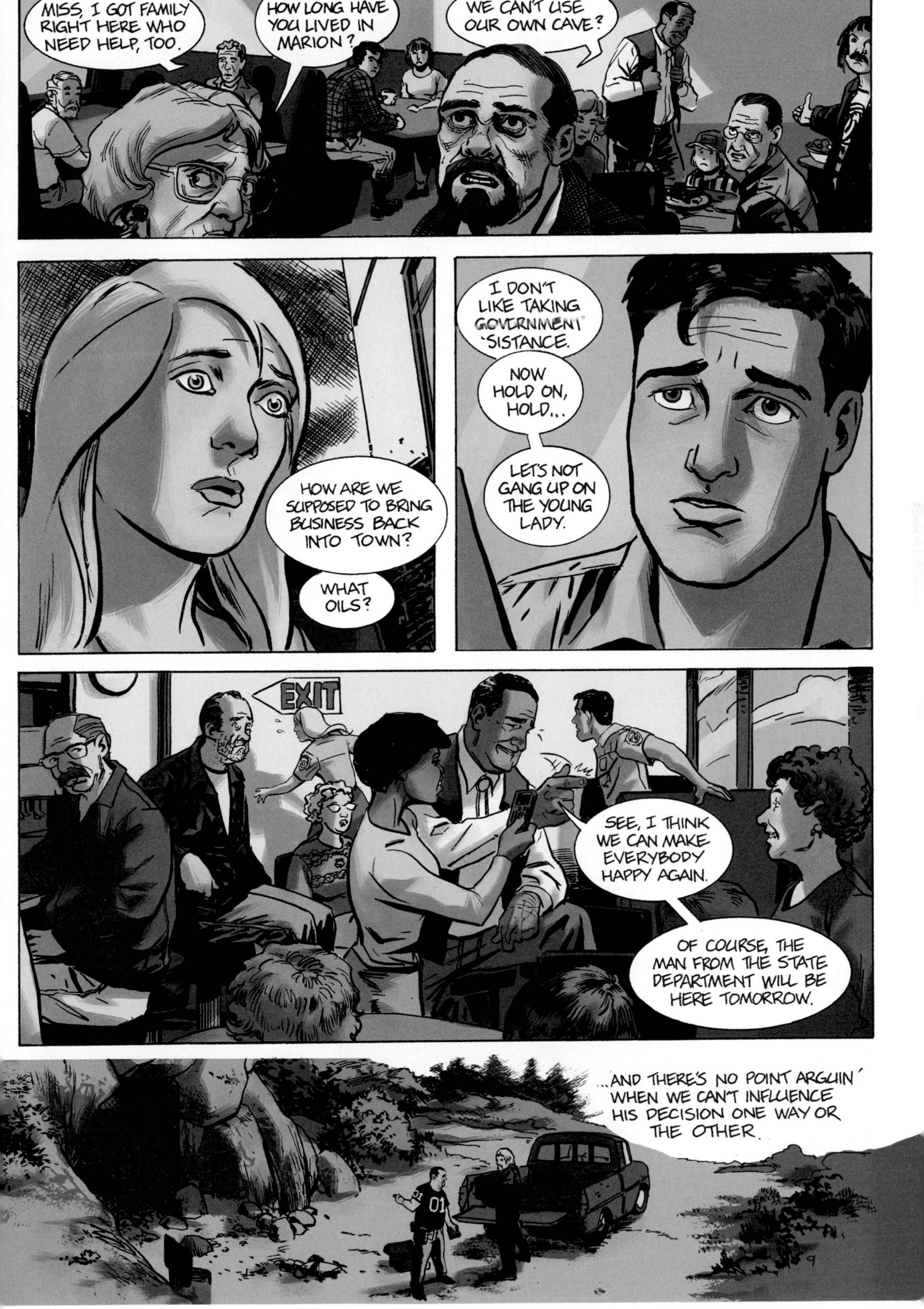
MISS, I GOT FAMILY RIGHT HERE WHO NEED HELP, TOO.
HOW LONG HAVE YOU LIVED IN MARION?
WE CAN'T USE OUR OWN CAVE?
I DON'T LIKE TAKING GOVERNMENT 'SISTANCE.
NOW HOLD ON, HOLD...
LET'S NOT GANG UP ON THE YOUNG LADY.
HOW ARE WE SUPPOSED TO BRING BUSINESS BACK INTO TOWN?
WHAT OILS?
EXIT
SEE, I THINK WE CAN MAKE EVERYBODY HAPPY AGAIN.
OF COURSE, THE MAN FROM THE STATE DEPARTMENT WILL BE HERE TOMORROW.
...AND THERE'S NO POINT ARGUIN' WHEN WE CAN'T INFLUENCE HIS DECISION ONE WAY OR THE OTHER.

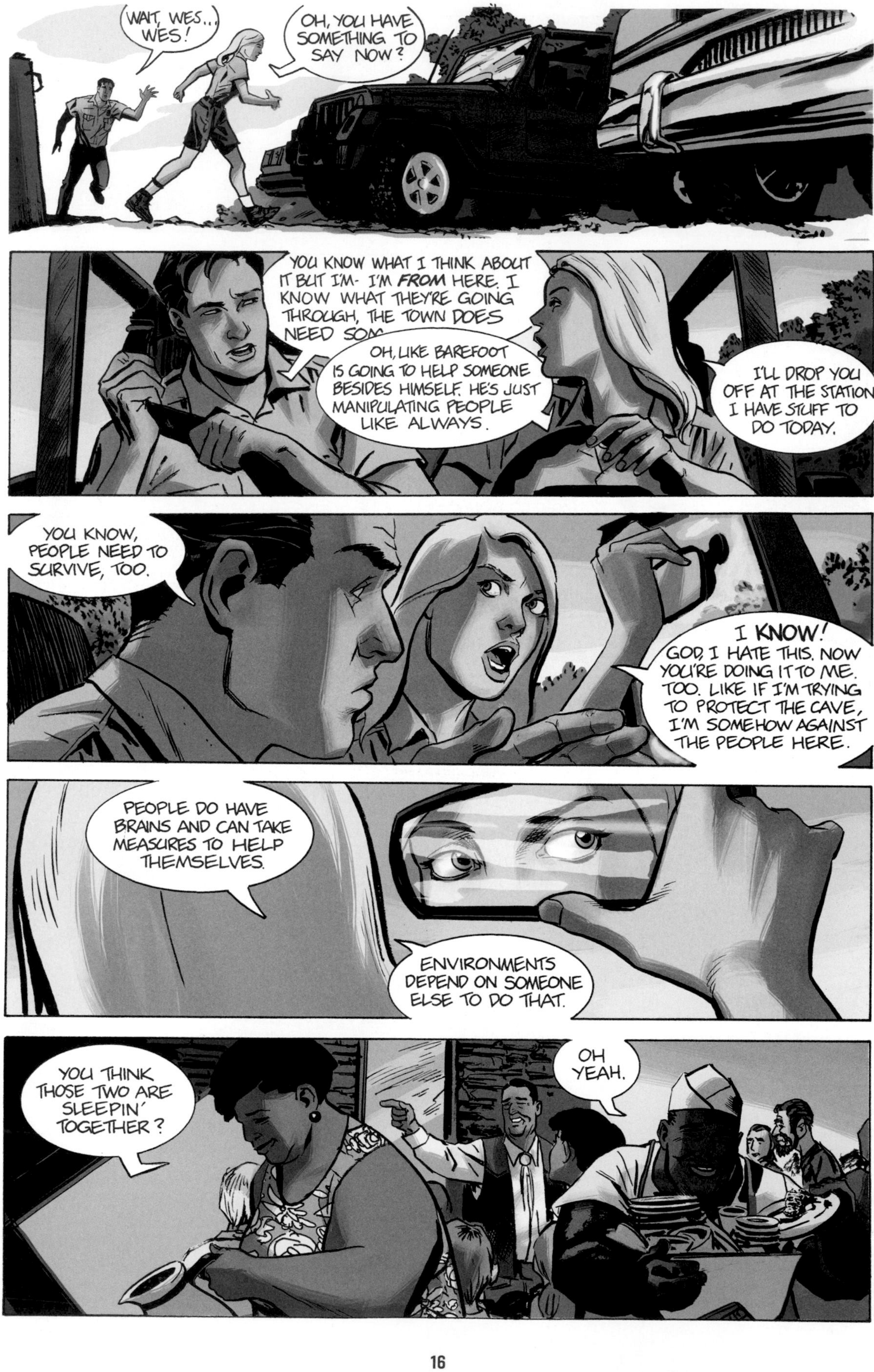
WAIT, WES...
WES!
OH, YOU HAVE SOMETHING TO SAY NOW?
YOU KNOW WHAT I THINK ABOUT IT BUT I'M- I'M FROM HERE. I KNOW WHAT THEY'RE GOING THROUGH, THE TOWN DOES NEED SOM
OH, LIKE BAREFOOT IS GOING TO HELP SOMEONE BESIDES HIMSELF. HE'S JUST MANIPULATING PEOPLE LIKE ALWAYS.
I'LL DROP YOU OFF AT THE STATION I HAVE STUFF TO DO TODAY.
YOU KNOW, PEOPLE NEED TO SURVIVE, TOO.
I KNOW! GOD, I HATE THIS. NOW YOU'RE DOING IT TO ME. TOO. LIKE IF I'M TRYING TO PROTECT THE CAVE, I'M SOMEHOW AGAINST THE PEOPLE HERE.
PEOPLE DO HAVE BRAINS AND CAN TAKE MEASURES TO HELP THEMSELVES.
ENVIRONMENTS DEPEND ON SOMEONE ELSE TO DO THAT.
YOU THINK THOSE TWO ARE SLEEPIN' TOGETHER?
OH YEAH.

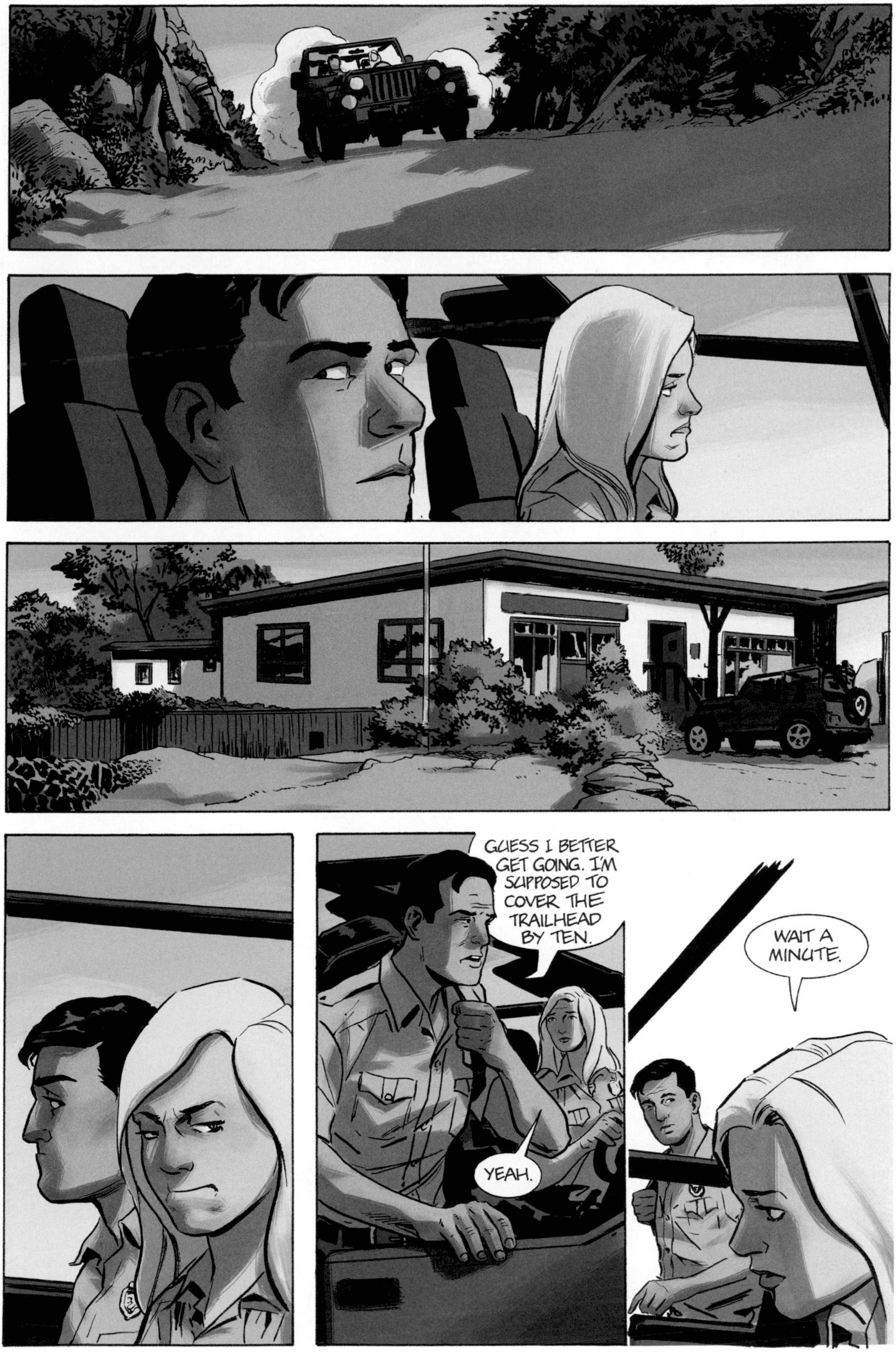
GUESS I BETTER GET GOING. I'M SUPPOSED TO COVER THE TRAILHEAD BY TEN.
YEAH.
WAIT A MINUTE.

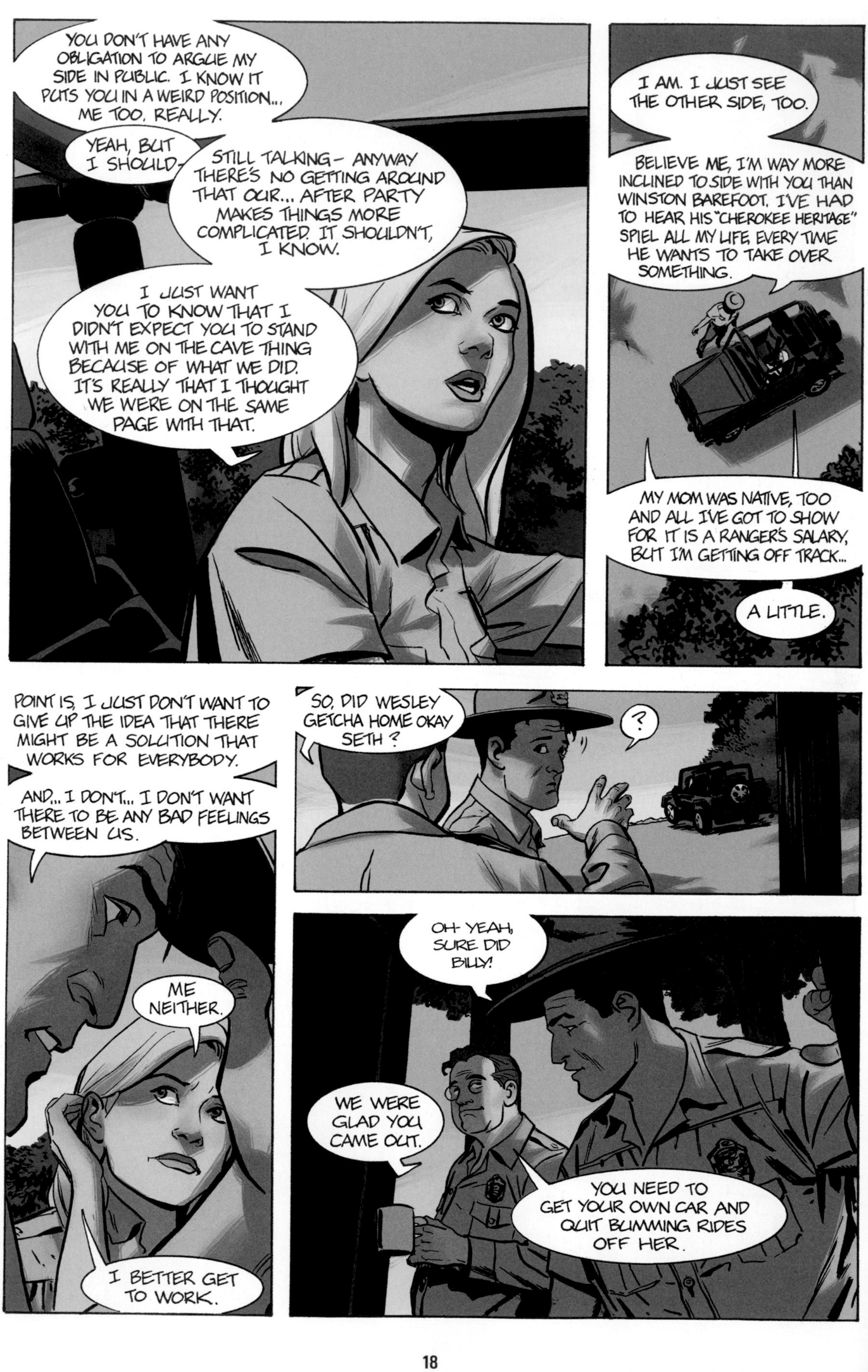
YOU DON'T HAVE ANY OBLIGATION TO ARGUE MY SIDE IN PUBLIC. I KNOW IT PUTS YOU IN A WEIRD POSITION... ME TOO, REALLY.
YEAH, BUT I SHOULD-
STILL TALKING- ANYWAY THERE'S NO GETTING AROUND THAT OUR... AFTER PARTY MAKES THINGS MORE COMPLICATED. IT SHOULDN'T, I KNOW.
I JUST WANT YOU TO KNOW THAT I DIDN'T EXPECT YOU TO STAND WITH ME ON THE CAVE THING BECAUSE OF WHAT WE DID. IT'S REALLY THAT I THOUGHT WE WERE ON THE SAME PAGE WITH THAT.
I AM. I JUST SEE THE OTHER SIDE, TOO.
BELIEVE ME, I'M WAY MORE INCLINED TO SIDE WITH YOU THAN WINSTON BAREFOOT. I'VE HAD TO HEAR HIS "CHEROKEE HERITAGE" SPIEL ALL MY LIFE, EVERY TIME HE WANTS TO TAKE OVER SOMETHING.
MY MOM WAS NATIVE, TOO AND ALL I'VE GOT TO SHOW FOR IT IS A RANGER'S SALARY, BUT I'M GETTING OFF TRACK...
A LITTLE.
POINT IS, I JUST DON'T WANT TO GIVE UP THE IDEA THAT THERE MIGHT BE A SOLUTION THAT WORKS FOR EVERYBODY.
AND... I DON'T... I DON'T WANT THERE TO BE ANY BAD FEELINGS BETWEEN US.
ME NEITHER.
I BETTER GET TO WORK.
SO, DID WESLEY GETCHA HOME OKAY SETH ?
?
OH- YEAH, SURE DID BILLY!
WE WERE GLAD YOU CAME OUT.
YOU NEED TO GET YOUR OWN CAR AND QUIT BUMMING RIDES OFF HER.

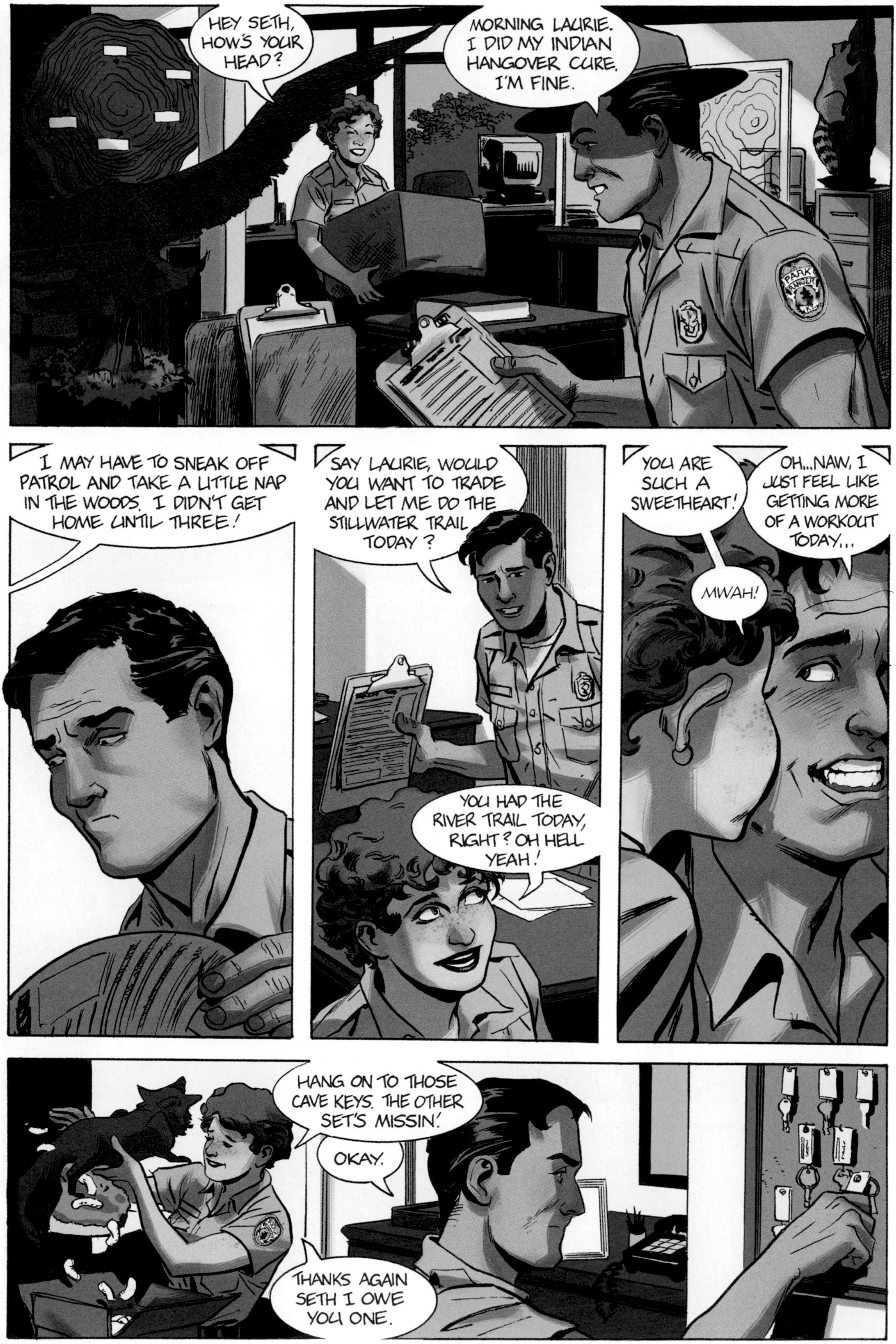
HEY SETH, HOW'S YOUR HEAD?
MORNING LAURIE. I DID MY INDIAN HANGOVER CURE. I'M FINE.
I MAY HAVE TO SNEAK OFF PATROL AND TAKE A LITTLE NAP IN THE WOODS. I DIDN'T GET HOME UNTIL THREE!
SAY LAURIE, WOULD YOU WANT TO TRADE AND LET ME DO THE STILLWATER TRAIL TODAY?
YOU HAD THE RIVER TRAIL TODAY, RIGHT? OH HELL YEAH!
YOU ARE SUCH A SWEETHEART!
MWAH!
OH...NAW, I JUST FEEL LIKE GETTING MORE OF A WORKOUT TODAY...
HANG ON TO THOSE CAVE KEYS. THE OTHER SET'S MISSIN'.
OKAY.
THANKS AGAIN SETH I OWE YOU ONE.

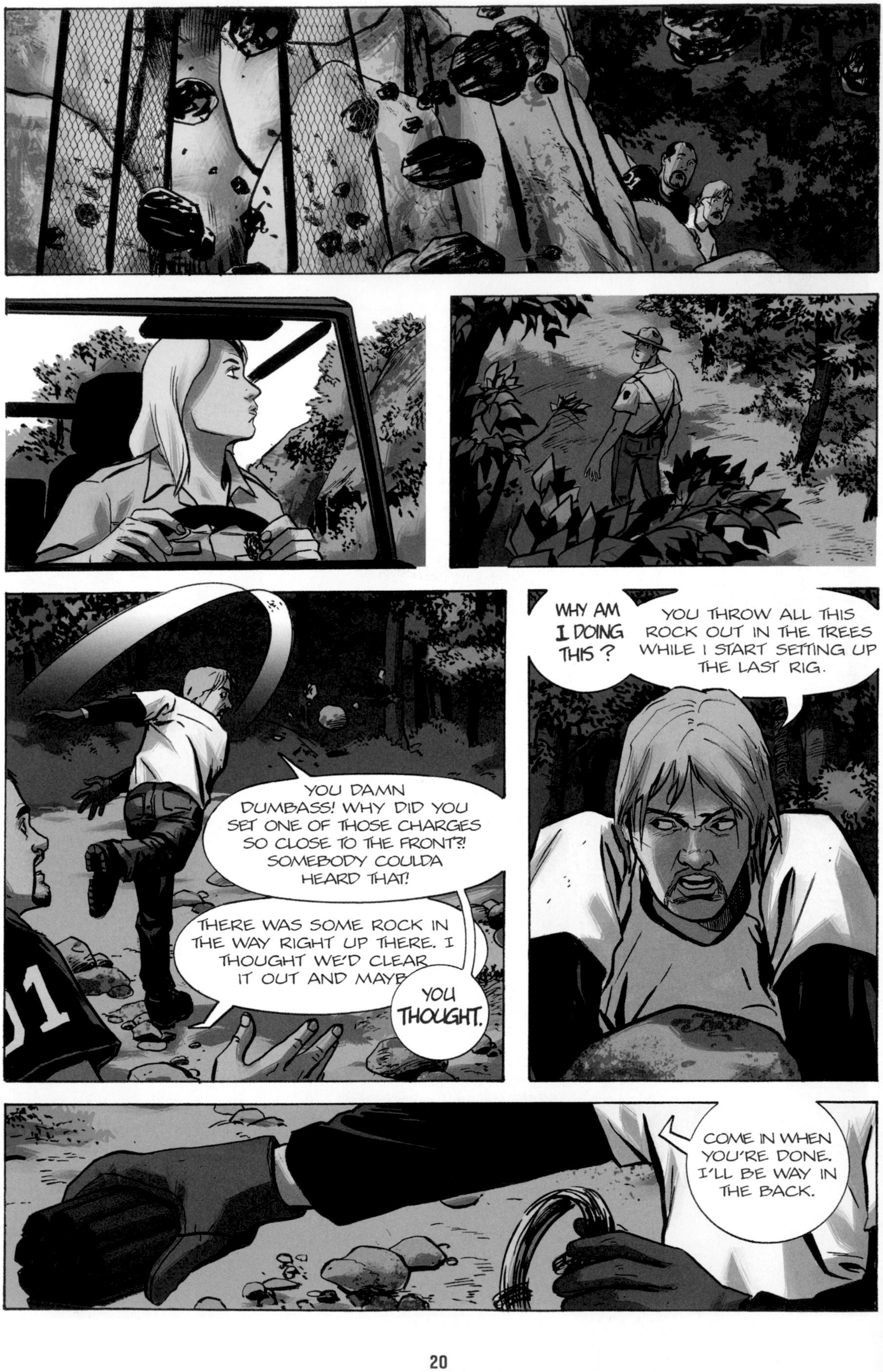
YOU DAMN DUMBASS! WHY DID YOU SET ONE OF THOSE CHARGES SO CLOSE TO THE FRONT?! SOMEBODY COULDA HEARD THAT!
THERE WAS SOME ROCK IN THE WAY RIGHT UP THERE. I THOUGHT WE'D CLEAR IT OUT AND MAYB
YOU THOUGHT.
WHY AM I DOING THIS?
YOU THROW ALL THIS ROCK OUT IN THE TREES WHILE I START SETTING UP THE LAST RIG.
COME IN WHEN YOU'RE DONE. I'LL BE WAY IN THE BACK.

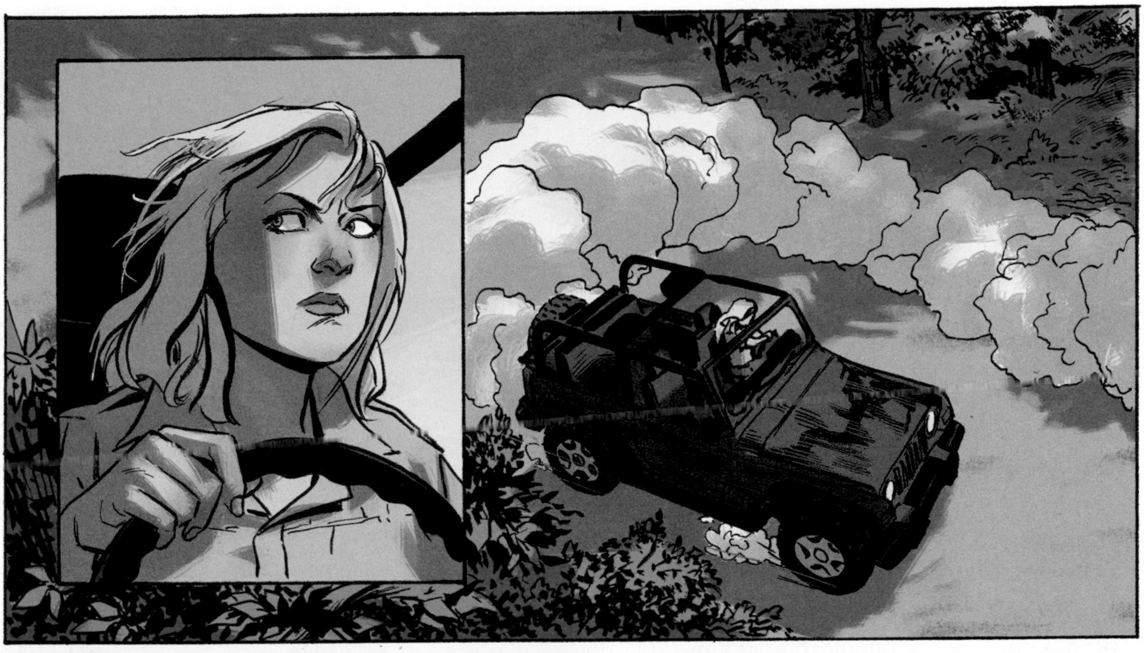

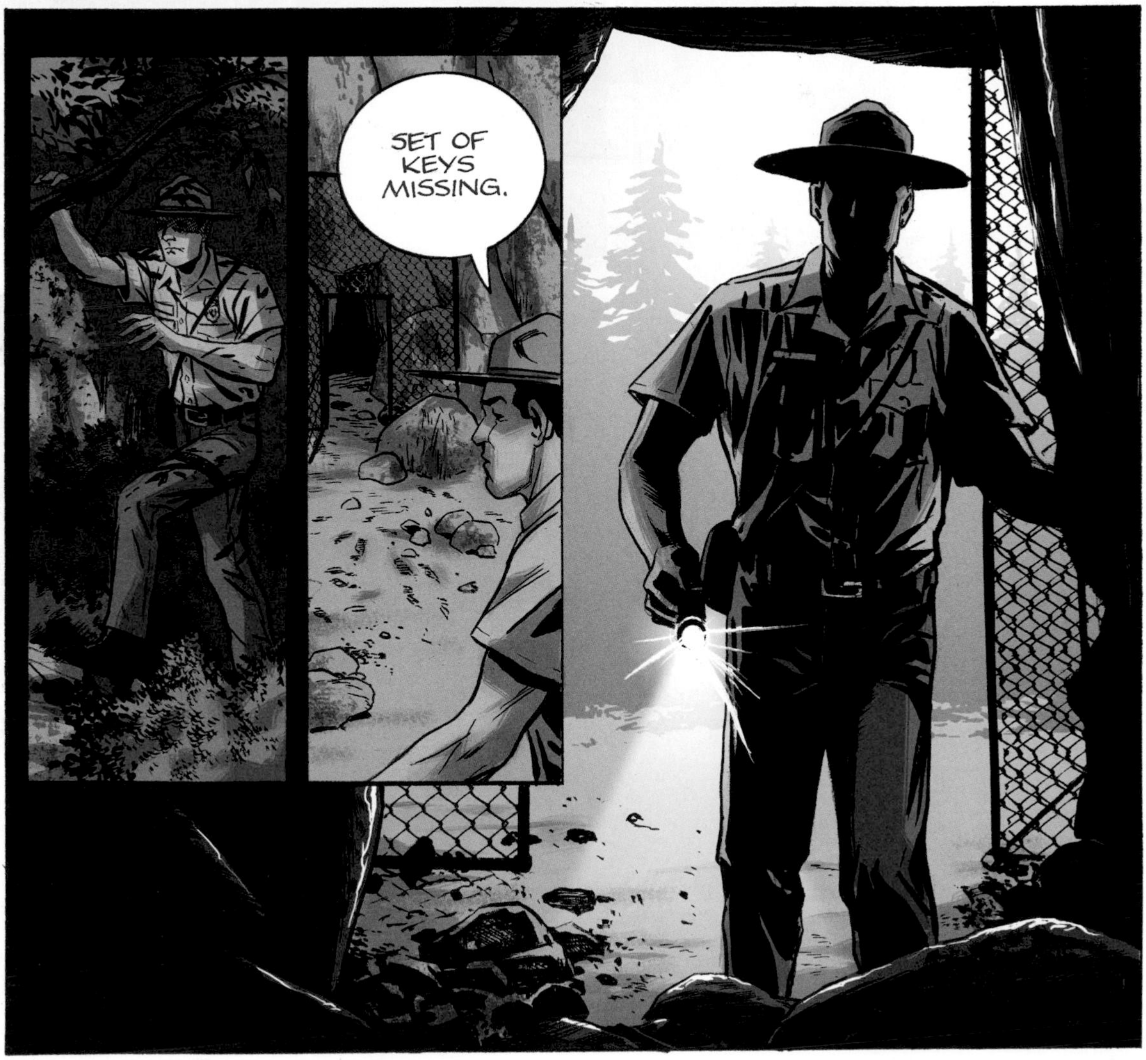
SET OF KEYS MISSING.

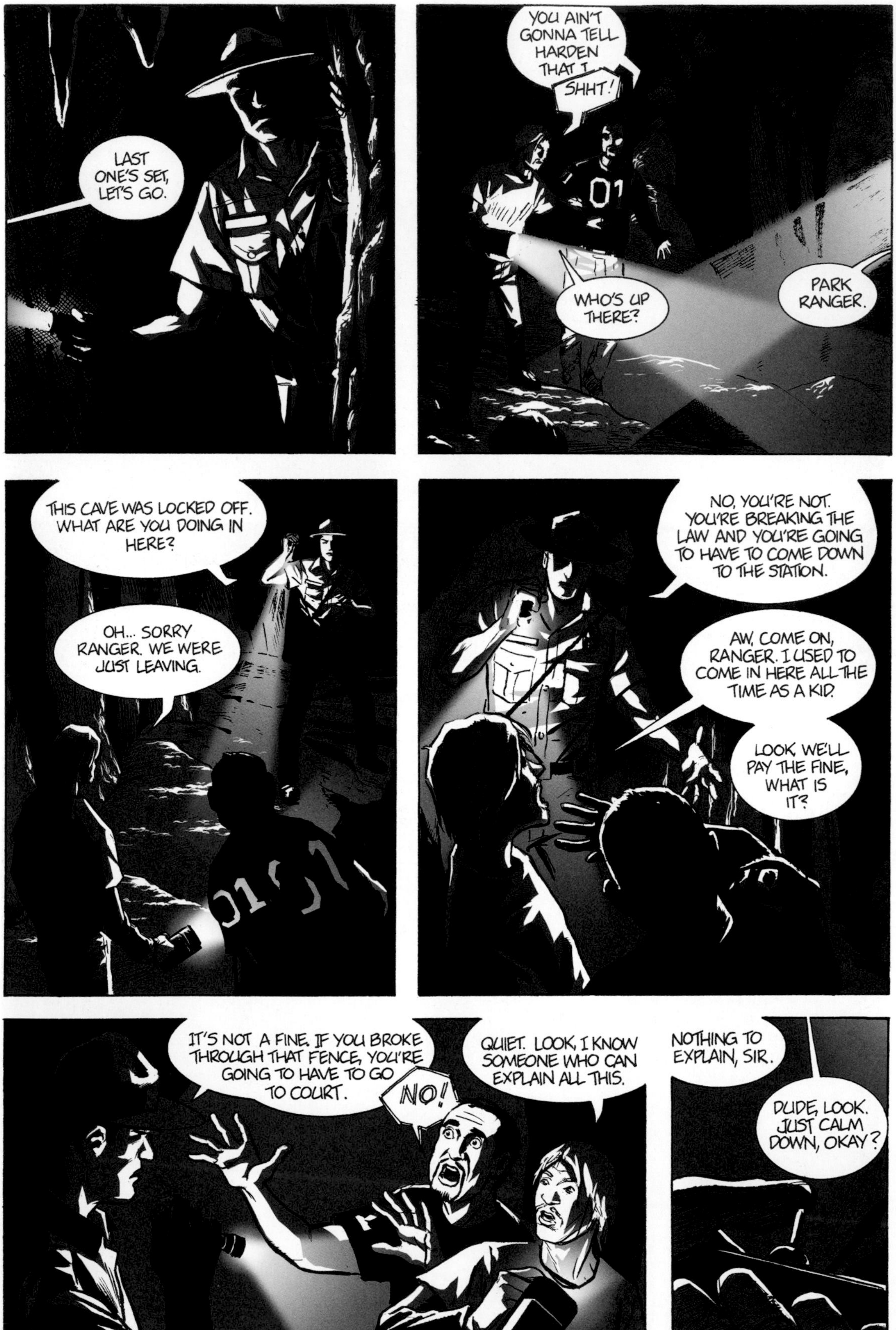
LAST ONE'S SET, LET'S GO.
YOU AIN'T GONNA TELL HARDEN THAT I
SHHT!
WHO'S UP THERE?
PARK RANGER.
THIS CAVE WAS LOCKED OFF. WHAT ARE YOU DOING IN HERE?
OH... SORRY RANGER. WE WERE JUST LEAVING.
NO, YOU'RE NOT. YOU'RE BREAKING THE LAW AND YOU'RE GOING TO HAVE TO COME DOWN TO THE STATION.
AW, COME ON, RANGER. I USED TO COME IN HERE ALL THE TIME AS A KID.
LOOK, WE'LL PAY THE FINE, WHAT IS IT?
IT'S NOT A FINE. IF YOU BROKE THROUGH THAT FENCE, YOU'RE GOING TO HAVE TO GO TO COURT.
NO!
QUIET. LOOK, I KNOW SOMEONE WHO CAN EXPLAIN ALL THIS.
NOTHING TO EXPLAIN, SIR.
DUDE, LOOK. JUST CALM DOWN, OKAY?

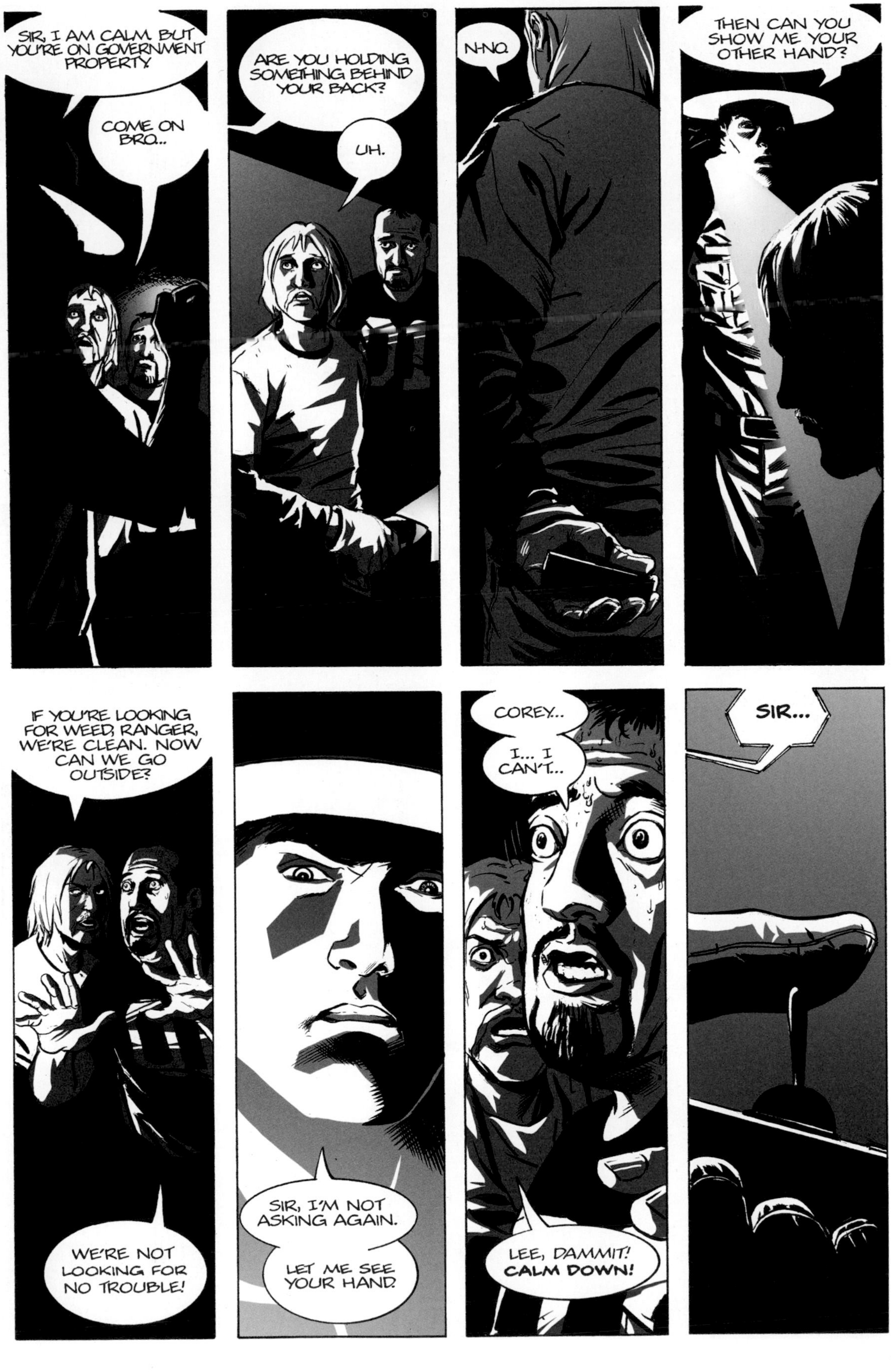

SIR, I AM CALM. BUT YOU'RE ON GOVERNMENT PROPERTY.
COME ON BRO...
ARE YOU HOLDING SOMETHING BEHIND YOUR BACK?
UH.
N-NO.
THEN CAN YOU SHOW ME YOUR OTHER HAND?
IF YOU'RE LOOKING FOR WEED, RANGER, WE'RE CLEAN. NOW CAN WE GO OUTSIDE?
WE'RE NOT LOOKING FOR NO TROUBLE!
SIR, I'M NOT ASKING AGAIN.
LET ME SEE YOUR HAND.
COREY...
I... I CAN'T...
LEE, DAMMIT! **CALM DOWN!**
SIR...

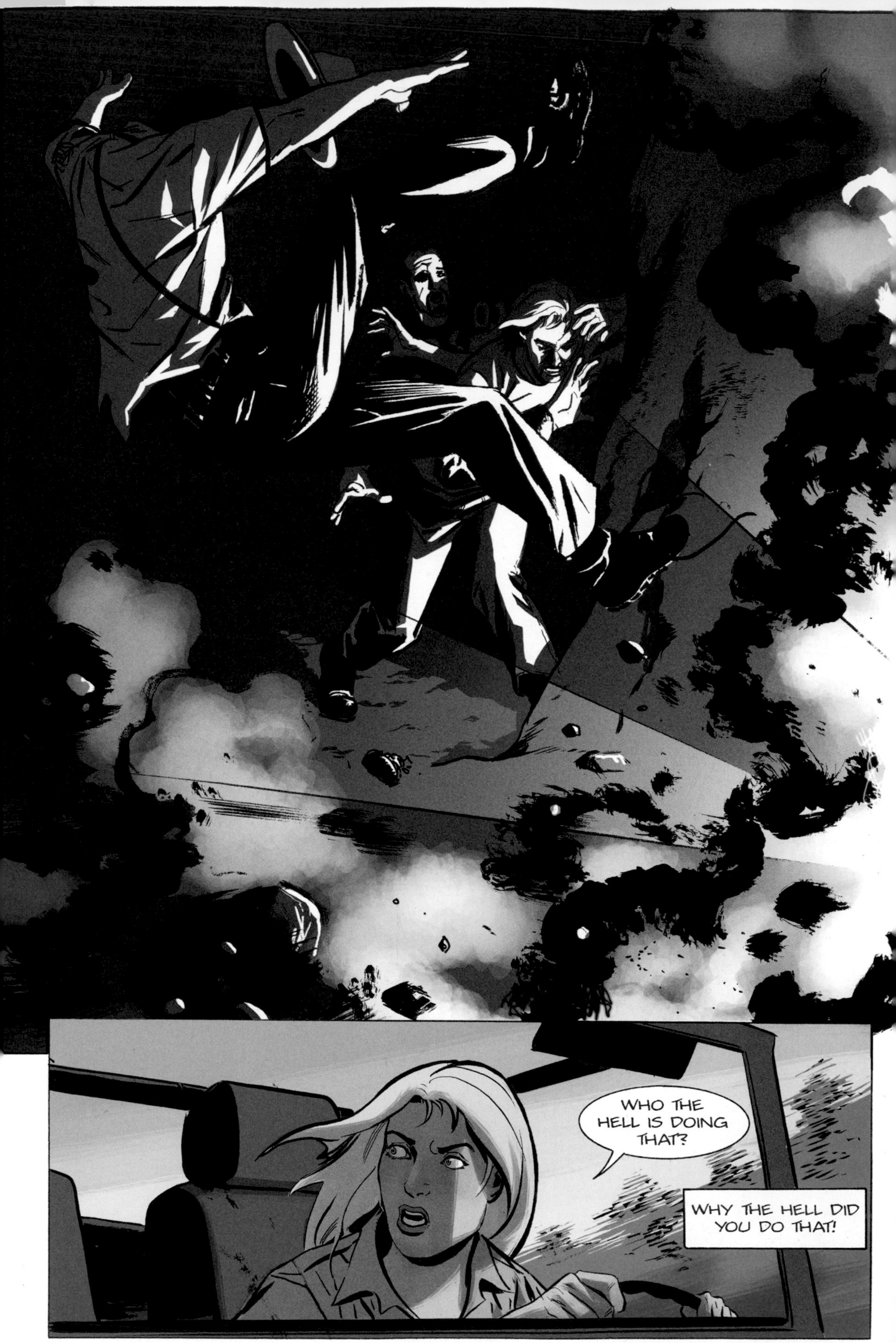
WHO THE HELL IS DOING THAT?
WHY THE HELL DID YOU DO THAT!

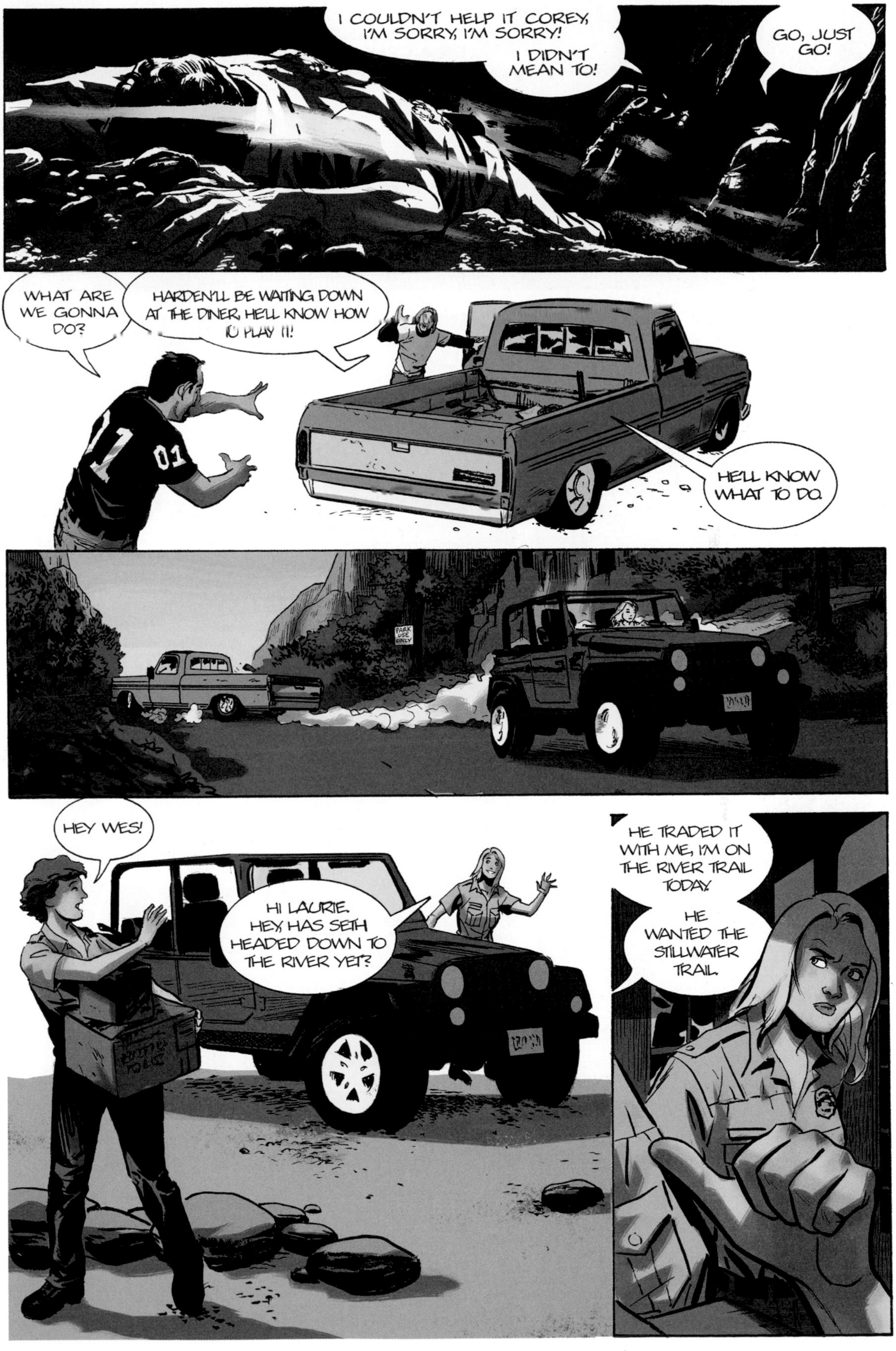
I COULDN'T HELP IT COREY, I'M SORRY, I'M SORRY!
I DIDN'T MEAN TO!
GO, JUST GO!
WHAT ARE WE GONNA DO?
HARDEN'LL BE WAITING DOWN AT THE DINER, HE'LL KNOW HOW TO PLAY IT!
HE'LL KNOW WHAT TO DO.
PARK USE ONLY
HEY WES!
HI LAURIE. HEY, HAS SETH HEADED DOWN TO THE RIVER YET?
HE TRADED IT WITH ME, I'M ON THE RIVER TRAIL TODAY.
HE WANTED THE STILLWATER TRAIL.

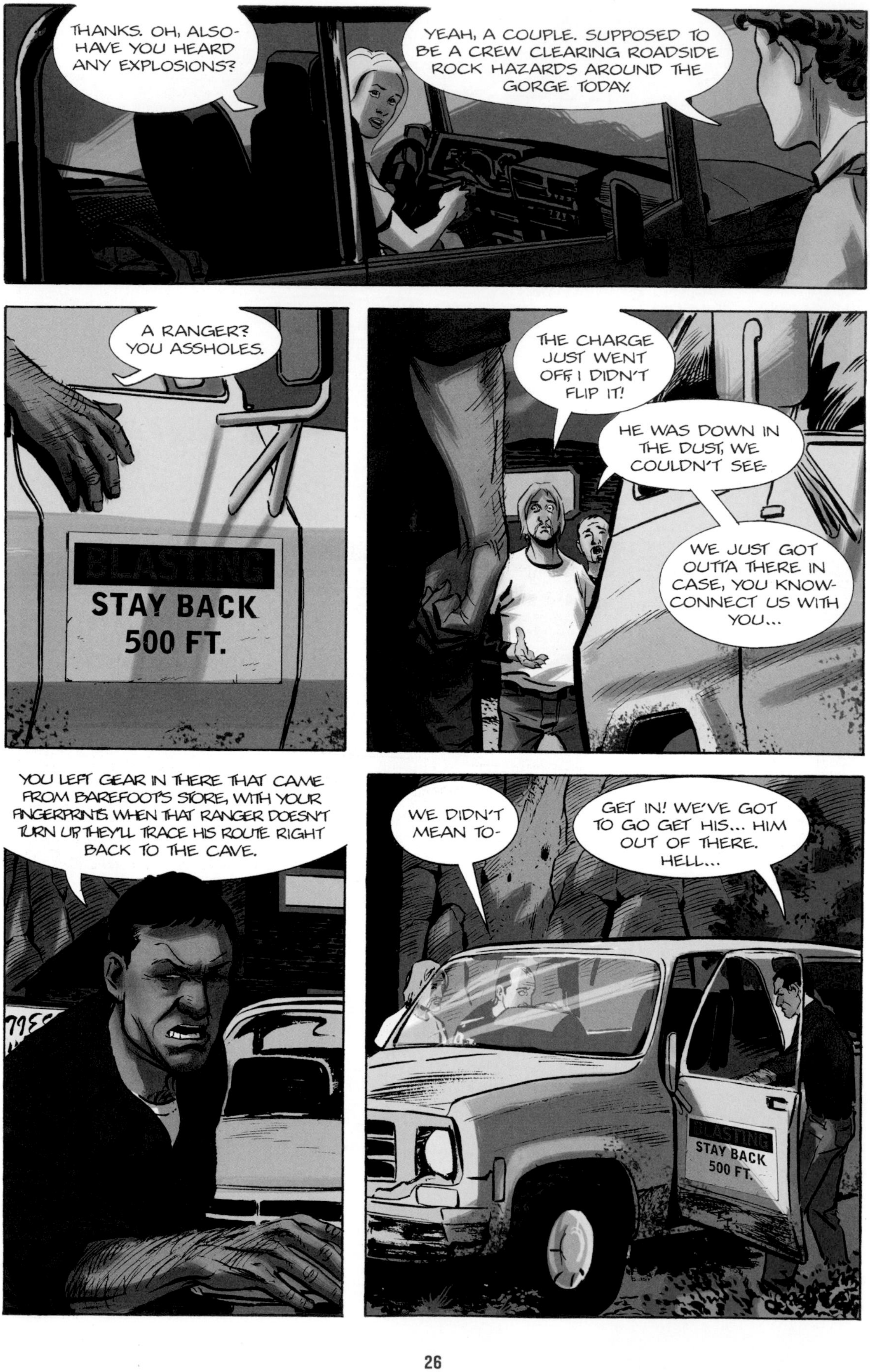
THANKS. OH, ALSO- HAVE YOU HEARD ANY EXPLOSIONS?
YEAH, A COUPLE. SUPPOSED TO BE A CREW CLEARING ROADSIDE ROCK HAZARDS AROUND THE GORGE TODAY.
A RANGER? YOU ASSHOLES.
BLASTING
STAY BACK 500 FT.
THE CHARGE JUST WENT OFF, I DIDN'T FLIP IT!
HE WAS DOWN IN THE DUST, WE COULDN'T SEE-
WE JUST GOT OUTTA THERE IN CASE, YOU KNOW- CONNECT US WITH YOU...
YOU LEFT GEAR IN THERE THAT CAME FROM BAREFOOT'S STORE, WITH YOUR FINGERPRINTS. WHEN THAT RANGER DOESN'T TURN UP THEY'LL TRACE HIS ROUTE RIGHT BACK TO THE CAVE.
WE DIDN'T MEAN TO-
GET IN! WE'VE GOT TO GO GET HIS... HIM OUT OF THERE. HELL...
BLASTING
STAY BACK 500 FT.

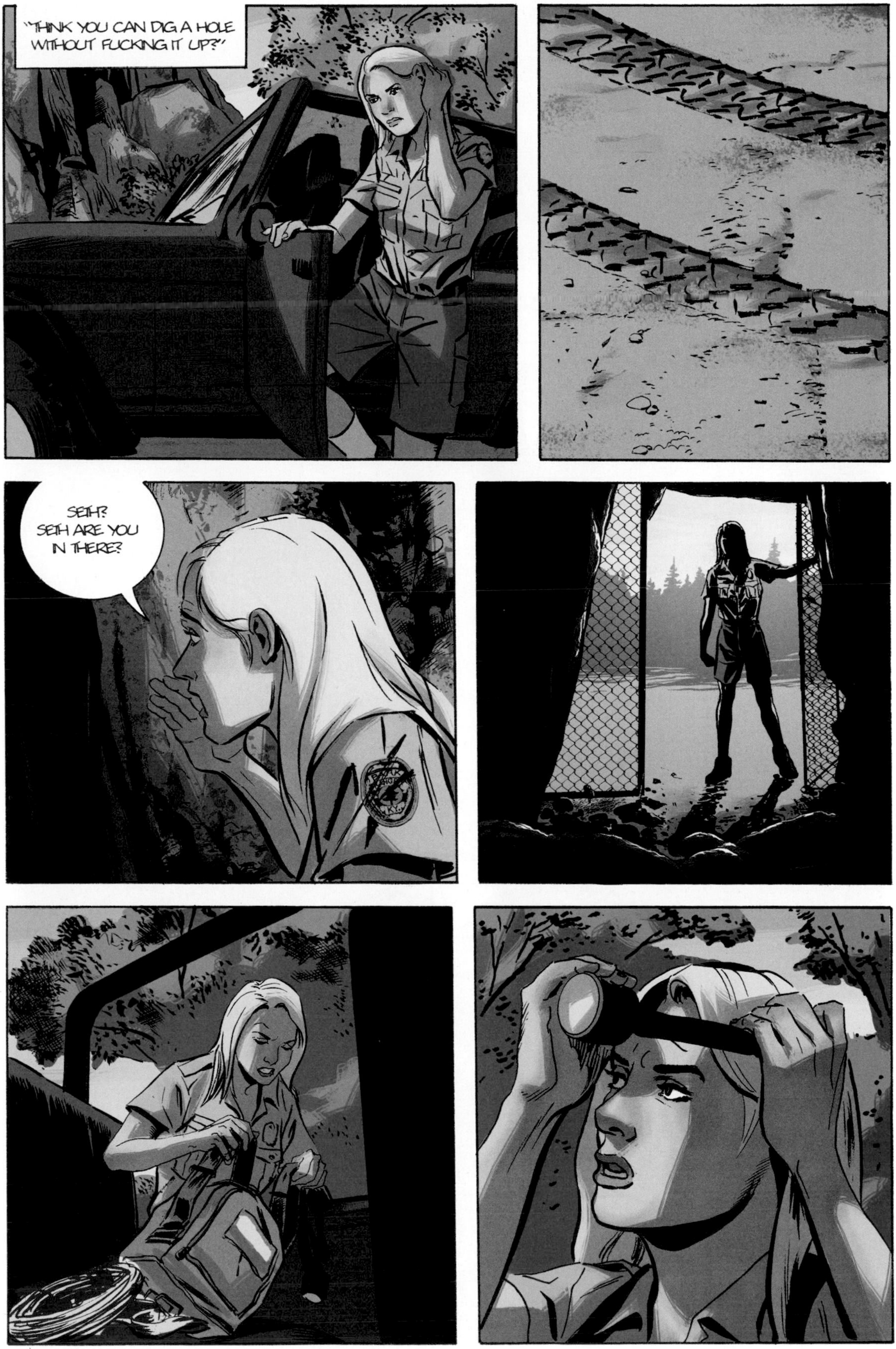
"THINK YOU CAN DIG A HOLE WITHOUT FUCKING IT UP?"
SETH?
SETH ARE YOU IN THERE?

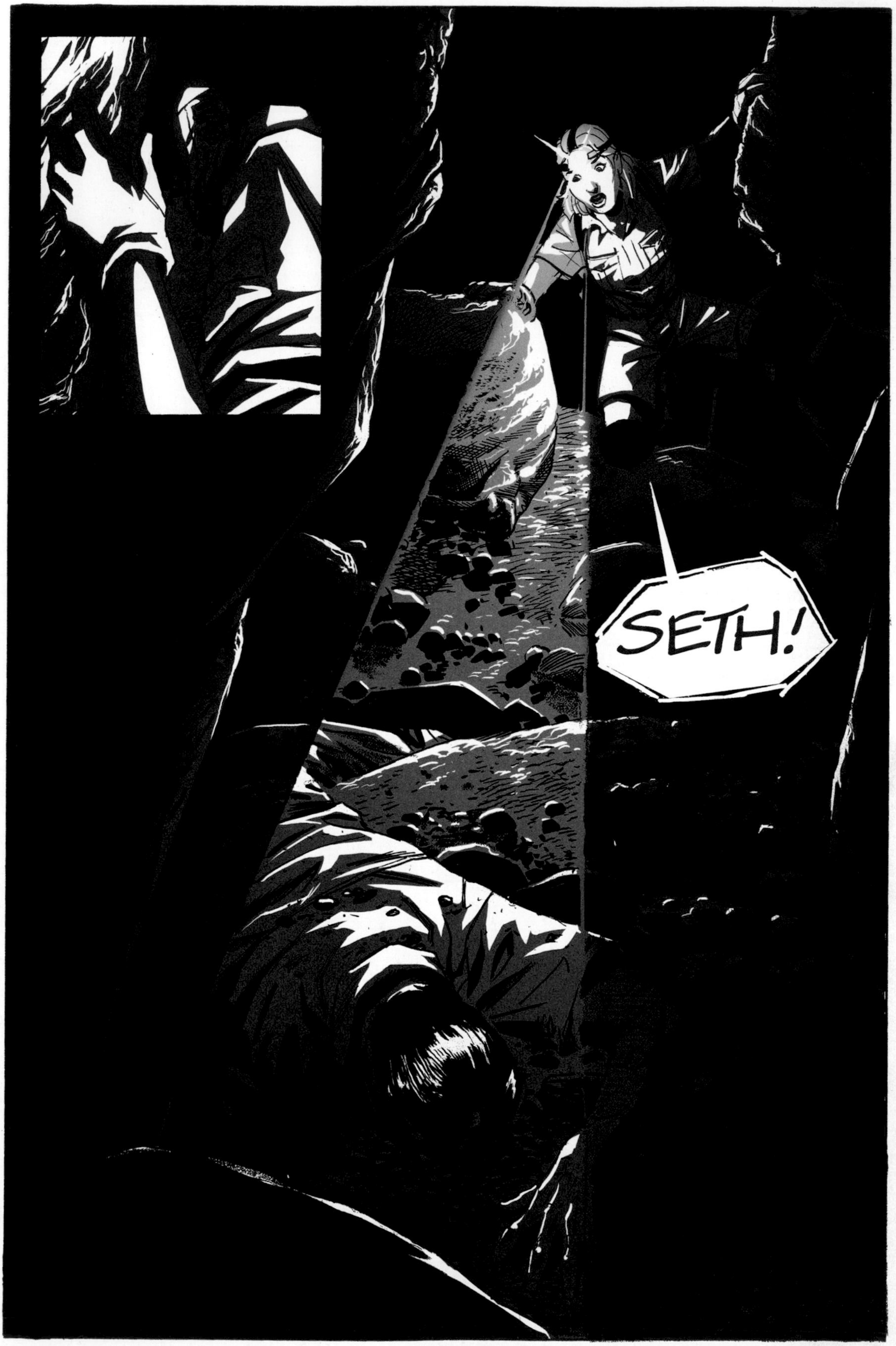
SETH!

CHAPTER TWO

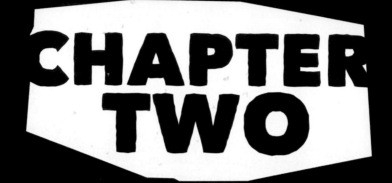

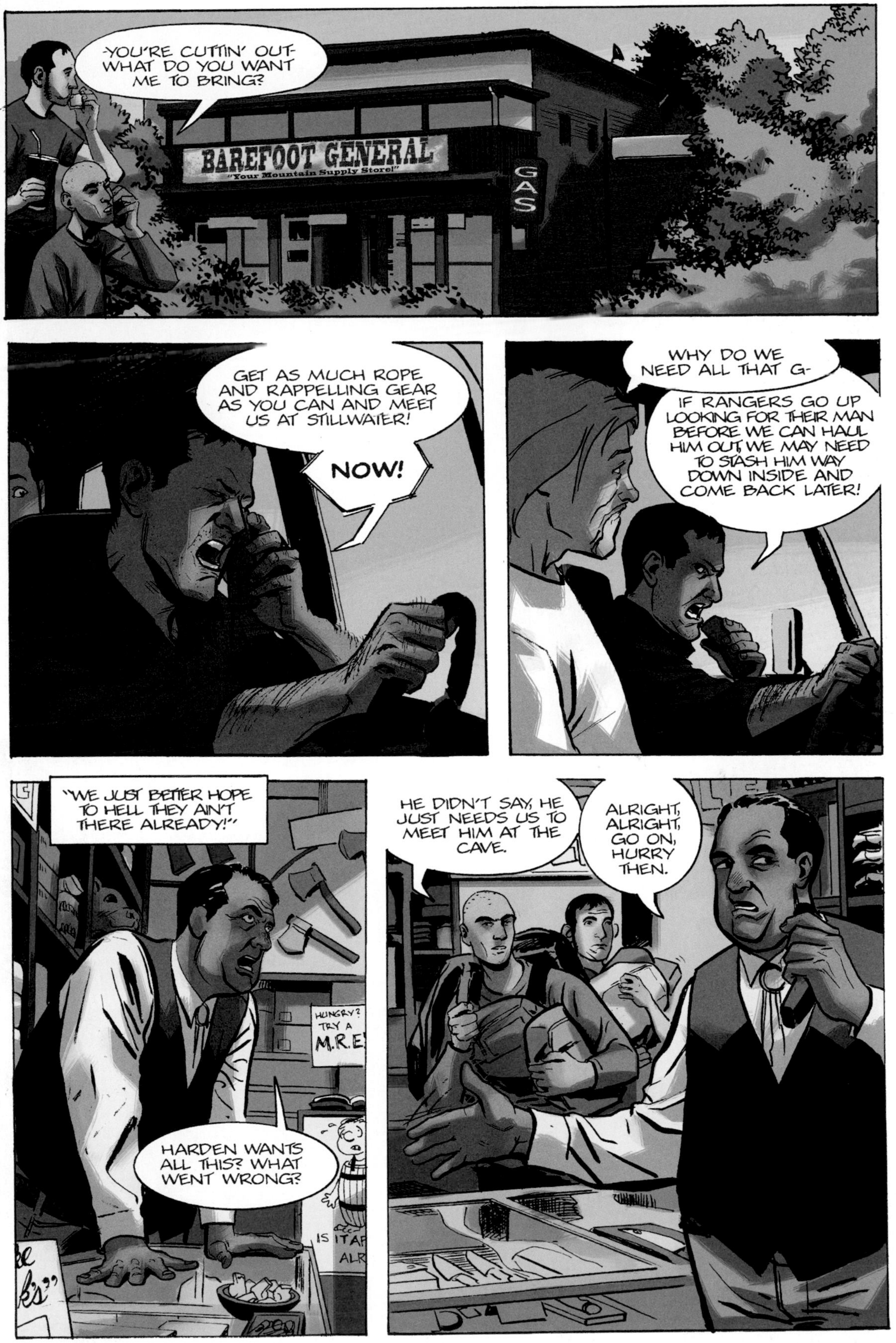

-YOU'RE CUTTIN' OUT- WHAT DO YOU WANT ME TO BRING?
BAREFOOT GENERAL
"Your Mountain Supply Store!"
GAS
GET AS MUCH ROPE AND RAPPELLING GEAR AS YOU CAN AND MEET US AT STILLWATER!
NOW!
WHY DO WE NEED ALL THAT G-
IF RANGERS GO UP LOOKING FOR THEIR MAN BEFORE WE CAN HAUL HIM OUT, WE MAY NEED TO STASH HIM WAY DOWN INSIDE AND COME BACK LATER!
"WE JUST BETTER HOPE TO HELL THEY AIN'T THERE ALREADY!"
HUNGRY? TRY A M.R.E.
HARDEN WANTS ALL THIS? WHAT WENT WRONG?
HE DIDN'T SAY, HE JUST NEEDS US TO MEET HIM AT THE CAVE.
ALRIGHT, ALRIGHT, GO ON, HURRY THEN.

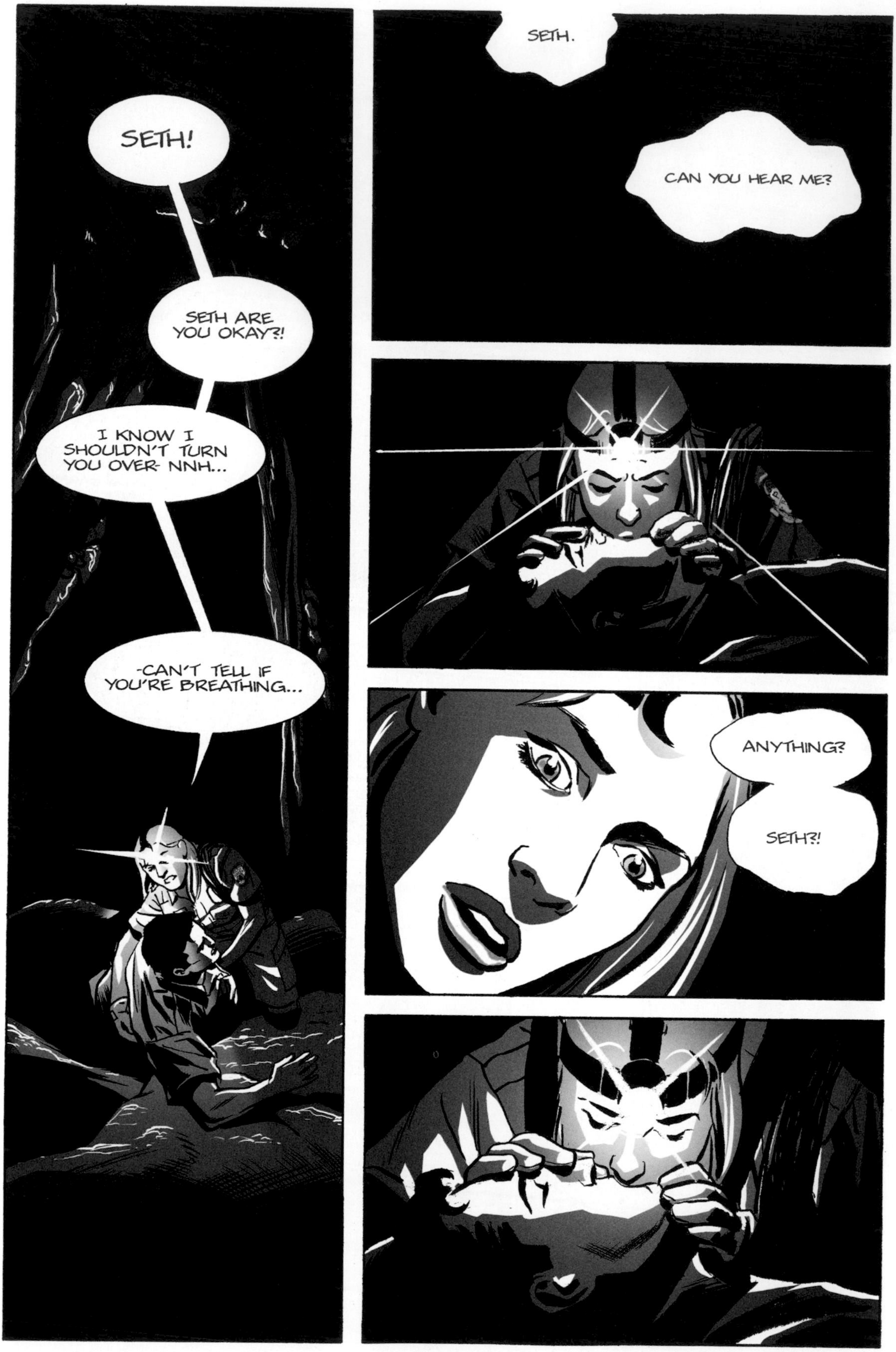
SETH!
SETH ARE YOU OKAY?!
I KNOW I SHOULDN'T TURN YOU OVER- NNH...
-CAN'T TELL IF YOU'RE BREATHING...
SETH.
CAN YOU HEAR ME?
ANYTHING?
SETH?!

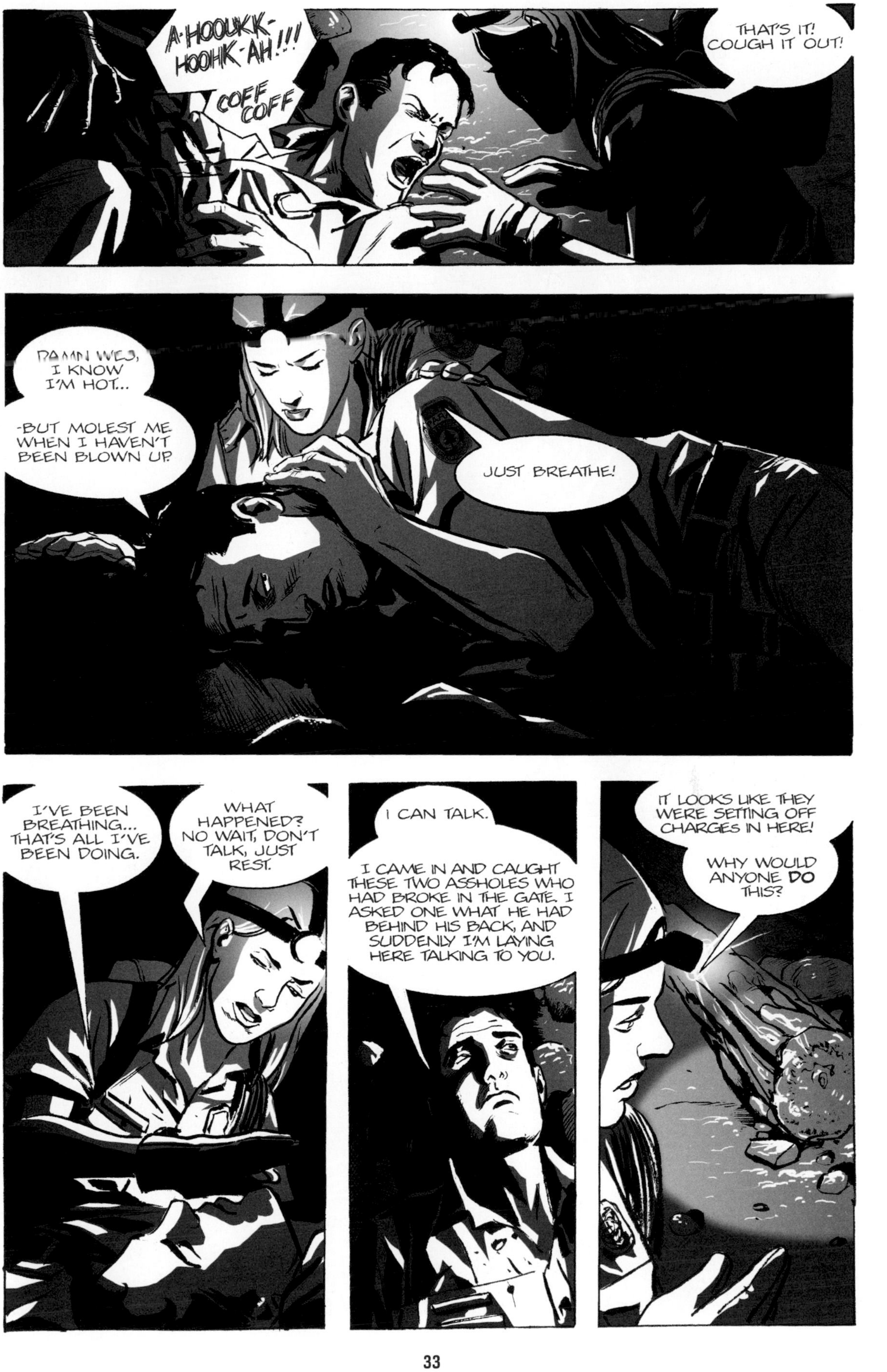
A-HOOUKK-HOOHK-AH!!!
COFF COFF
THAT'S IT! COUGH IT OUT!
DAMN WES, I KNOW I'M HOT...
-BUT MOLEST ME WHEN I HAVEN'T BEEN BLOWN UP.
JUST BREATHE!
I'VE BEEN BREATHING... THAT'S ALL I'VE BEEN DOING.
WHAT HAPPENED? NO WAIT, DON'T TALK, JUST REST.
I CAN TALK.
I CAME IN AND CAUGHT THESE TWO ASSHOLES WHO HAD BROKE IN THE GATE. I ASKED ONE WHAT HE HAD BEHIND HIS BACK, AND SUDDENLY I'M LAYING HERE TALKING TO YOU.
IT LOOKS LIKE THEY WERE SETTING OFF CHARGES IN HERE!
WHY WOULD ANYONE **DO** THIS?

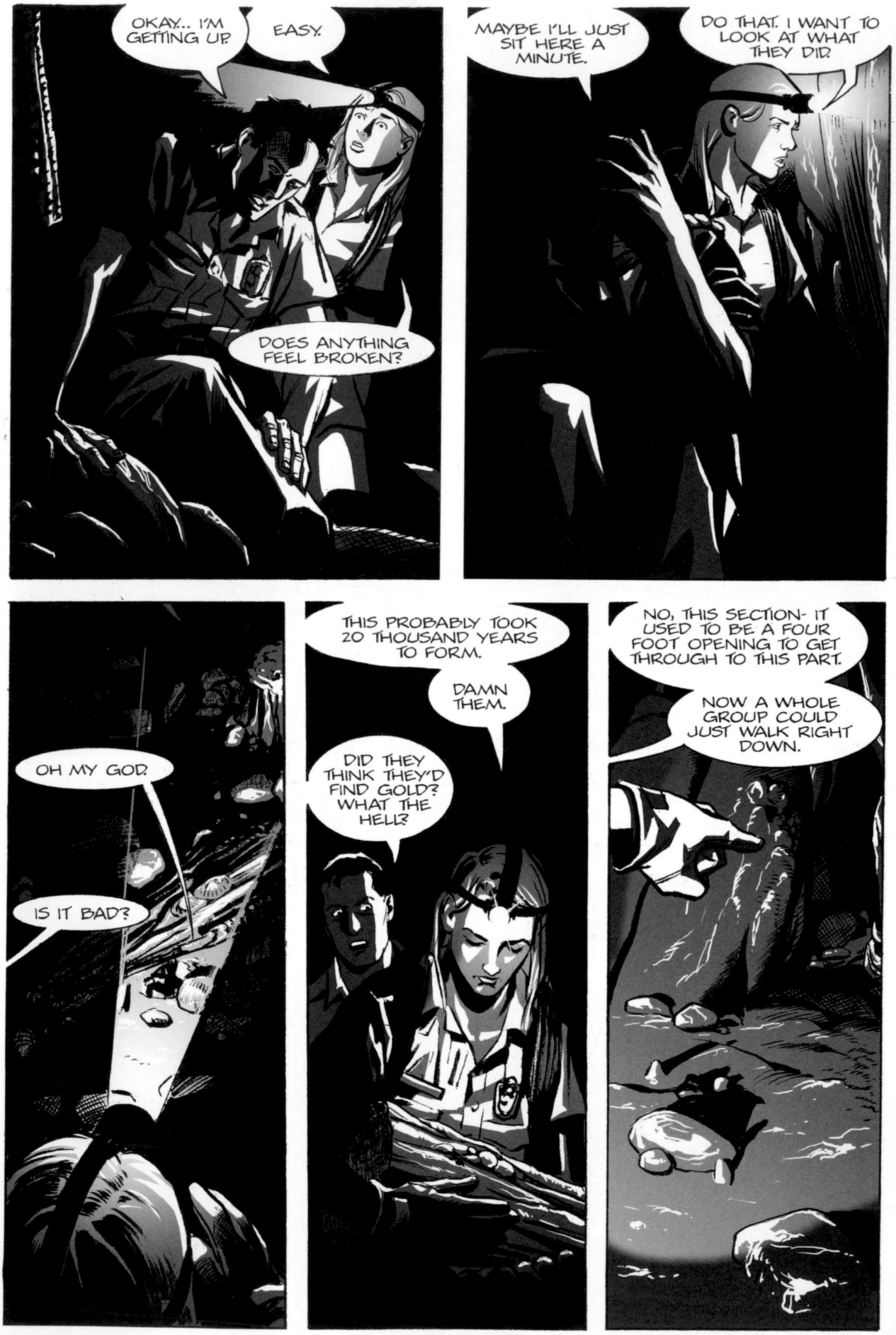
OKAY... I'M GETTING UP.
EASY.
DOES ANYTHING FEEL BROKEN?
MAYBE I'LL JUST SIT HERE A MINUTE.
DO THAT. I WANT TO LOOK AT WHAT THEY DID.
OH MY GOD.
IS IT BAD?
THIS PROBABLY TOOK 20 THOUSAND YEARS TO FORM.
DAMN THEM.
DID THEY THINK THEY'D FIND GOLD? WHAT THE HELL?
NO, THIS SECTION- IT USED TO BE A FOUR FOOT OPENING TO GET THROUGH TO THIS PART.
NOW A WHOLE GROUP COULD JUST WALK RIGHT DOWN.

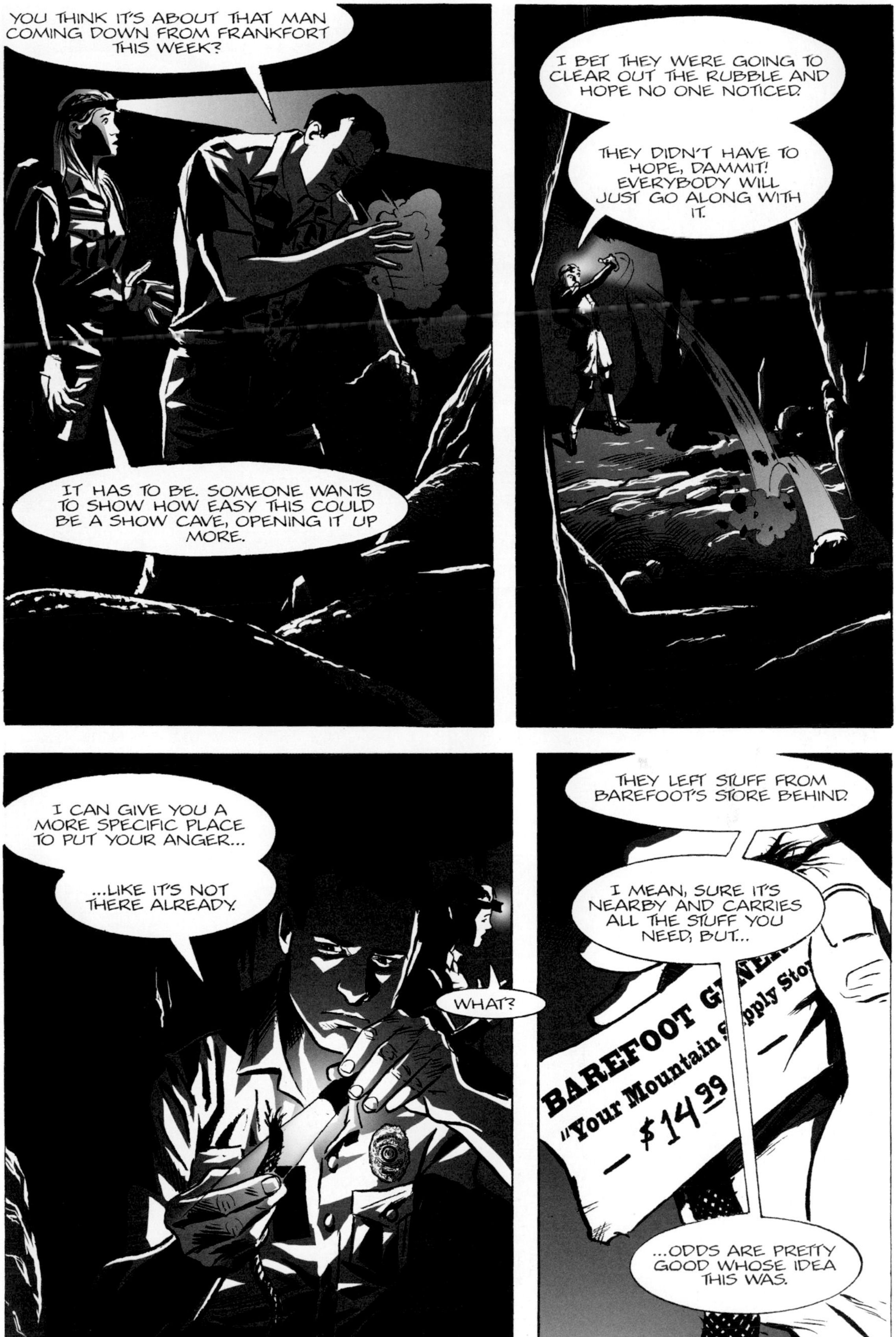
YOU THINK IT'S ABOUT THAT MAN COMING DOWN FROM FRANKFORT THIS WEEK?
IT HAS TO BE. SOMEONE WANTS TO SHOW HOW EASY THIS COULD BE A SHOW CAVE, OPENING IT UP MORE.
I BET THEY WERE GOING TO CLEAR OUT THE RUBBLE AND HOPE NO ONE NOTICED.
THEY DIDN'T HAVE TO HOPE, DAMMIT! EVERYBODY WILL JUST GO ALONG WITH IT.
I CAN GIVE YOU A MORE SPECIFIC PLACE TO PUT YOUR ANGER...
...LIKE IT'S NOT THERE ALREADY.
WHAT?
THEY LEFT STUFF FROM BAREFOOT'S STORE BEHIND.
I MEAN, SURE IT'S NEARBY AND CARRIES ALL THE STUFF YOU NEED, BUT...
BAREFOOT
"Your Mountain
— $14.99
...ODDS ARE PRETTY GOOD WHOSE IDEA THIS WAS.

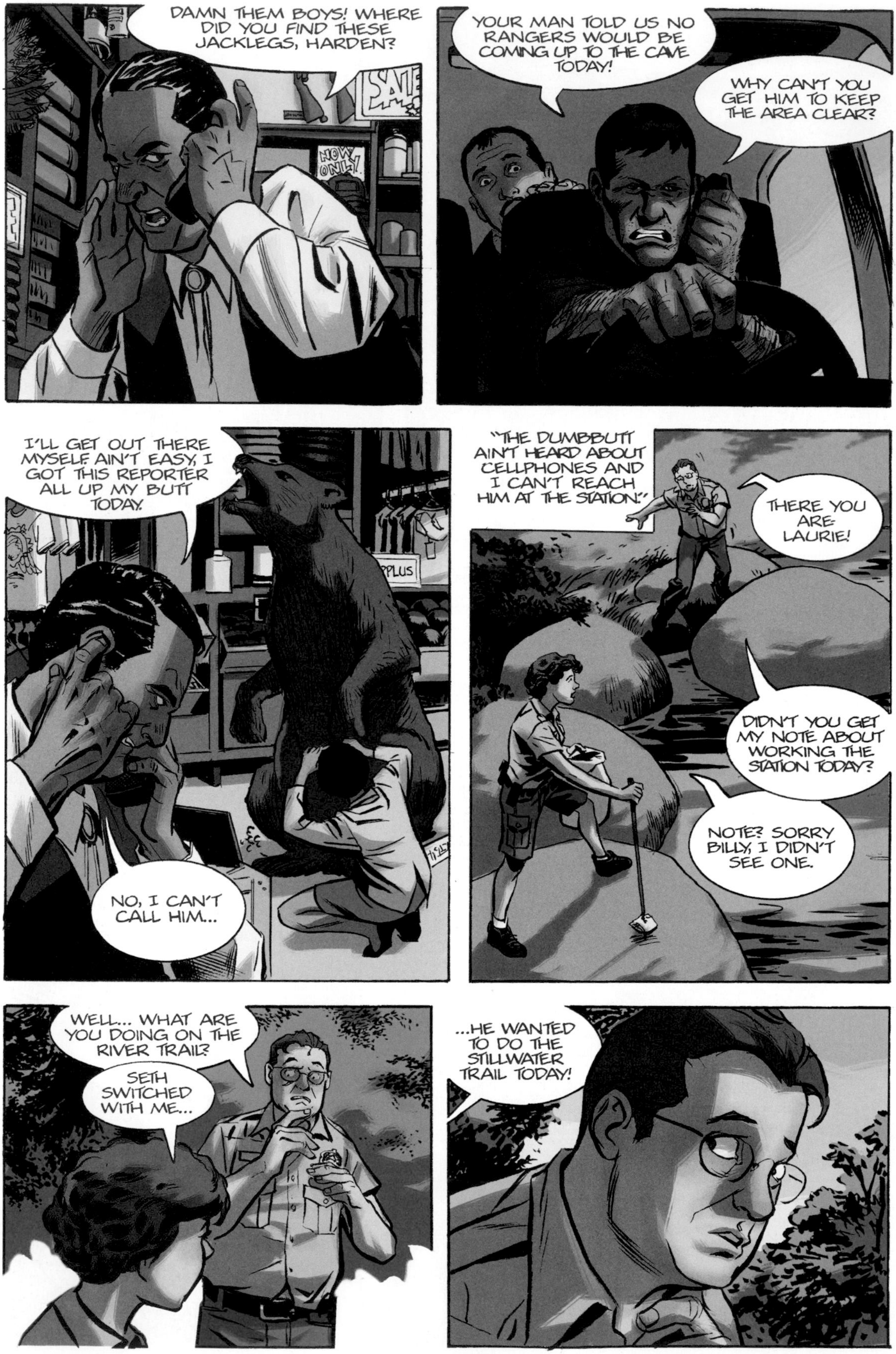

DAMN THEM BOYS! WHERE DID YOU FIND THESE JACKLEGS, HARDEN?
SALE
NOW ONLY!
YOUR MAN TOLD US NO RANGERS WOULD BE COMING UP TO THE CAVE TODAY!
WHY CAN'T YOU GET HIM TO KEEP THE AREA CLEAR?
I'LL GET OUT THERE MYSELF. AIN'T EASY, I GOT THIS REPORTER ALL UP MY BUTT TODAY.
NO, I CAN'T CALL HIM...
"THE DUMBBUTT AIN'T HEARD ABOUT CELLPHONES AND I CAN'T REACH HIM AT THE STATION."
THERE YOU ARE LAURIE!
DIDN'T YOU GET MY NOTE ABOUT WORKING THE STATION TODAY?
NOTE? SORRY BILLY, I DIDN'T SEE ONE.
WELL... WHAT ARE YOU DOING ON THE RIVER TRAIL?
SETH SWITCHED WITH ME...
...HE WANTED TO DO THE STILLWATER TRAIL TODAY!

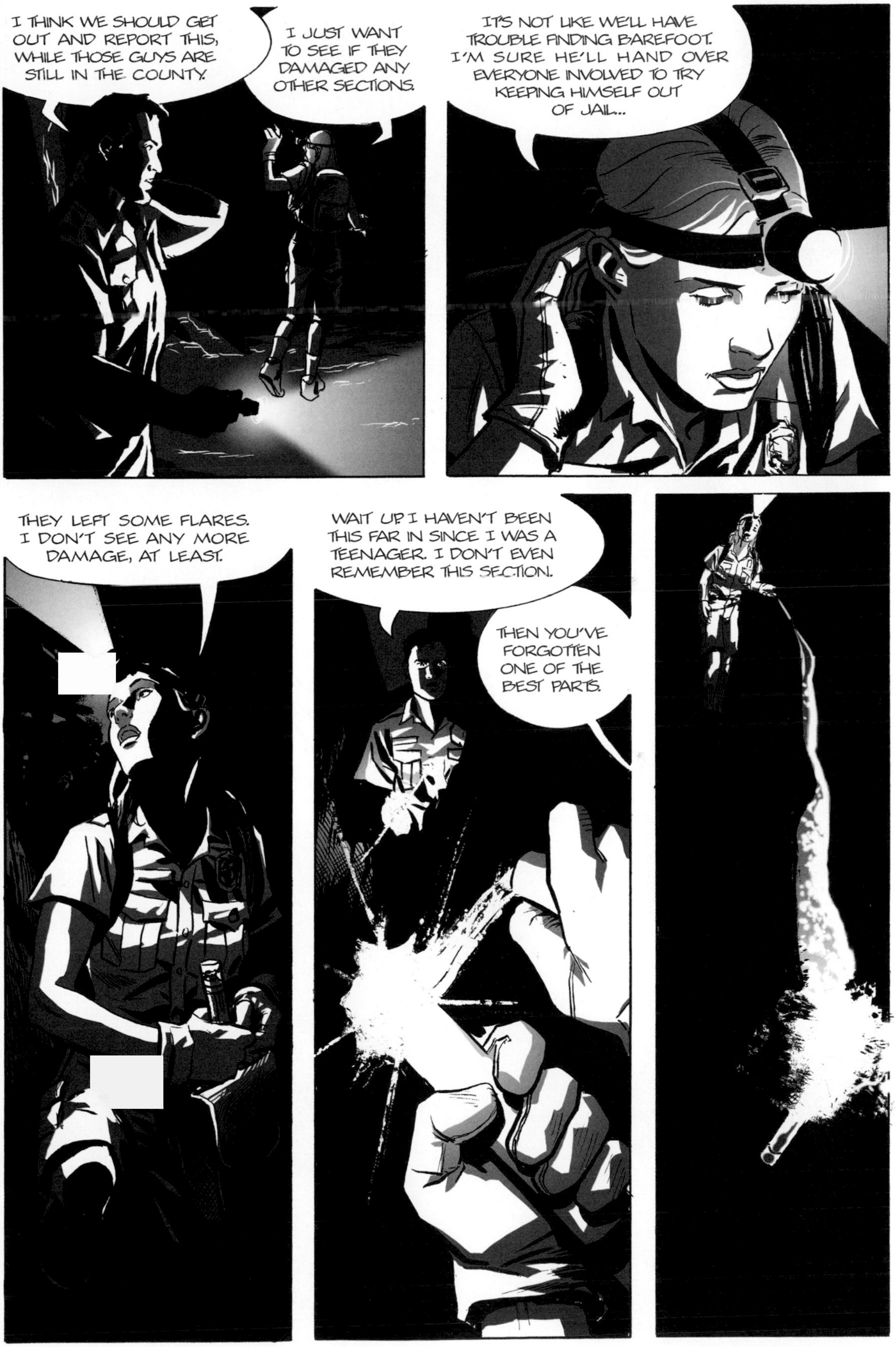
I THINK WE SHOULD GET OUT AND REPORT THIS, WHILE THOSE GUYS ARE STILL IN THE COUNTY.
I JUST WANT TO SEE IF THEY DAMAGED ANY OTHER SECTIONS.
IT'S NOT LIKE WE'LL HAVE TROUBLE FINDING BAREFOOT. I'M SURE HE'LL HAND OVER EVERYONE INVOLVED TO TRY KEEPING HIMSELF OUT OF JAIL...
THEY LEFT SOME FLARES. I DON'T SEE ANY MORE DAMAGE, AT LEAST.
WAIT UP. I HAVEN'T BEEN THIS FAR IN SINCE I WAS A TEENAGER. I DON'T EVEN REMEMBER THIS SECTION.
THEN YOU'VE FORGOTTEN ONE OF THE BEST PARTS.

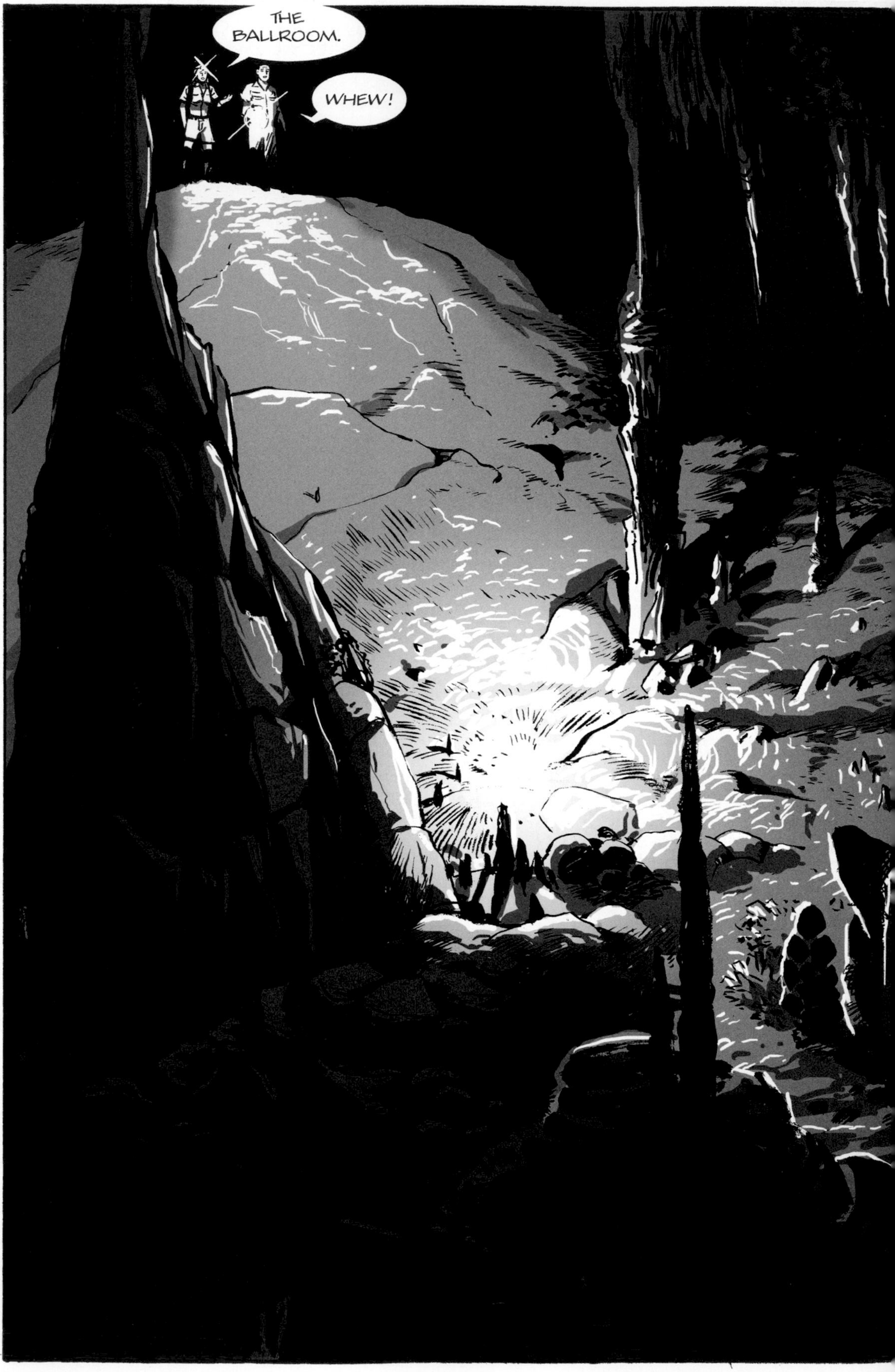
THE BALLROOM.
WHEW!

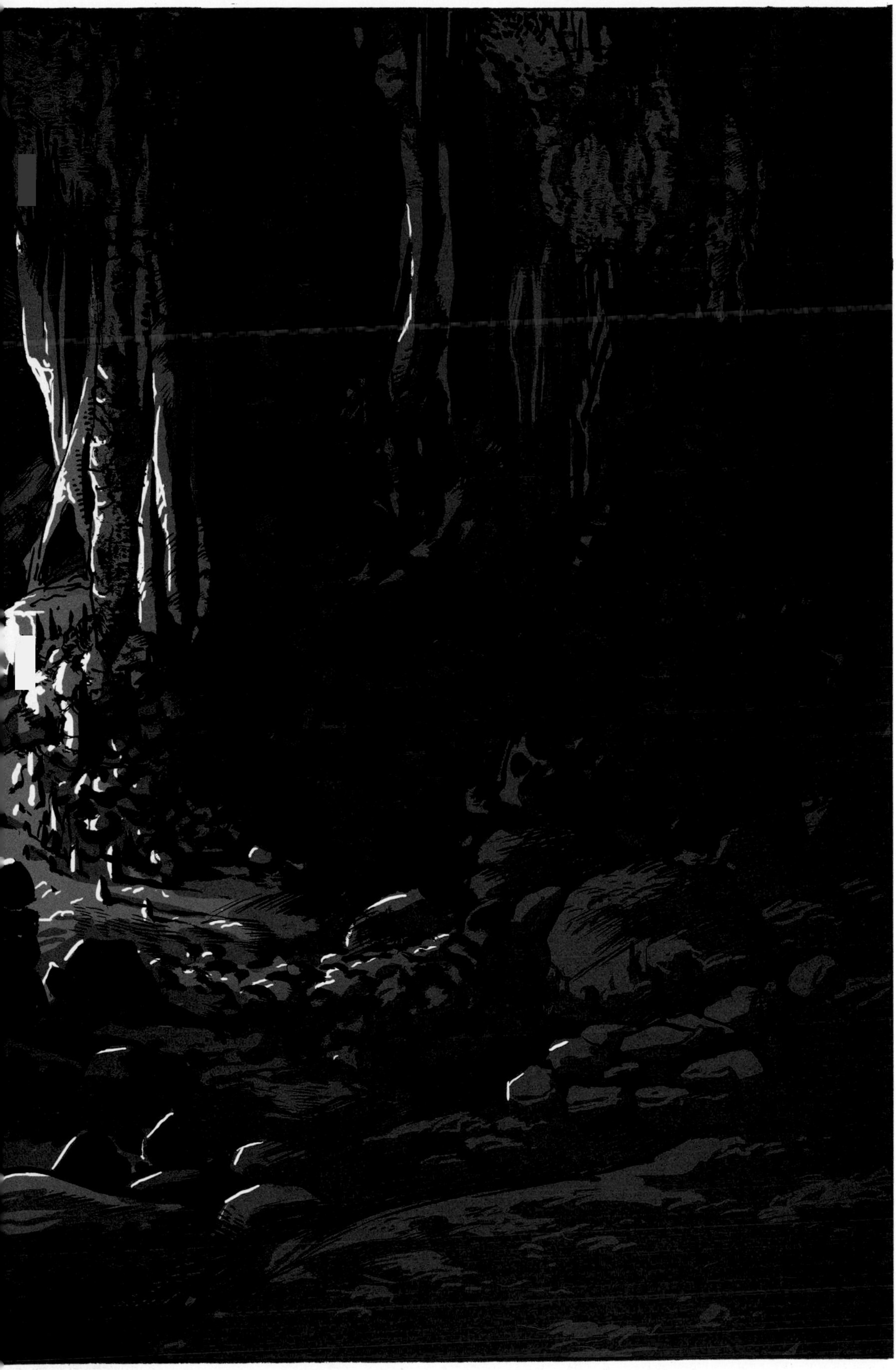

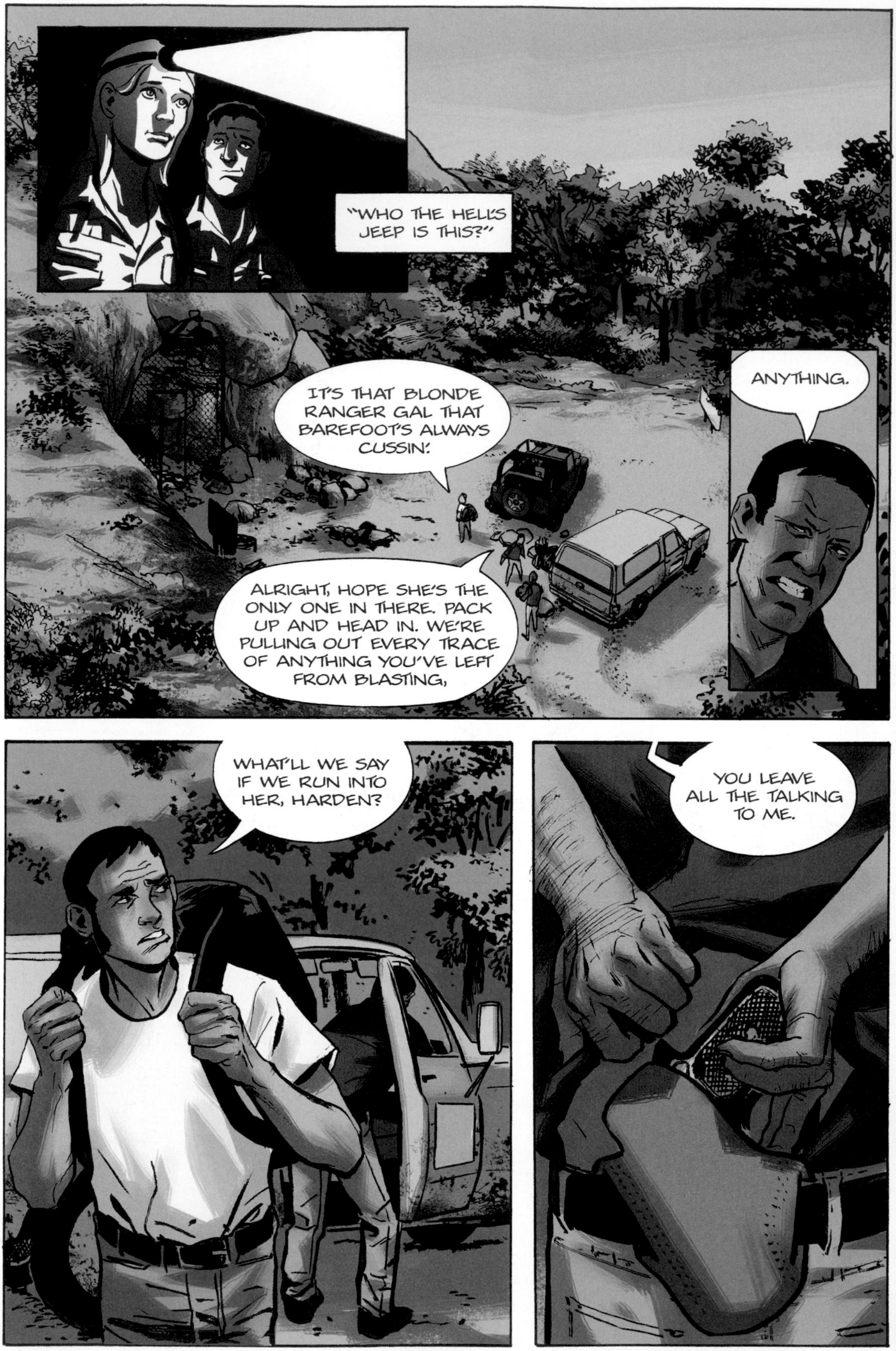
"WHO THE HELL'S JEEP IS THIS?"
IT'S THAT BLONDE RANGER GAL THAT BAREFOOT'S ALWAYS CUSSIN'.
ALRIGHT, HOPE SHE'S THE ONLY ONE IN THERE. PACK UP AND HEAD IN. WE'RE PULLING OUT EVERY TRACE OF ANYTHING YOU'VE LEFT FROM BLASTING,
ANYTHING.
WHAT'LL WE SAY IF WE RUN INTO HER, HARDEN?
YOU LEAVE ALL THE TALKING TO ME.

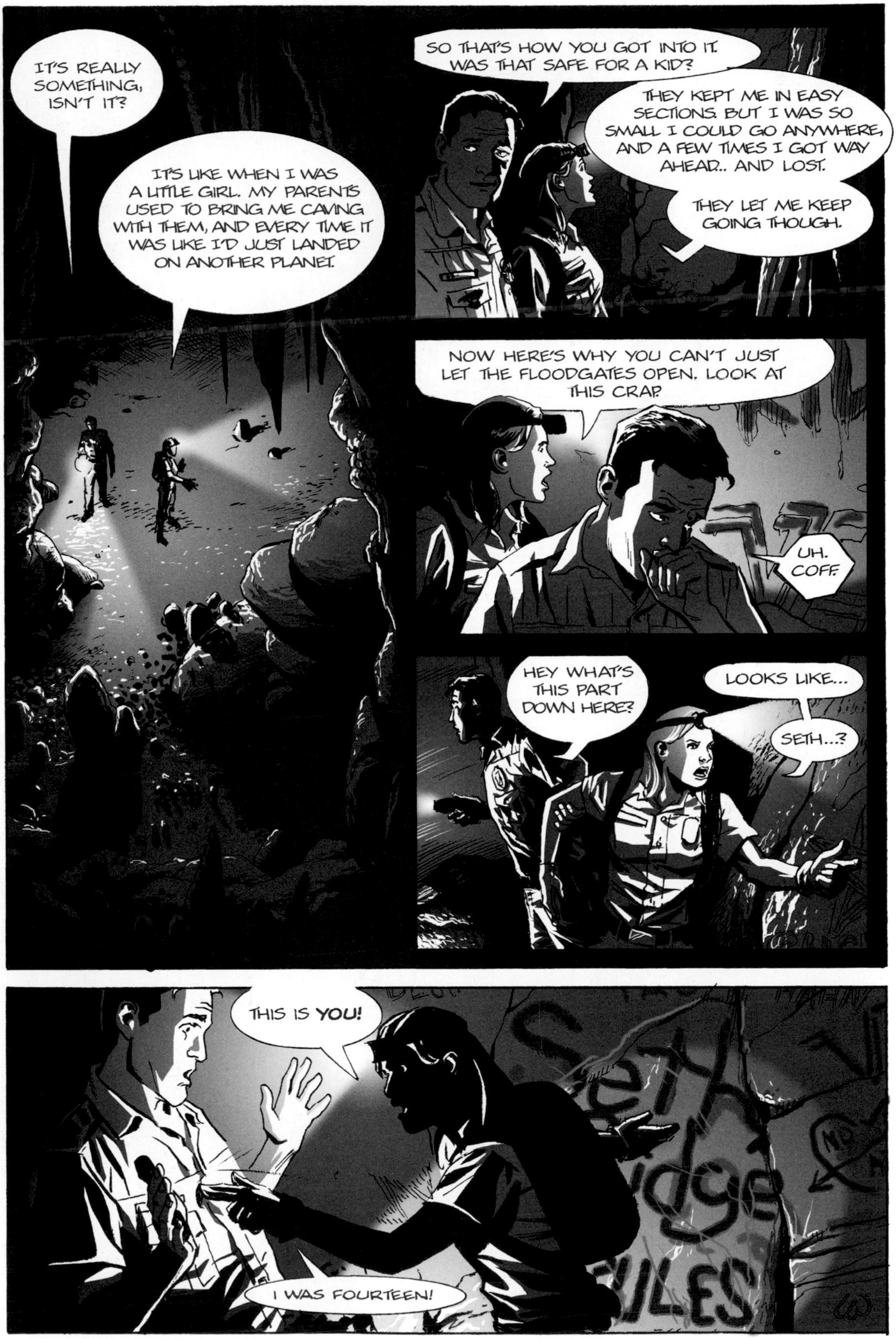
IT'S REALLY SOMETHING, ISN'T IT?
IT'S LIKE WHEN I WAS A LITTLE GIRL. MY PARENTS USED TO BRING ME CAVING WITH THEM, AND EVERY TIME IT WAS LIKE I'D JUST LANDED ON ANOTHER PLANET.
SO THAT'S HOW YOU GOT INTO IT. WAS THAT SAFE FOR A KID?
THEY KEPT ME IN EASY SECTIONS. BUT I WAS SO SMALL I COULD GO ANYWHERE, AND A FEW TIMES I GOT WAY AHEAD.. AND LOST.
THEY LET ME KEEP GOING THOUGH.
NOW HERE'S WHY YOU CAN'T JUST LET THE FLOODGATES OPEN. LOOK AT THIS CRAP.
UH. COFF.
HEY WHAT'S THIS PART DOWN HERE?
LOOKS LIKE...
SETH...?
THIS IS YOU!
I WAS FOURTEEN!
LES

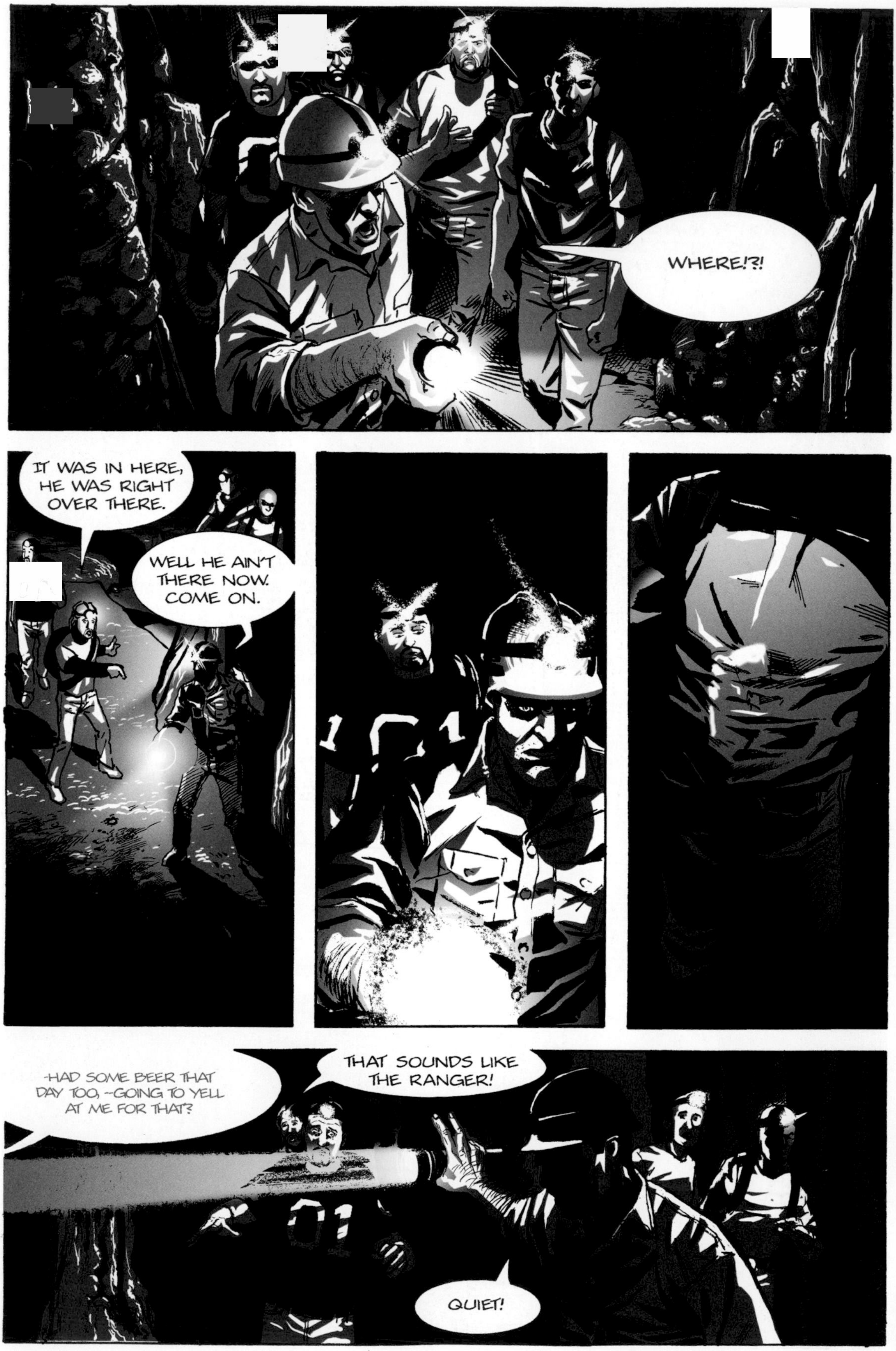
WHERE!?!
IT WAS IN HERE, HE WAS RIGHT OVER THERE.
WELL HE AIN'T THERE NOW. COME ON.
-HAD SOME BEER THAT DAY TOO, --GOING TO YELL AT ME FOR THAT?
THAT SOUNDS LIKE THE RANGER!
QUIET!

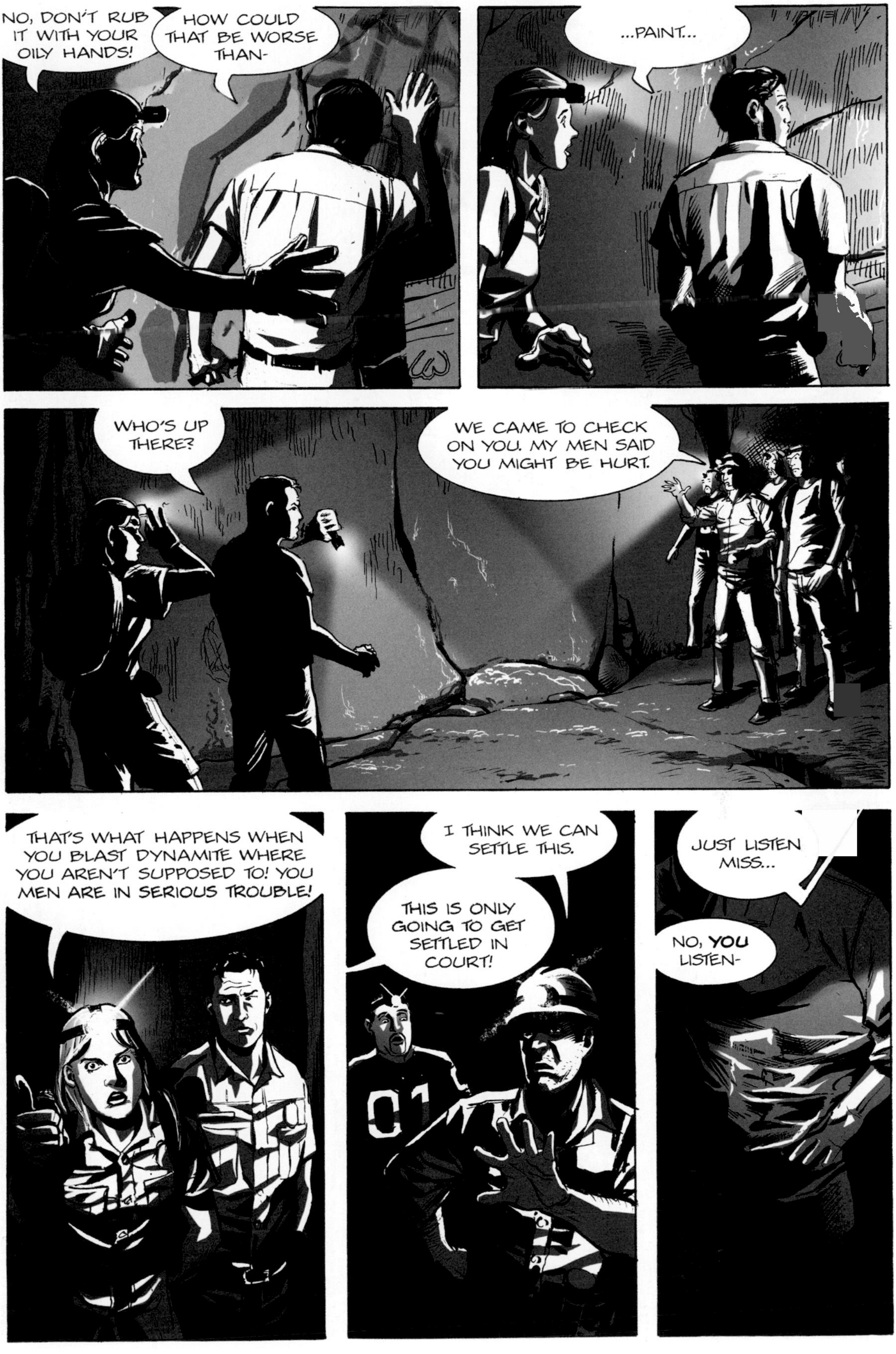
NO, DON'T RUB IT WITH YOUR OILY HANDS!
HOW COULD THAT BE WORSE THAN-
...PAINT...
WHO'S UP THERE?
WE CAME TO CHECK ON YOU. MY MEN SAID YOU MIGHT BE HURT.
THAT'S WHAT HAPPENS WHEN YOU BLAST DYNAMITE WHERE YOU AREN'T SUPPOSED TO! YOU MEN ARE IN SERIOUS TROUBLE!
I THINK WE CAN SETTLE THIS.
THIS IS ONLY GOING TO GET SETTLED IN COURT!
JUST LISTEN MISS...
NO, **YOU** LISTEN-

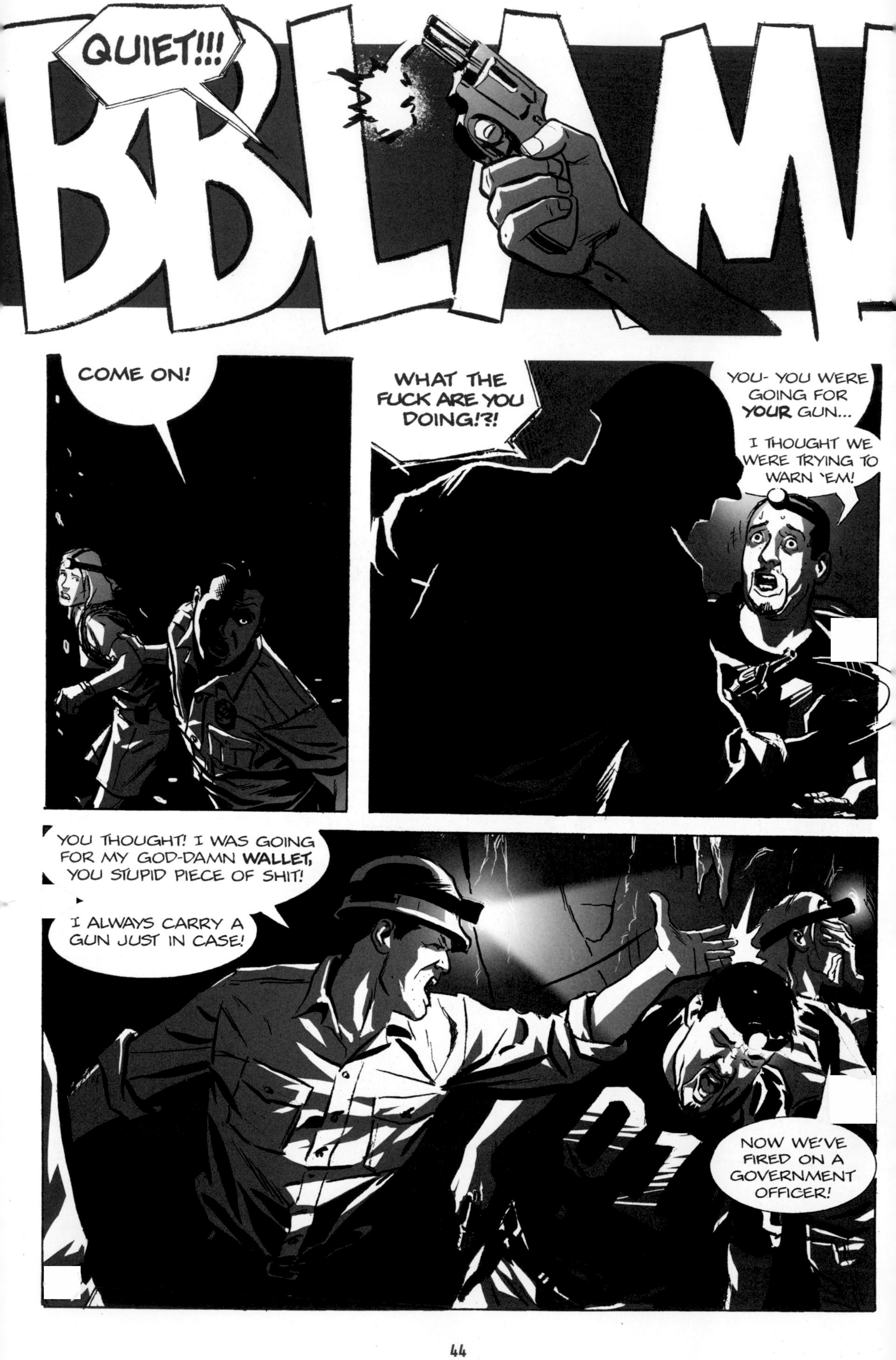

QUIET!!!
BBLAM!
COME ON!
WHAT THE FUCK ARE YOU DOING!?!
YOU- YOU WERE GOING FOR YOUR GUN...
I THOUGHT WE WERE TRYING TO WARN 'EM!
YOU THOUGHT! I WAS GOING FOR MY GOD-DAMN WALLET, YOU STUPID PIECE OF SHIT!
I ALWAYS CARRY A GUN JUST IN CASE!
NOW WE'VE FIRED ON A GOVERNMENT OFFICER!

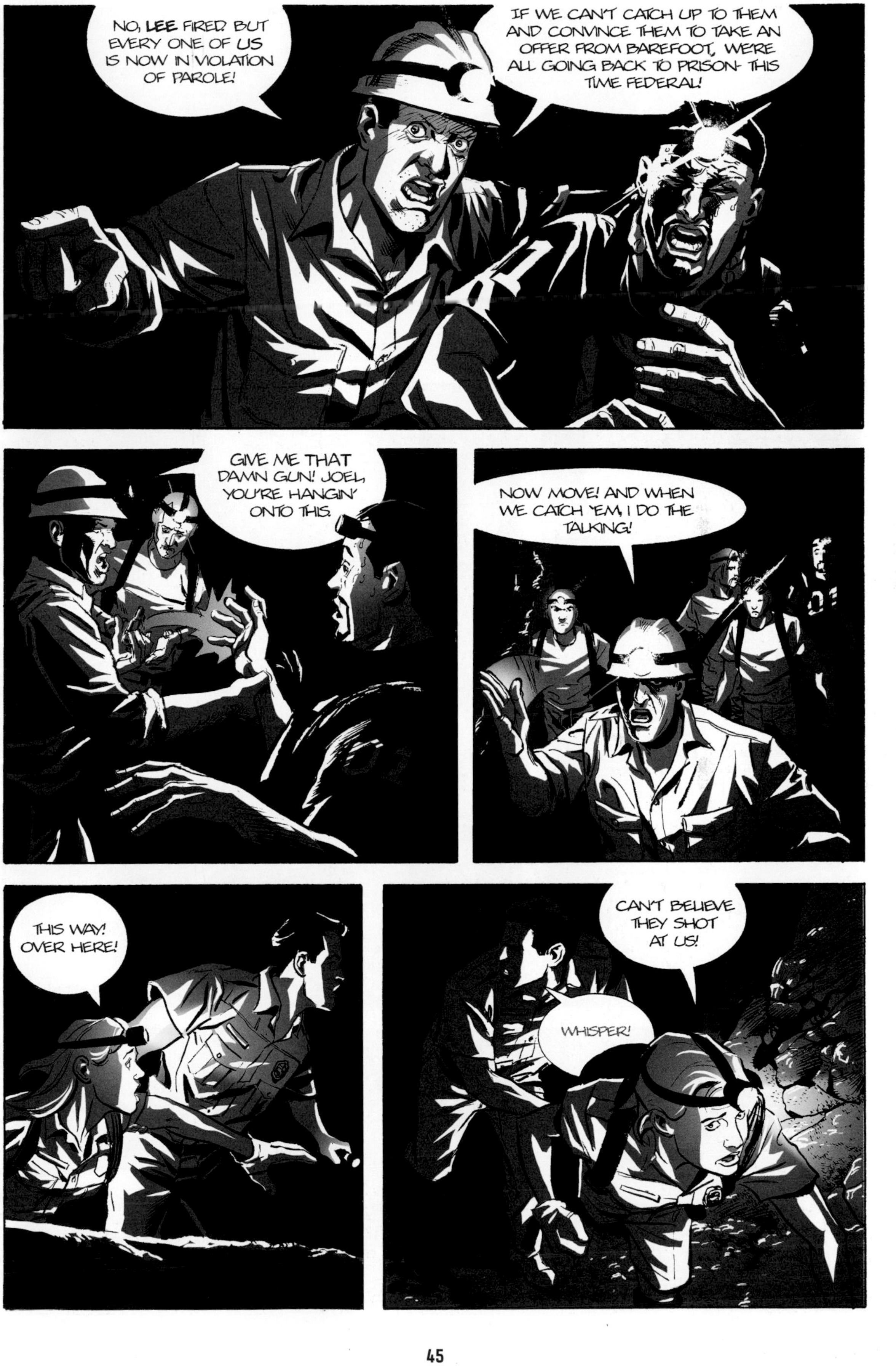

NO, LEE FIRED! BUT EVERY ONE OF US IS NOW IN VIOLATION OF PAROLE!
IF WE CAN'T CATCH UP TO THEM AND CONVINCE THEM TO TAKE AN OFFER FROM BAREFOOT, WE'RE ALL GOING BACK TO PRISON- THIS TIME FEDERAL!
GIVE ME THAT DAMN GUN! JOEL, YOU'RE HANGIN' ONTO THIS.
NOW MOVE! AND WHEN WE CATCH 'EM, I DO THE TALKING!
THIS WAY! OVER HERE!
CAN'T BELIEVE THEY SHOT AT US!
WHISPER!

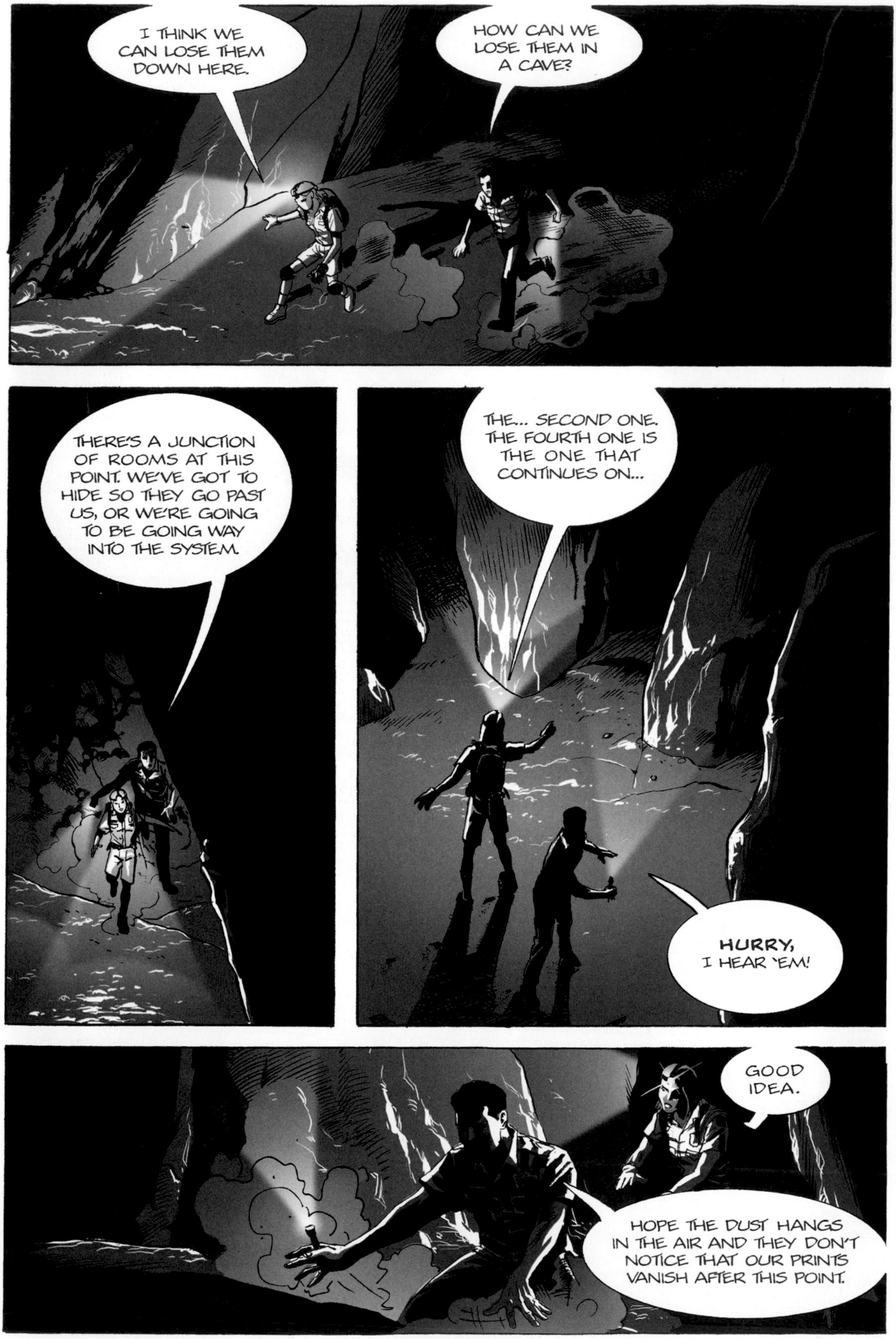
I THINK WE CAN LOSE THEM DOWN HERE.
HOW CAN WE LOSE THEM IN A CAVE?
THERE'S A JUNCTION OF ROOMS AT THIS POINT. WE'VE GOT TO HIDE SO THEY GO PAST US, OR WE'RE GOING TO BE GOING WAY INTO THE SYSTEM.
THE... SECOND ONE. THE FOURTH ONE IS THE ONE THAT CONTINUES ON...
HURRY, I HEAR 'EM!
GOOD IDEA.
HOPE THE DUST HANGS IN THE AIR AND THEY DON'T NOTICE THAT OUR PRINTS VANISH AFTER THIS POINT.

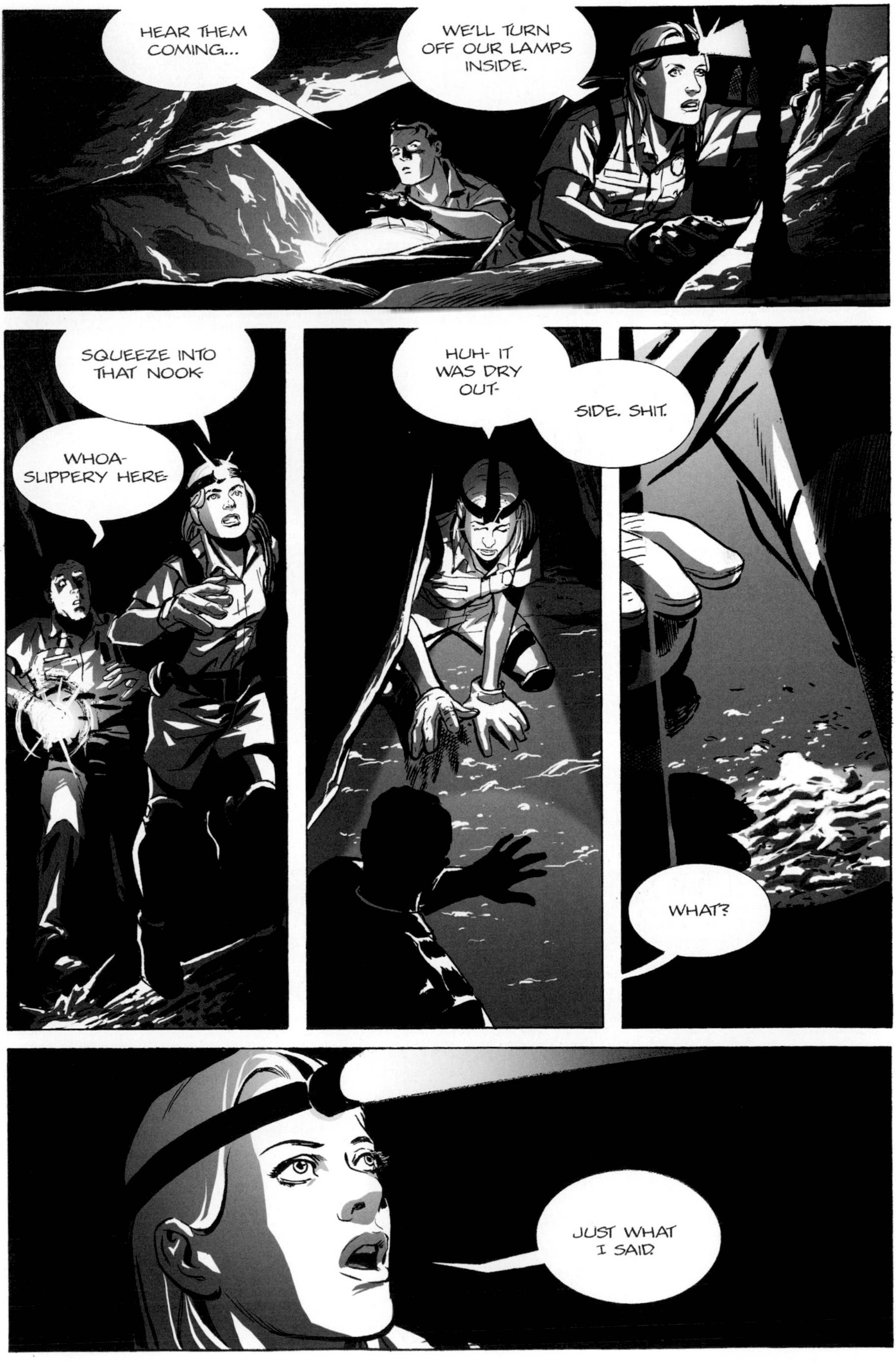
HEAR THEM COMING...
WE'LL TURN OFF OUR LAMPS INSIDE.
SQUEEZE INTO THAT NOOK-
WHOA- SLIPPERY HERE-
HUH- IT WAS DRY OUT-
-SIDE. SHIT.
WHAT?
JUST WHAT I SAID.

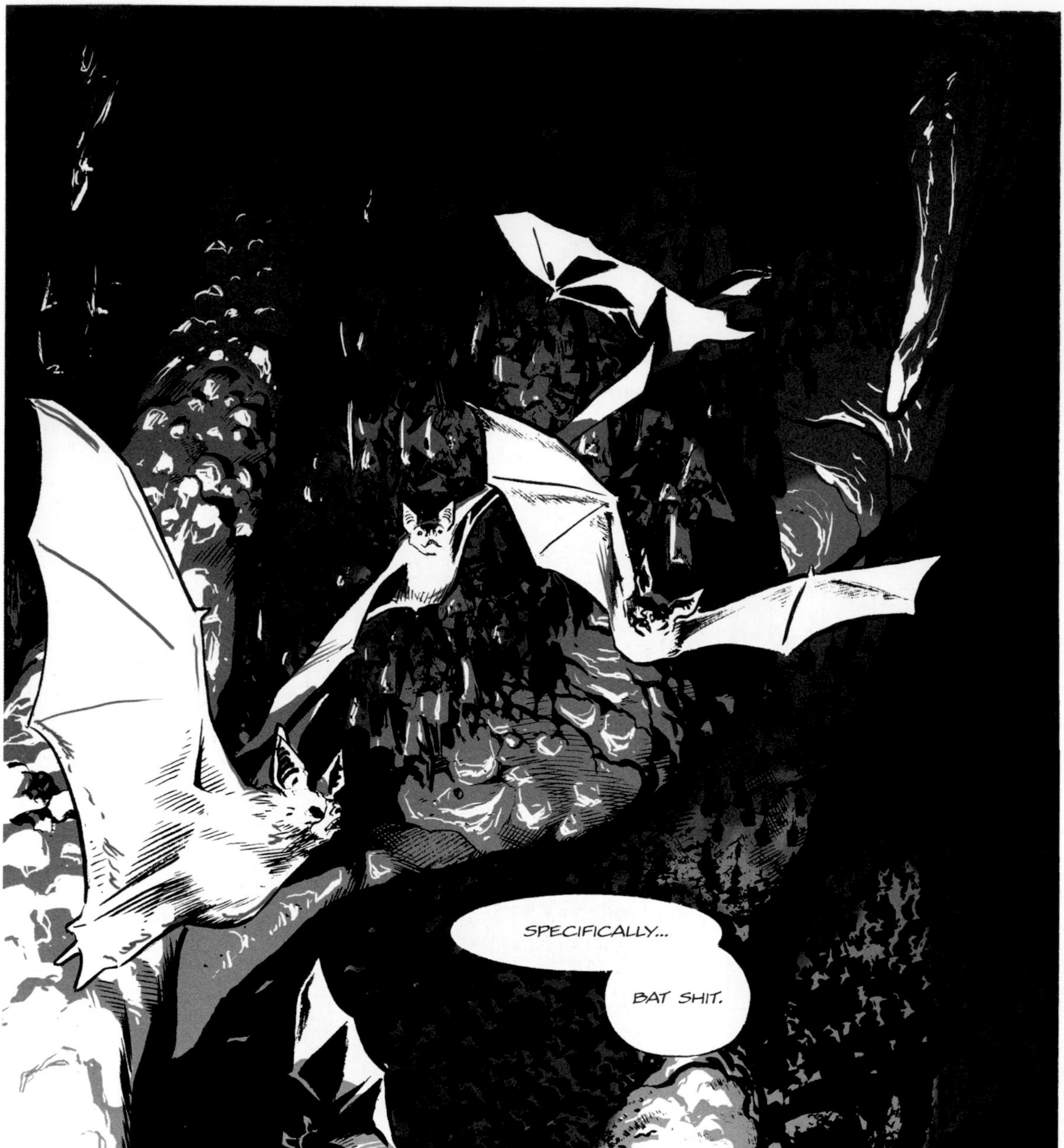
SPECIFICALLY...
BAT SHIT.

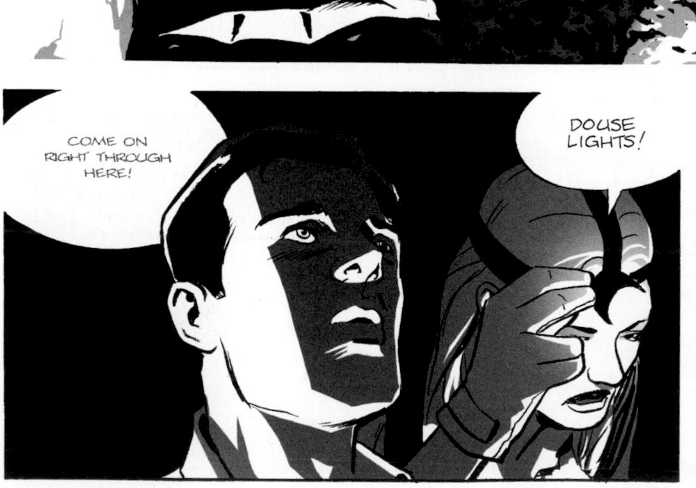
COME ON RIGHT THROUGH HERE!
DOUSE LIGHTS!

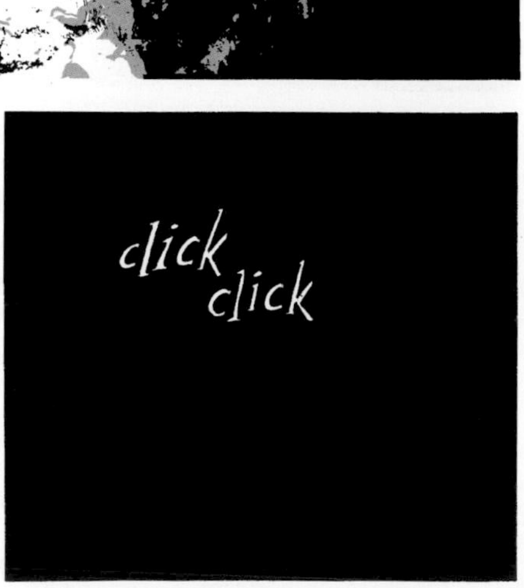
click
click

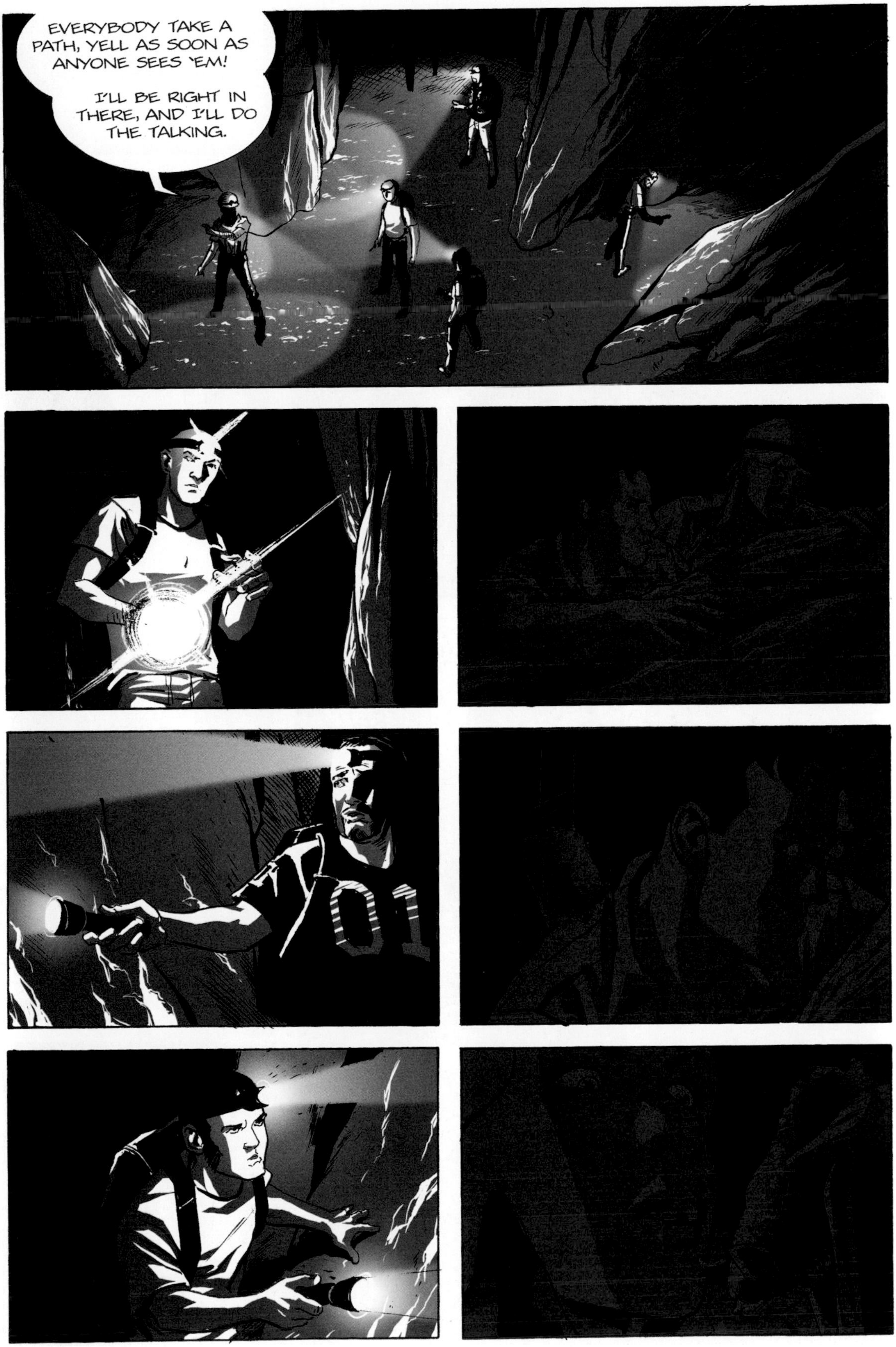
EVERYBODY TAKE A PATH, YELL AS SOON AS ANYONE SEES 'EM!
I'LL BE RIGHT IN THERE, AND I'LL DO THE TALKING.

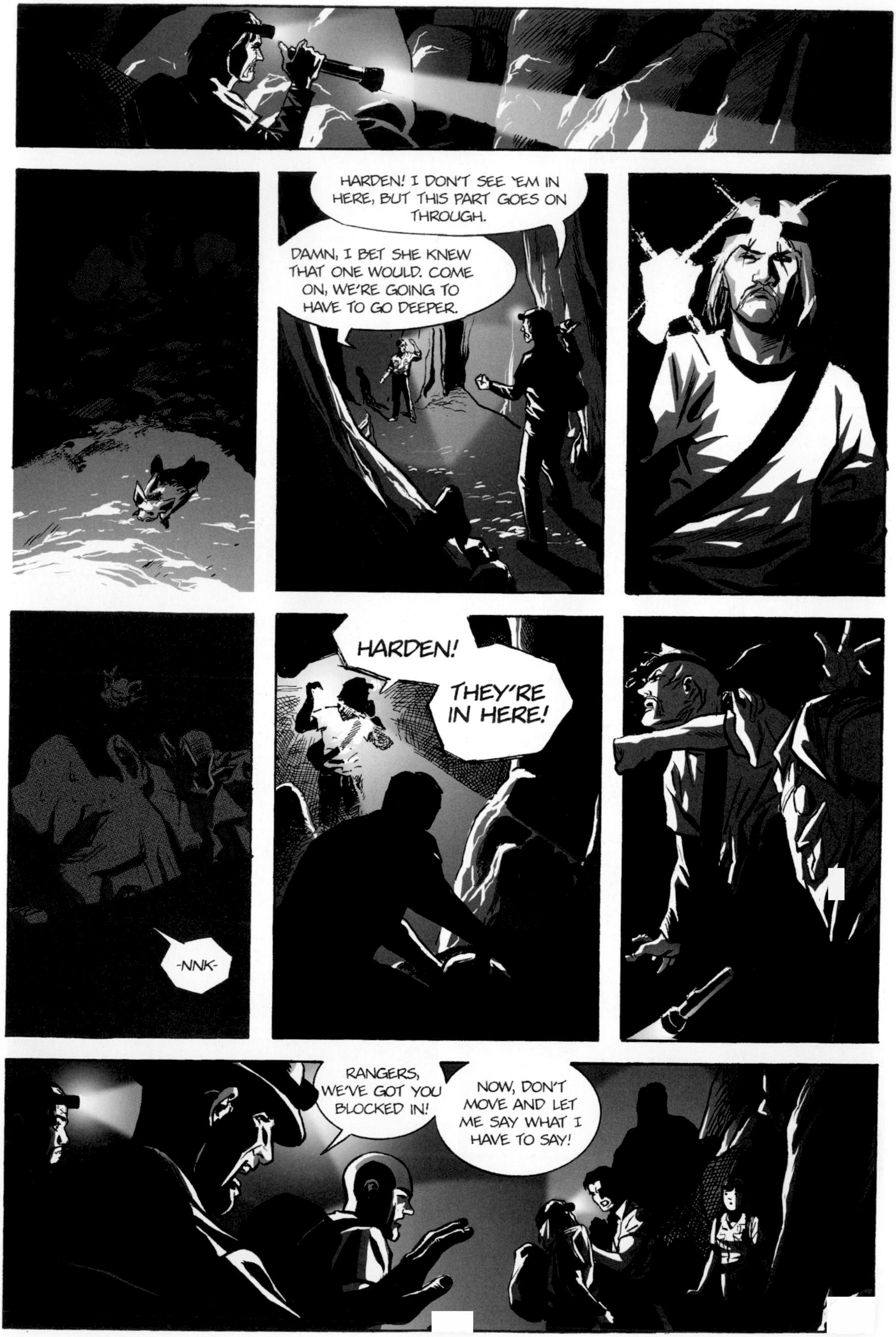
HARDEN! I DON'T SEE 'EM IN HERE, BUT THIS PART GOES ON THROUGH.
DAMN, I BET SHE KNEW THAT ONE WOULD. COME ON, WE'RE GOING TO HAVE TO GO DEEPER.
-NNK-
HARDEN!
THEY'RE IN HERE!
RANGERS, WE'VE GOT YOU BLOCKED IN!
NOW, DON'T MOVE AND LET ME SAY WHAT I HAVE TO SAY!

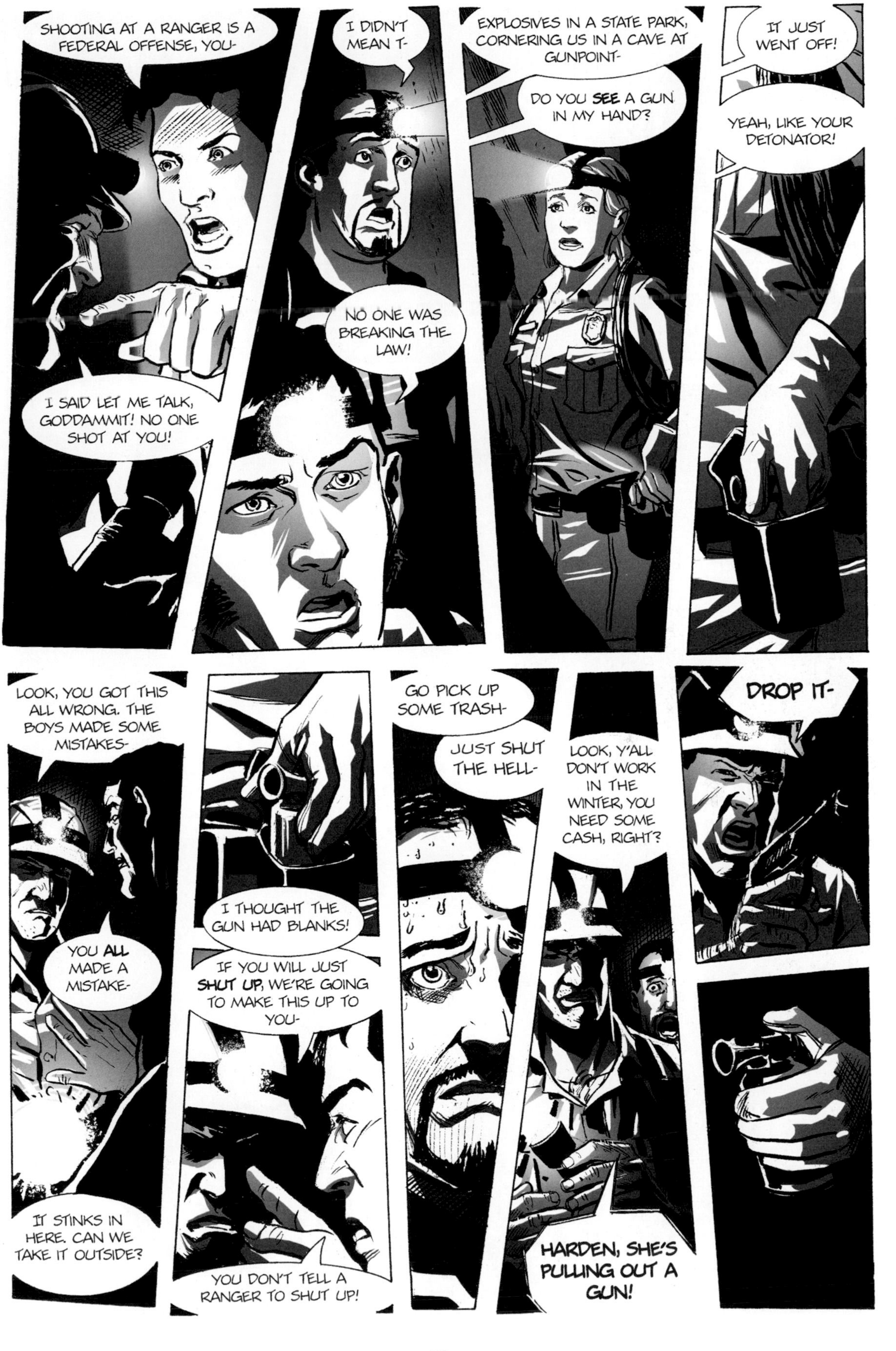
SHOOTING AT A RANGER IS A FEDERAL OFFENSE, YOU-
I SAID LET ME TALK, GODDAMMIT! NO ONE SHOT AT YOU!
I DIDN'T MEAN T-
NO ONE WAS BREAKING THE LAW!
EXPLOSIVES IN A STATE PARK, CORNERING US IN A CAVE AT GUNPOINT-
DO YOU SEE A GUN IN MY HAND?
IT JUST WENT OFF!
YEAH, LIKE YOUR DETONATOR!
LOOK, YOU GOT THIS ALL WRONG. THE BOYS MADE SOME MISTAKES-
YOU ALL MADE A MISTAKE-
IT STINKS IN HERE. CAN WE TAKE IT OUTSIDE?
I THOUGHT THE GUN HAD BLANKS!
IF YOU WILL JUST SHUT UP, WE'RE GOING TO MAKE THIS UP TO YOU-
YOU DON'T TELL A RANGER TO SHUT UP!
GO PICK UP SOME TRASH-
JUST SHUT THE HELL-
LOOK, Y'ALL DON'T WORK IN THE WINTER, YOU NEED SOME CASH, RIGHT?
HARDEN, SHE'S PULLING OUT A GUN!
DROP IT-

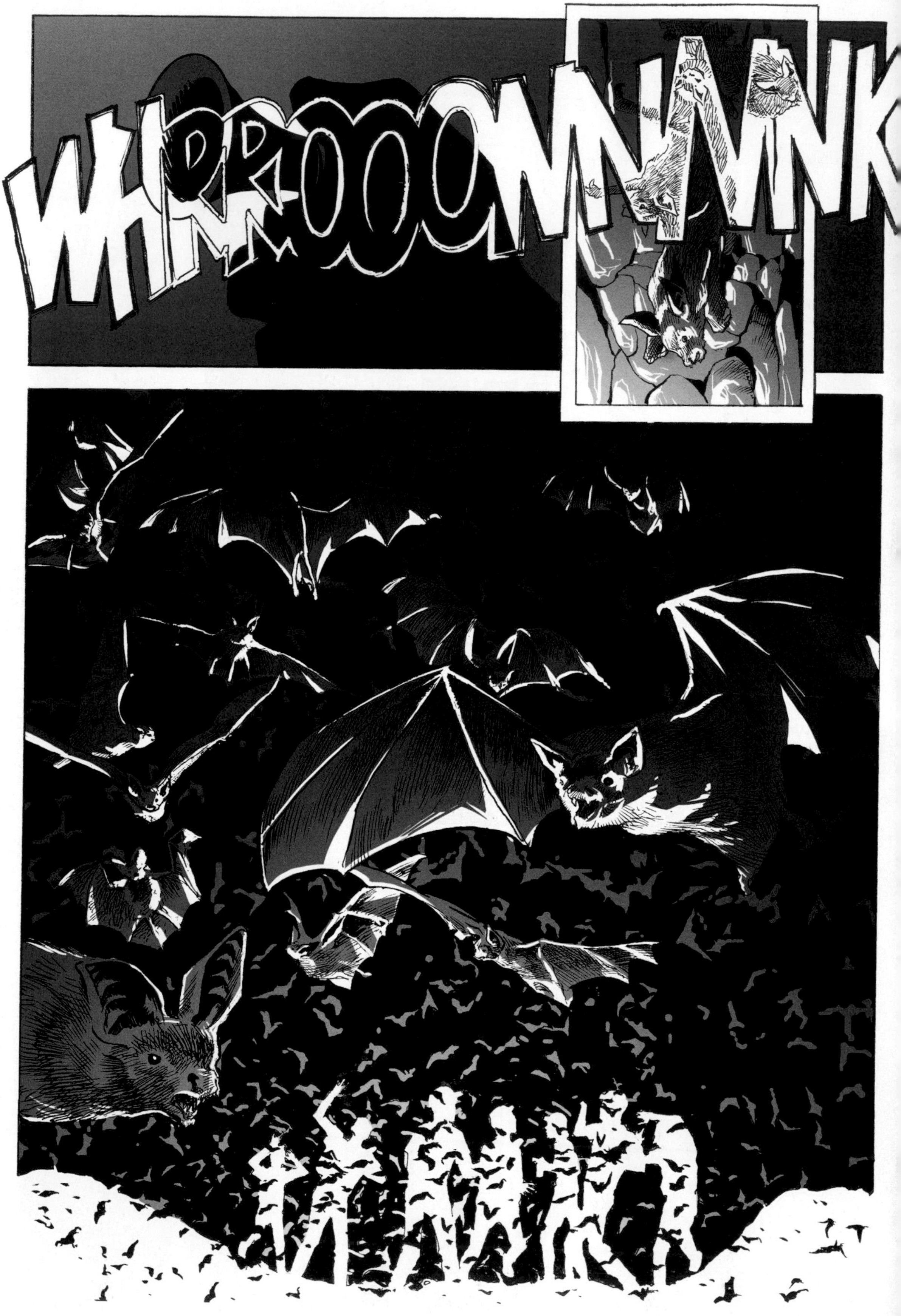
WHRROOOOMNNNK

CHAPTER THREE

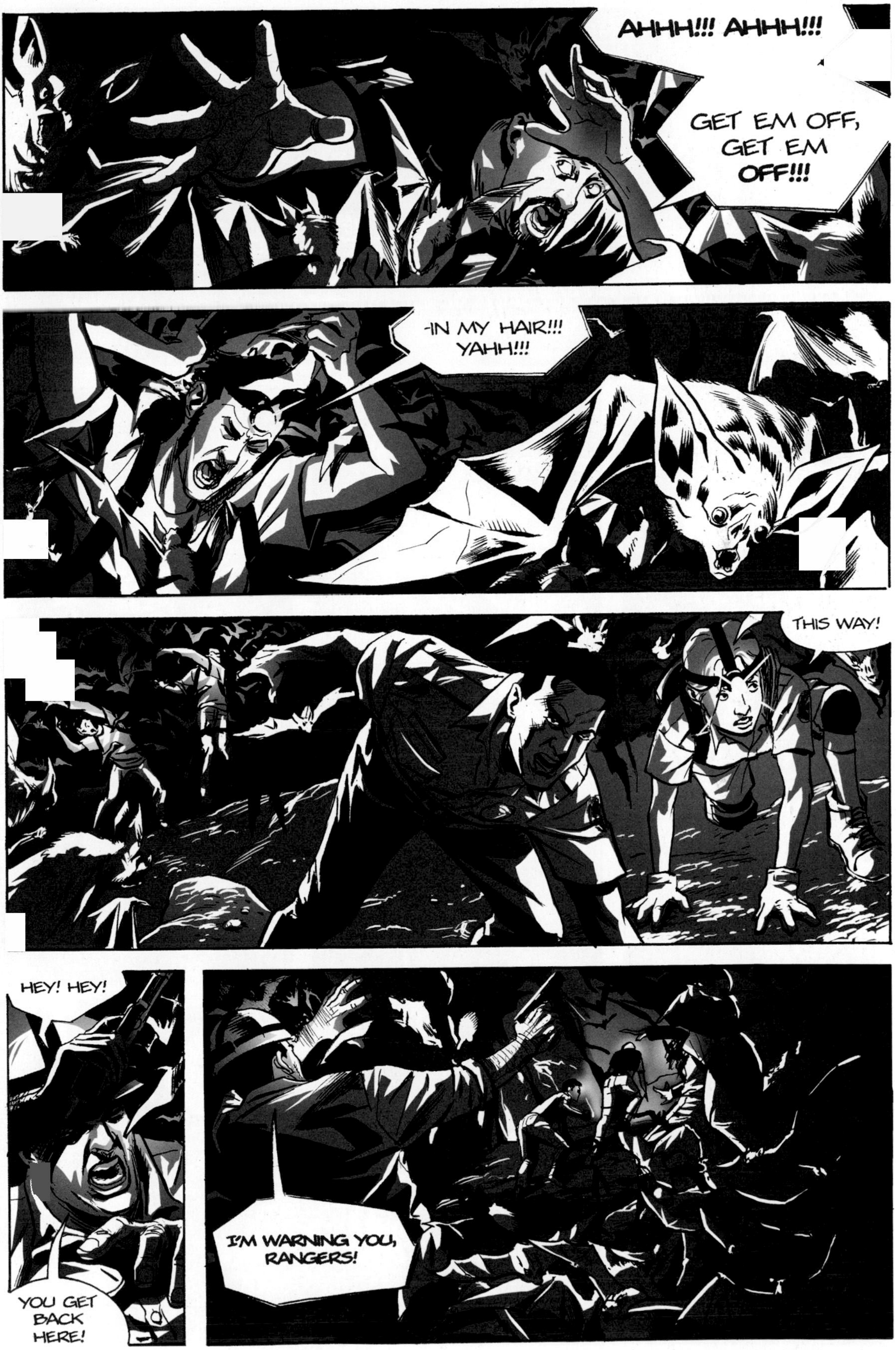
AHHH!!! AHHH!!!
GET EM OFF, GET EM OFF!!!
-IN MY HAIR!!! YAHH!!!
THIS WAY!
HEY! HEY!
YOU GET BACK HERE!
I'M WARNING YOU, RANGERS!

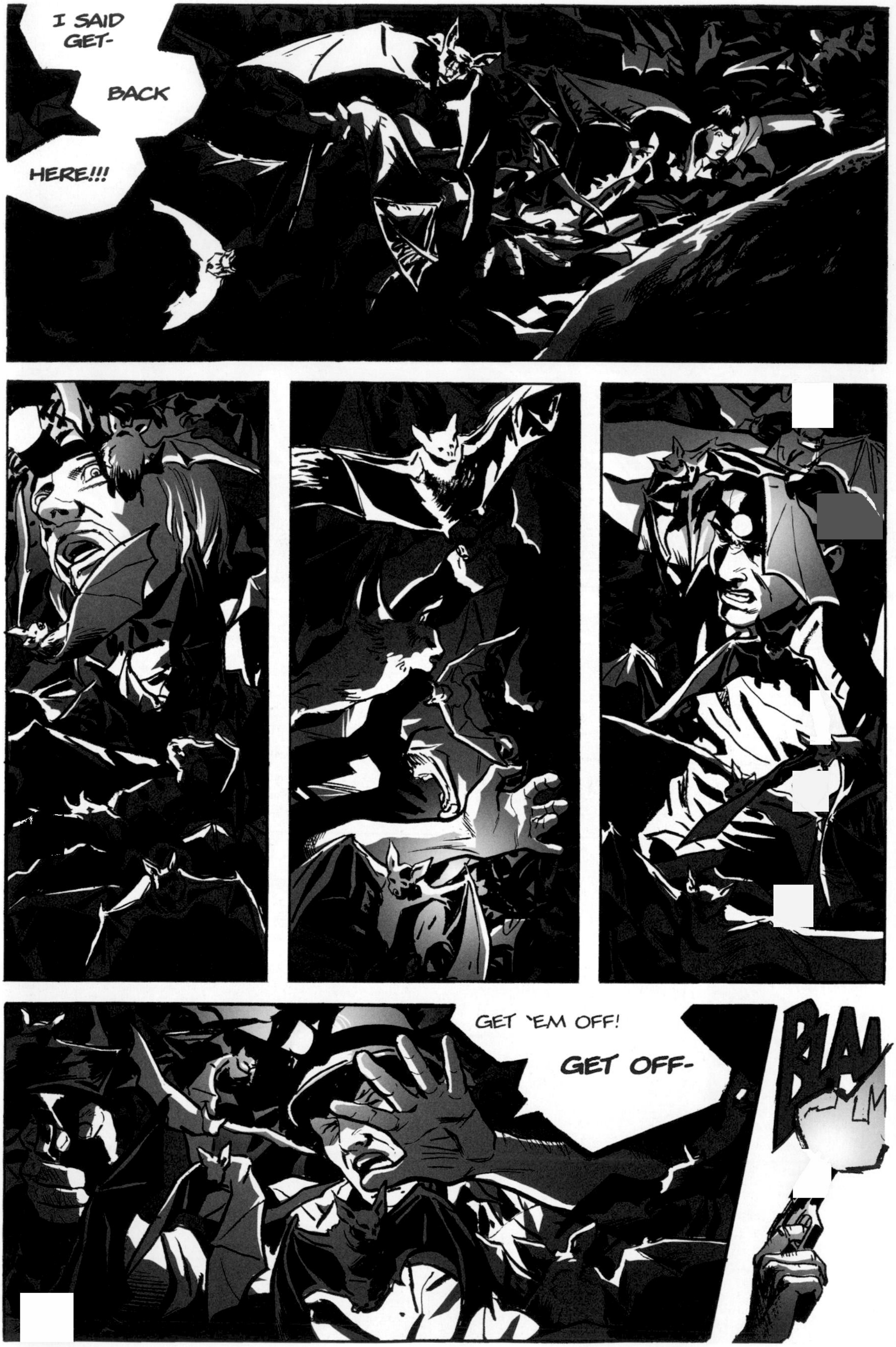
I SAID GET-
BACK
HERE!!!
GET 'EM OFF!
GET OFF-
BLAM

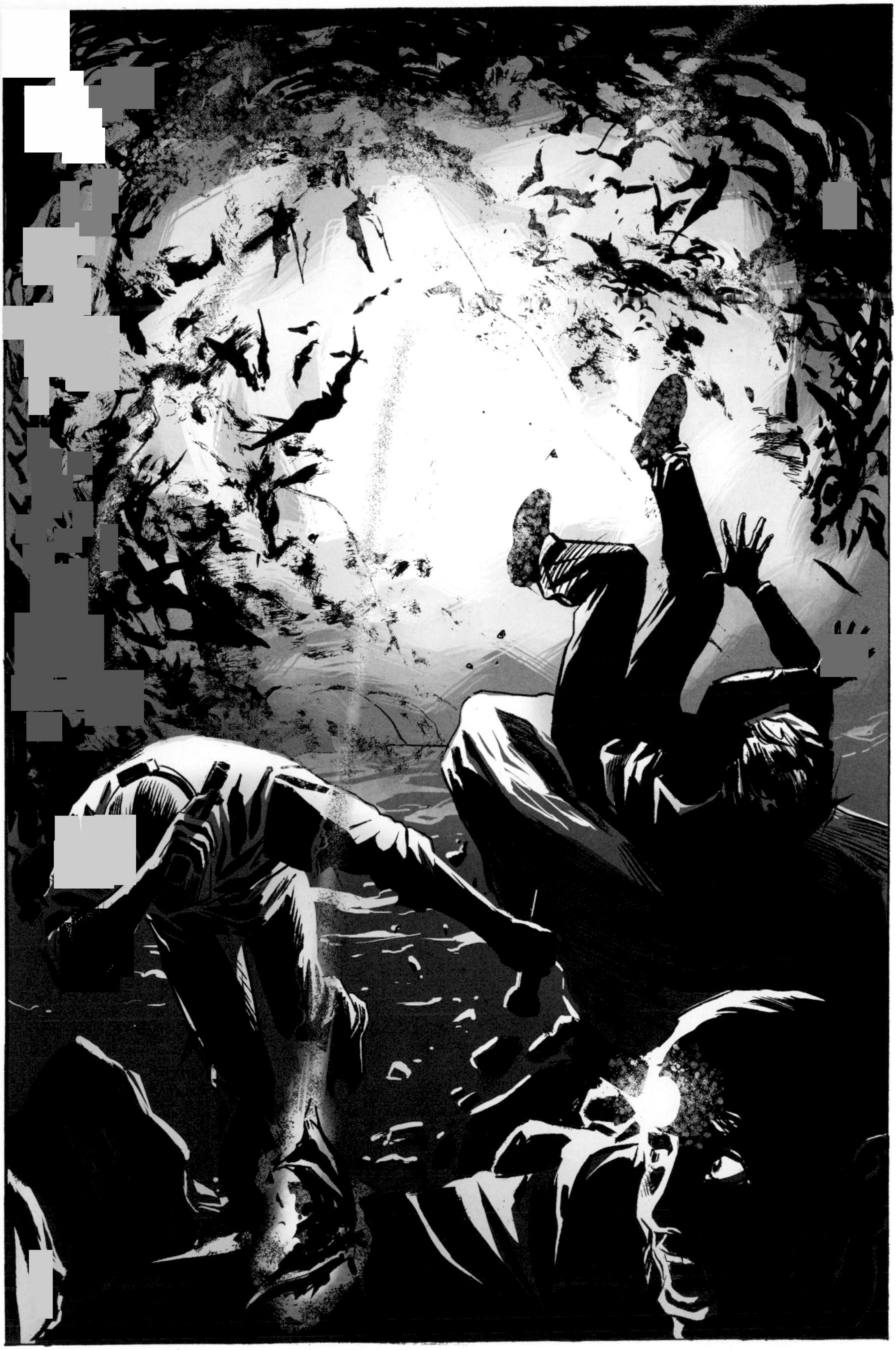

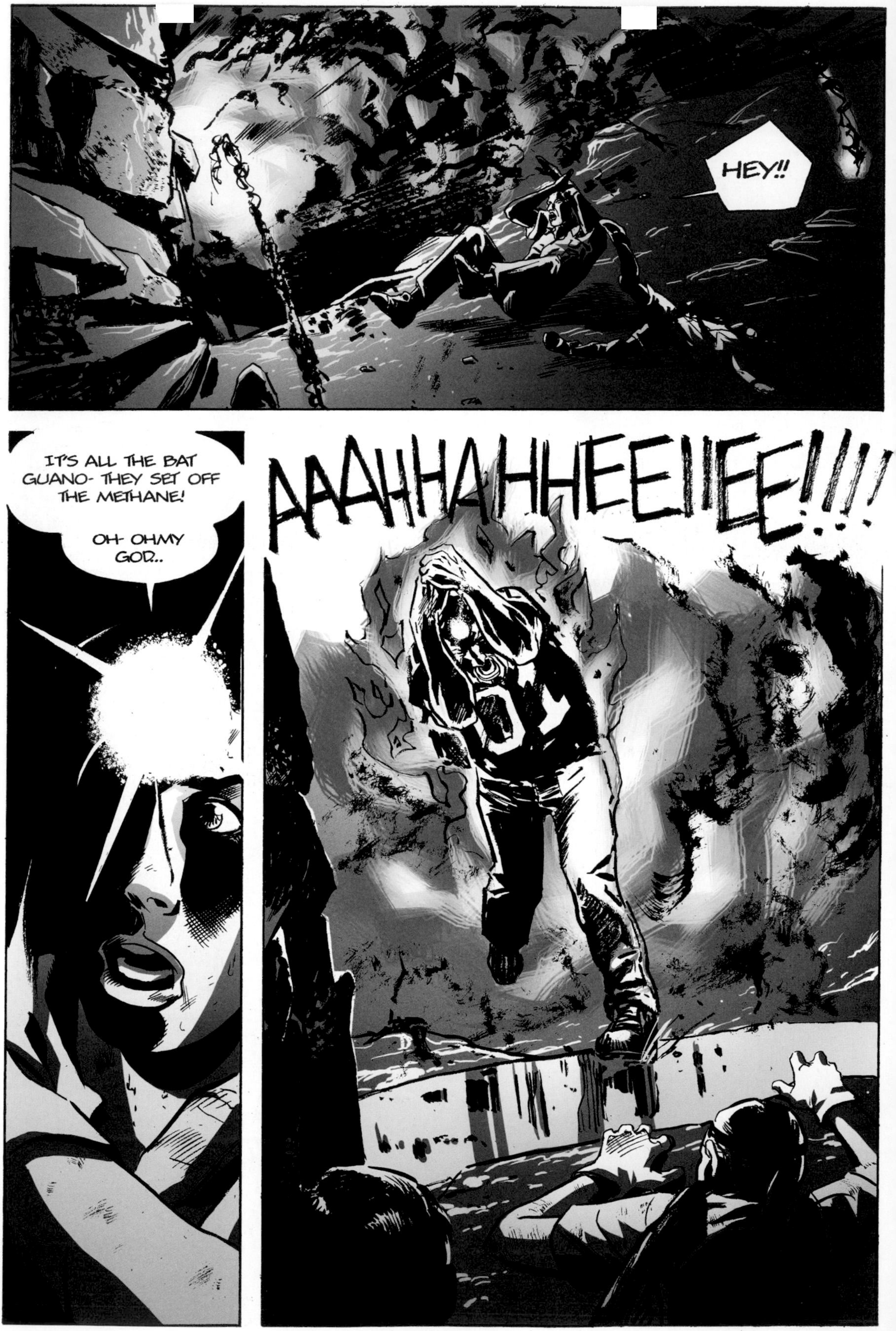
HEY!!
IT'S ALL THE BAT GUANO- THEY SET OFF THE METHANE!
OH- OH MY GOD..
AAAHHAHHEEIIEE!!!!

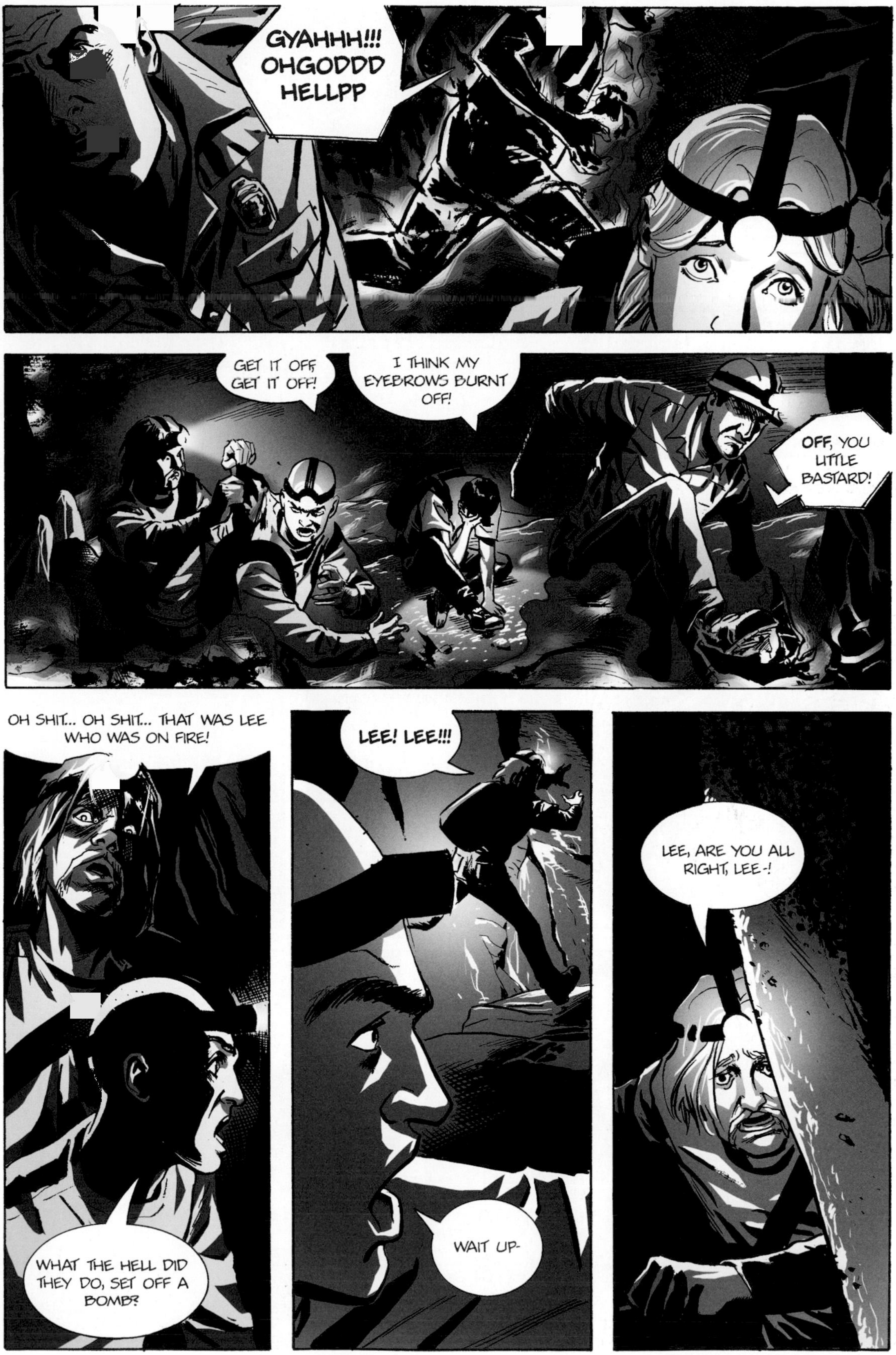
GYAHHH!!! OHGODDD HELLPP
GET IT OFF, GET IT OFF!
I THINK MY EYEBROWS BURNT OFF!
OFF, YOU LITTLE BASTARD!
OH SHIT... OH SHIT... THAT WAS LEE WHO WAS ON FIRE!
WHAT THE HELL DID THEY DO, SET OFF A BOMB?
LEE! LEE!!!
WAIT UP-
LEE, ARE YOU ALL RIGHT, LEE-!

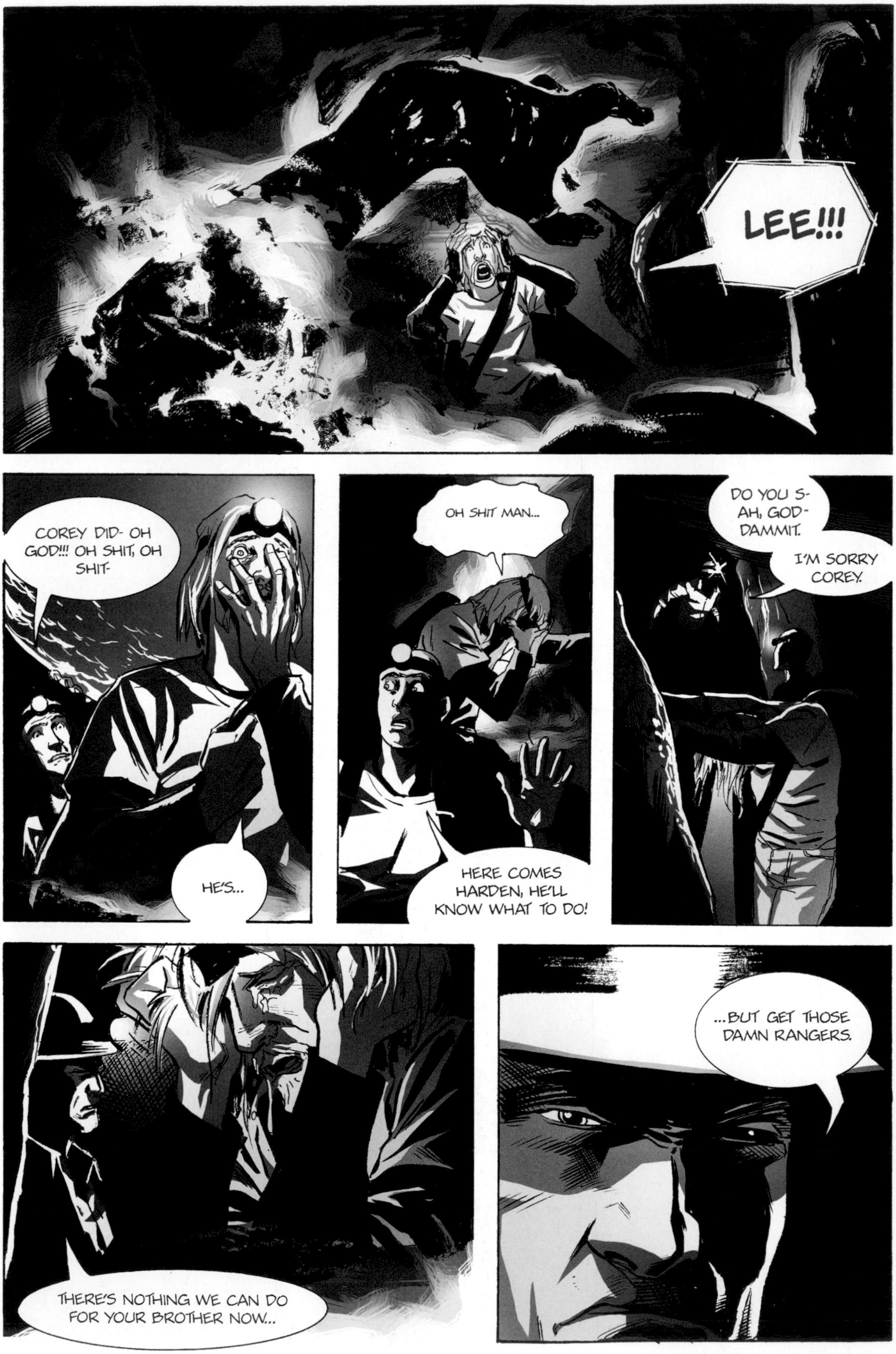
LEE!!!
COREY DID- OH GOD!!! OH SHIT, OH SHIT-
HE'S...
OH SHIT MAN...
HERE COMES HARDEN, HE'LL KNOW WHAT TO DO!
DO YOU S- AH, GOD-DAMMIT.
I'M SORRY COREY.
THERE'S NOTHING WE CAN DO FOR YOUR BROTHER NOW...
...BUT GET THOSE DAMN RANGERS.

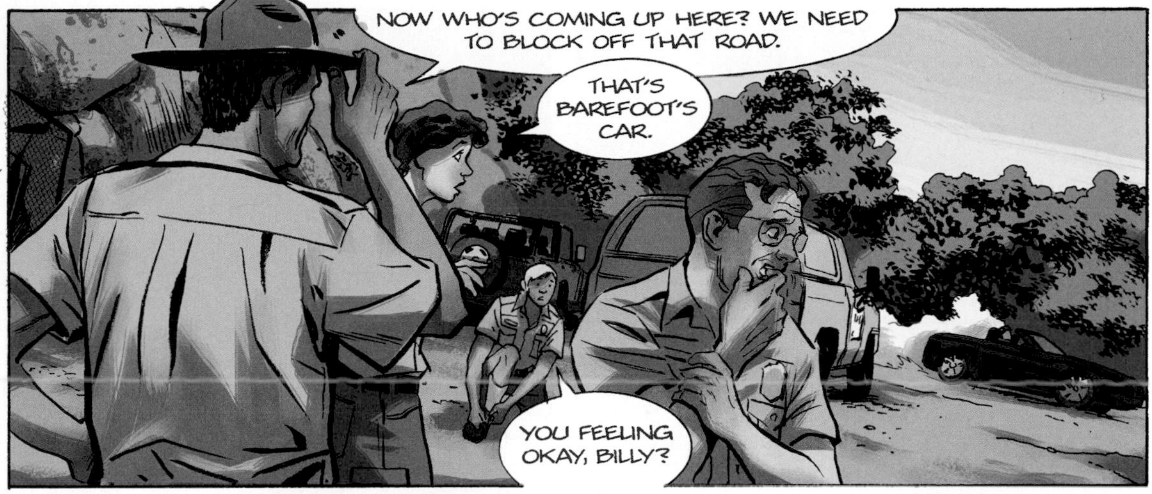
NOW WHO'S COMING UP HERE? WE NEED TO BLOCK OFF THAT ROAD.
THAT'S BAREFOOT'S CAR.
YOU FEELING OKAY, BILLY?

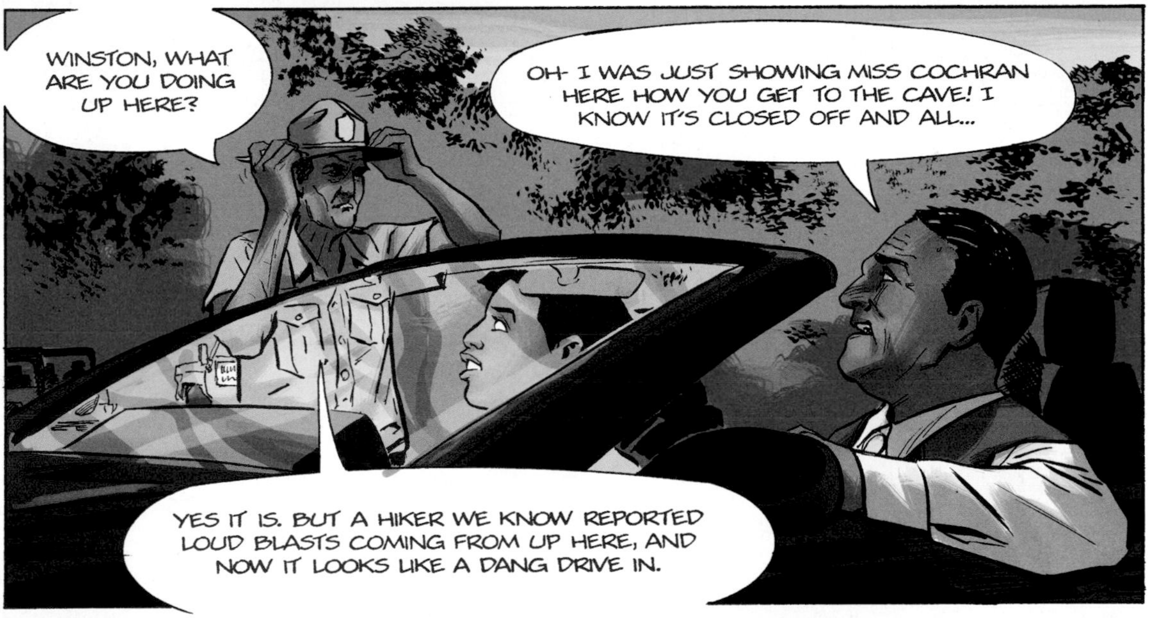
WINSTON, WHAT ARE YOU DOING UP HERE?
OH- I WAS JUST SHOWING MISS COCHRAN HERE HOW YOU GET TO THE CAVE! I KNOW IT'S CLOSED OFF AND ALL...
YES IT IS. BUT A HIKER WE KNOW REPORTED LOUD BLASTS COMING FROM UP HERE, AND NOW IT LOOKS LIKE A DANG DRIVE IN.

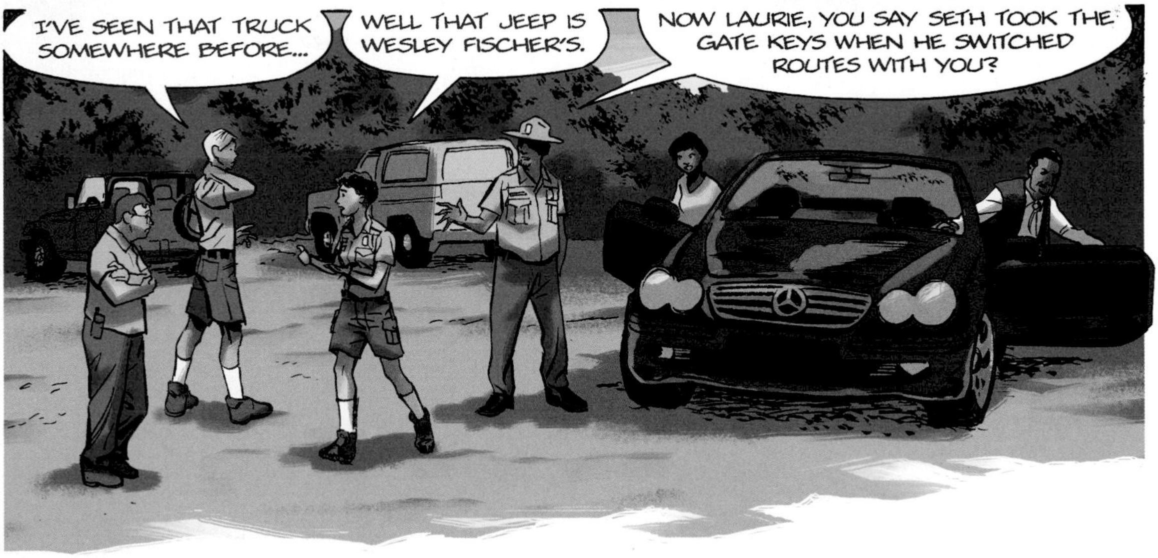
I'VE SEEN THAT TRUCK SOMEWHERE BEFORE...
WELL THAT JEEP IS WESLEY FISCHER'S.
NOW LAURIE, YOU SAY SETH TOOK THE GATE KEYS WHEN HE SWITCHED ROUTES WITH YOU?

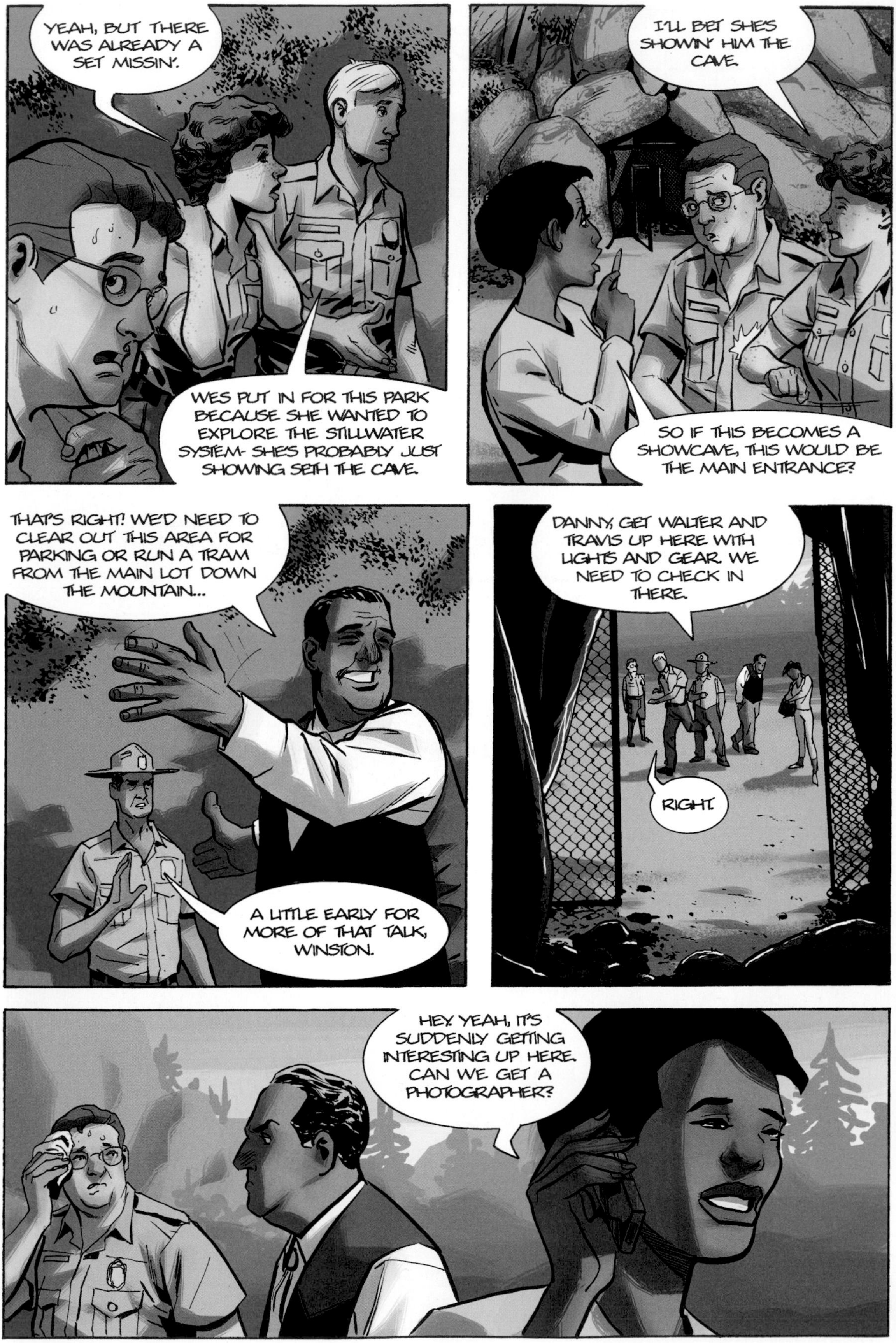

YEAH, BUT THERE WAS ALREADY A SET MISSIN'.
WES PUT IN FOR THIS PARK BECAUSE SHE WANTED TO EXPLORE THE STILLWATER SYSTEM- SHE'S PROBABLY JUST SHOWING SETH THE CAVE.
I'LL BET SHE'S SHOWIN' HIM THE CAVE.
SO IF THIS BECOMES A SHOWCAVE, THIS WOULD BE THE MAIN ENTRANCE?
THAT'S RIGHT! WE'D NEED TO CLEAR OUT THIS AREA FOR PARKING OR RUN A TRAM FROM THE MAIN LOT DOWN THE MOUNTAIN...
A LITTLE EARLY FOR MORE OF THAT TALK, WINSTON.
DANNY, GET WALTER AND TRAVIS UP HERE WITH LIGHTS AND GEAR. WE NEED TO CHECK IN THERE.
RIGHT.
HEY. YEAH, IT'S SUDDENLY GETTING INTERESTING UP HERE. CAN WE GET A PHOTOGRAPHER?

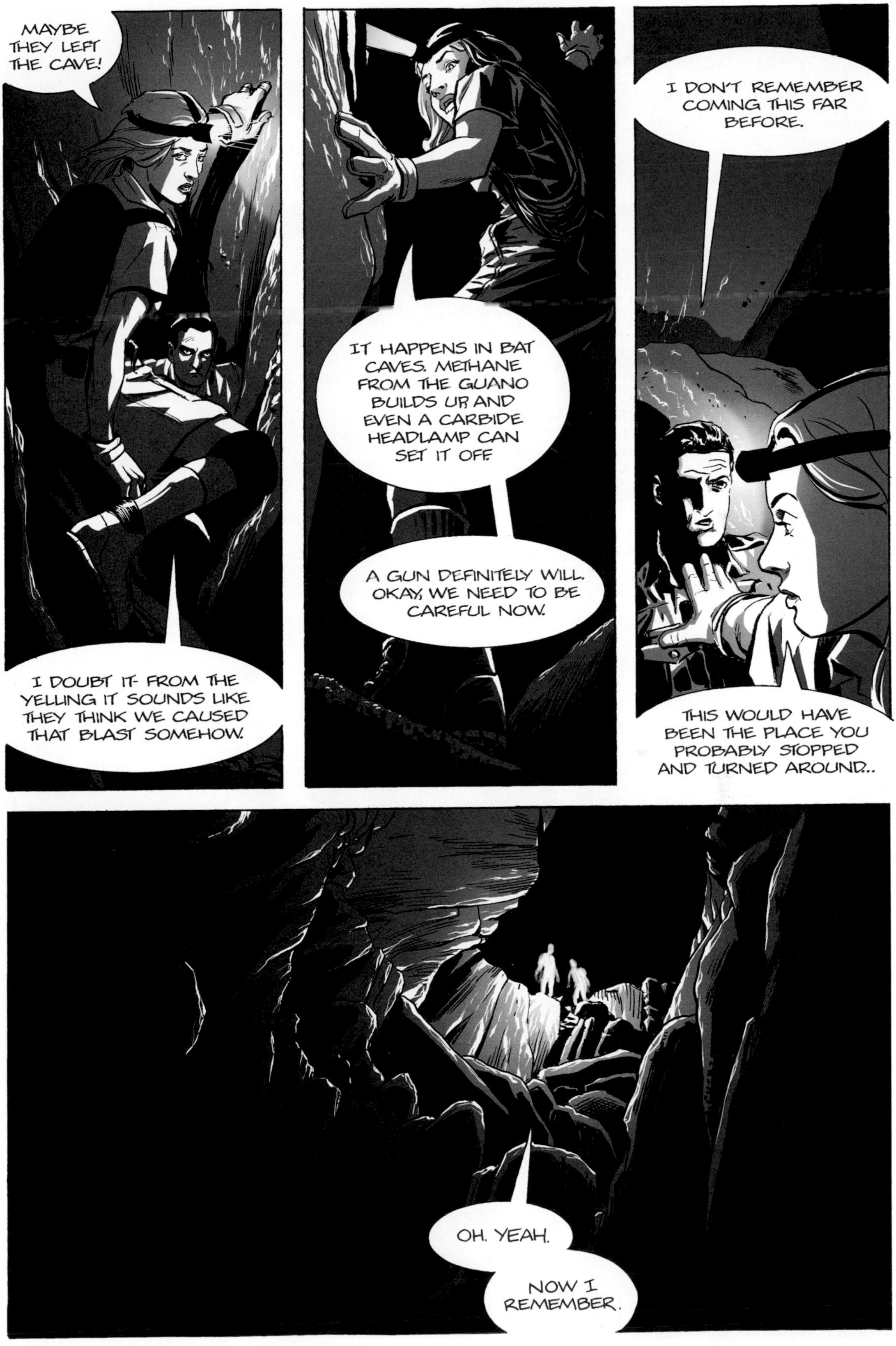
MAYBE THEY LEFT THE CAVE!
I DOUBT IT- FROM THE YELLING IT SOUNDS LIKE THEY THINK WE CAUSED THAT BLAST SOMEHOW.
IT HAPPENS IN BAT CAVES. METHANE FROM THE GUANO BUILDS UP, AND EVEN A CARBIDE HEADLAMP CAN SET IT OFF.
A GUN DEFINITELY WILL. OKAY, WE NEED TO BE CAREFUL NOW.
I DON'T REMEMBER COMING THIS FAR BEFORE.
THIS WOULD HAVE BEEN THE PLACE YOU PROBABLY STOPPED AND TURNED AROUND..
OH. YEAH.
NOW I REMEMBER.

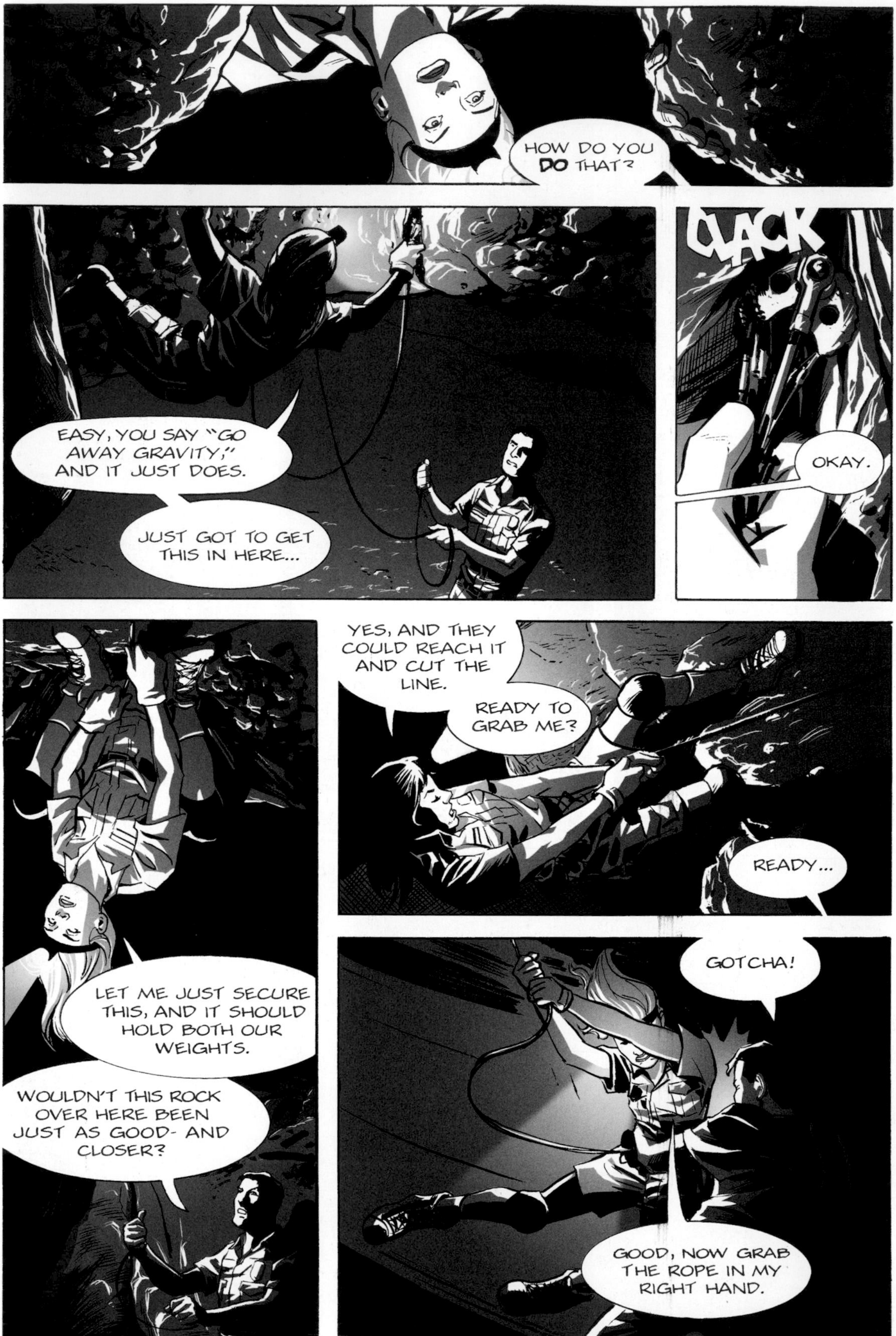
HOW DO YOU DO THAT?
EASY, YOU SAY "GO AWAY GRAVITY," AND IT JUST DOES.
JUST GOT TO GET THIS IN HERE...
CLACK
OKAY.
LET ME JUST SECURE THIS, AND IT SHOULD HOLD BOTH OUR WEIGHTS.
WOULDN'T THIS ROCK OVER HERE BEEN JUST AS GOOD- AND CLOSER?
YES, AND THEY COULD REACH IT AND CUT THE LINE.
READY TO GRAB ME?
READY...
GOTCHA!
GOOD, NOW GRAB THE ROPE IN MY RIGHT HAND.

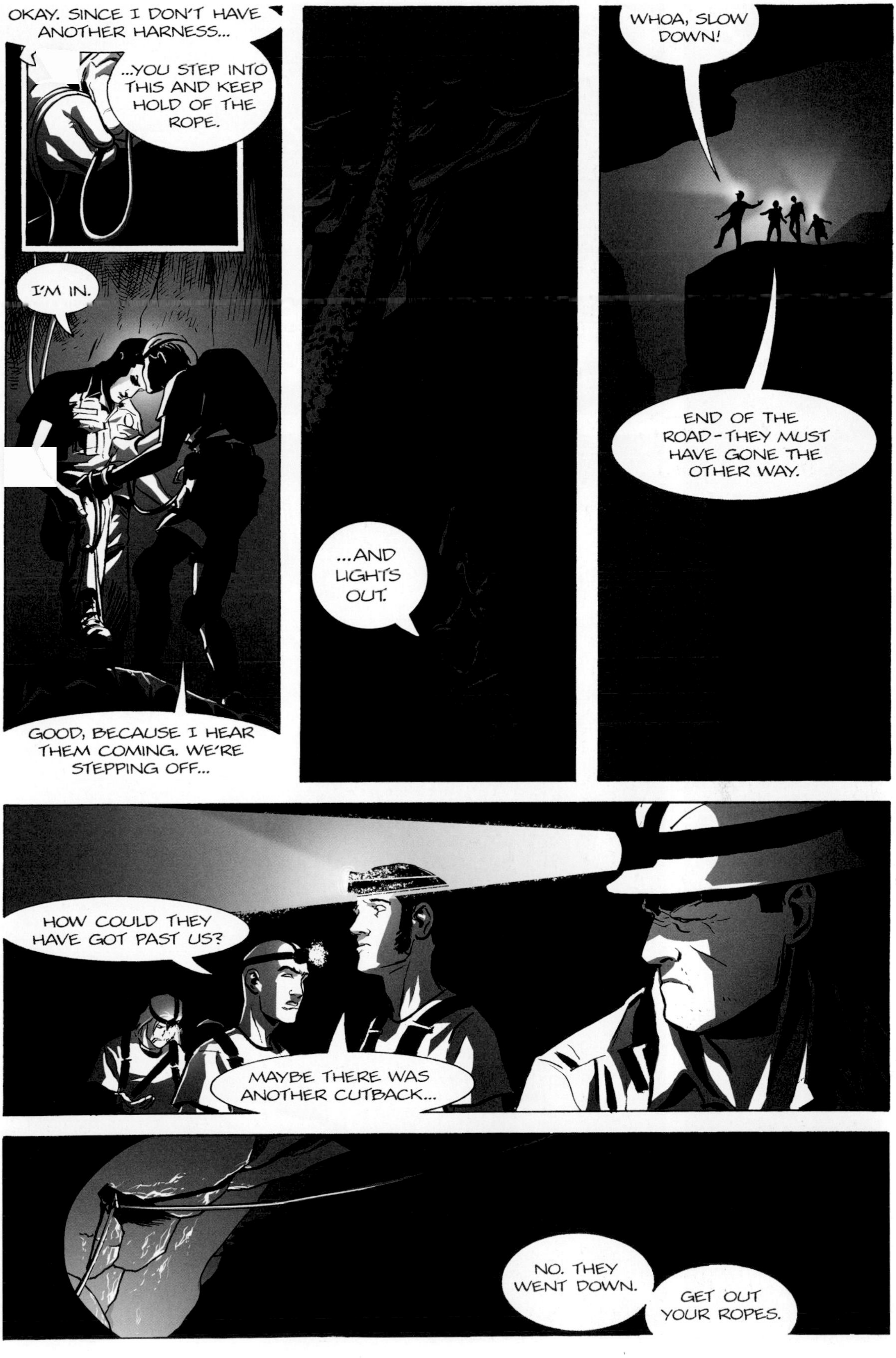
OKAY. SINCE I DON'T HAVE ANOTHER HARNESS...
...YOU STEP INTO THIS AND KEEP HOLD OF THE ROPE.
I'M IN.
GOOD, BECAUSE I HEAR THEM COMING. WE'RE STEPPING OFF...
...AND LIGHTS OUT.
WHOA, SLOW DOWN!
END OF THE ROAD - THEY MUST HAVE GONE THE OTHER WAY.
HOW COULD THEY HAVE GOT PAST US?
MAYBE THERE WAS ANOTHER CUTBACK...
NO. THEY WENT DOWN.
GET OUT YOUR ROPES.

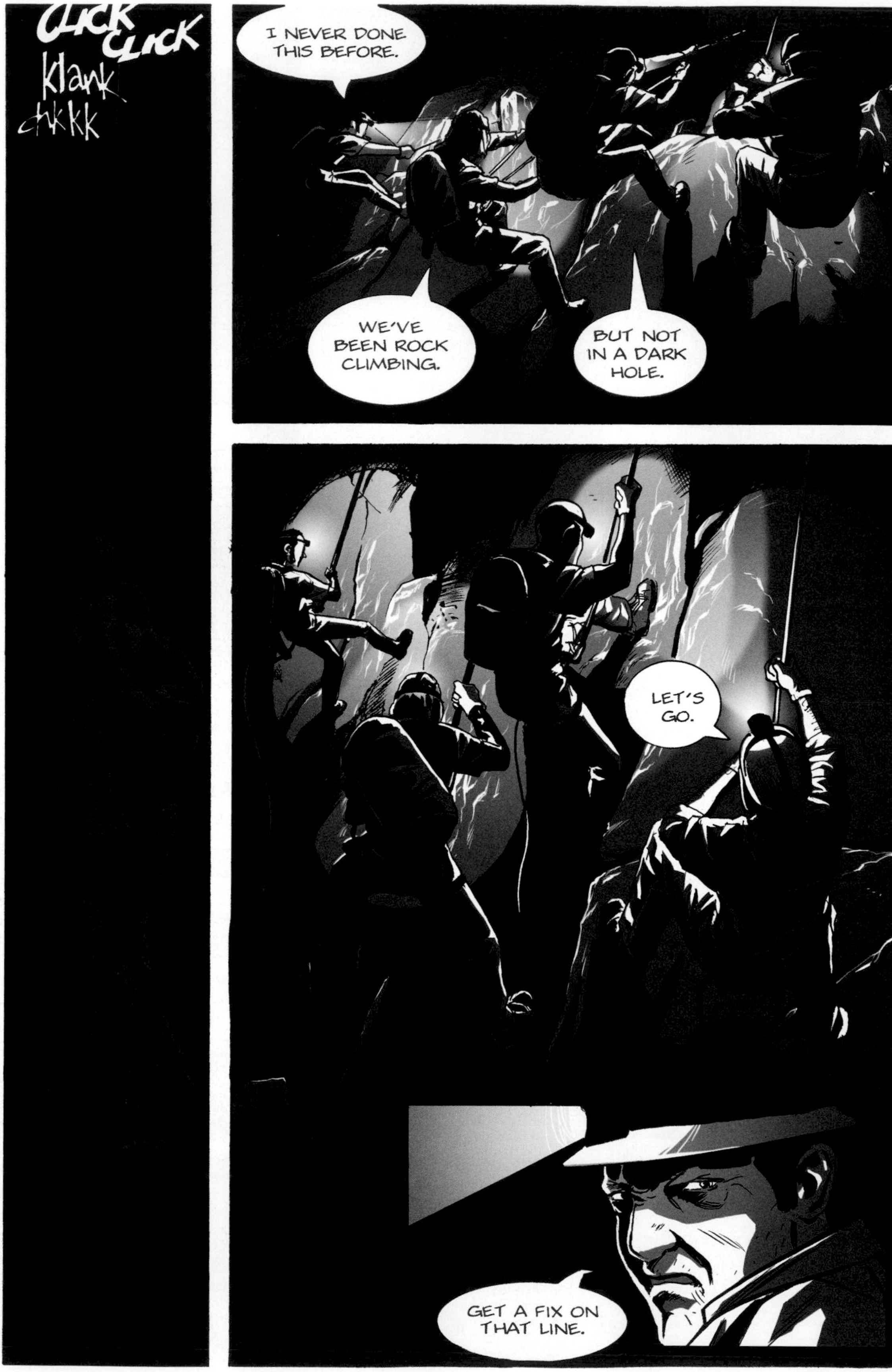
CLICK CLICK
klank
chkkk
I NEVER DONE THIS BEFORE.
WE'VE BEEN ROCK CLIMBING.
BUT NOT IN A DARK HOLE.
LET'S GO.
GET A FIX ON THAT LINE.

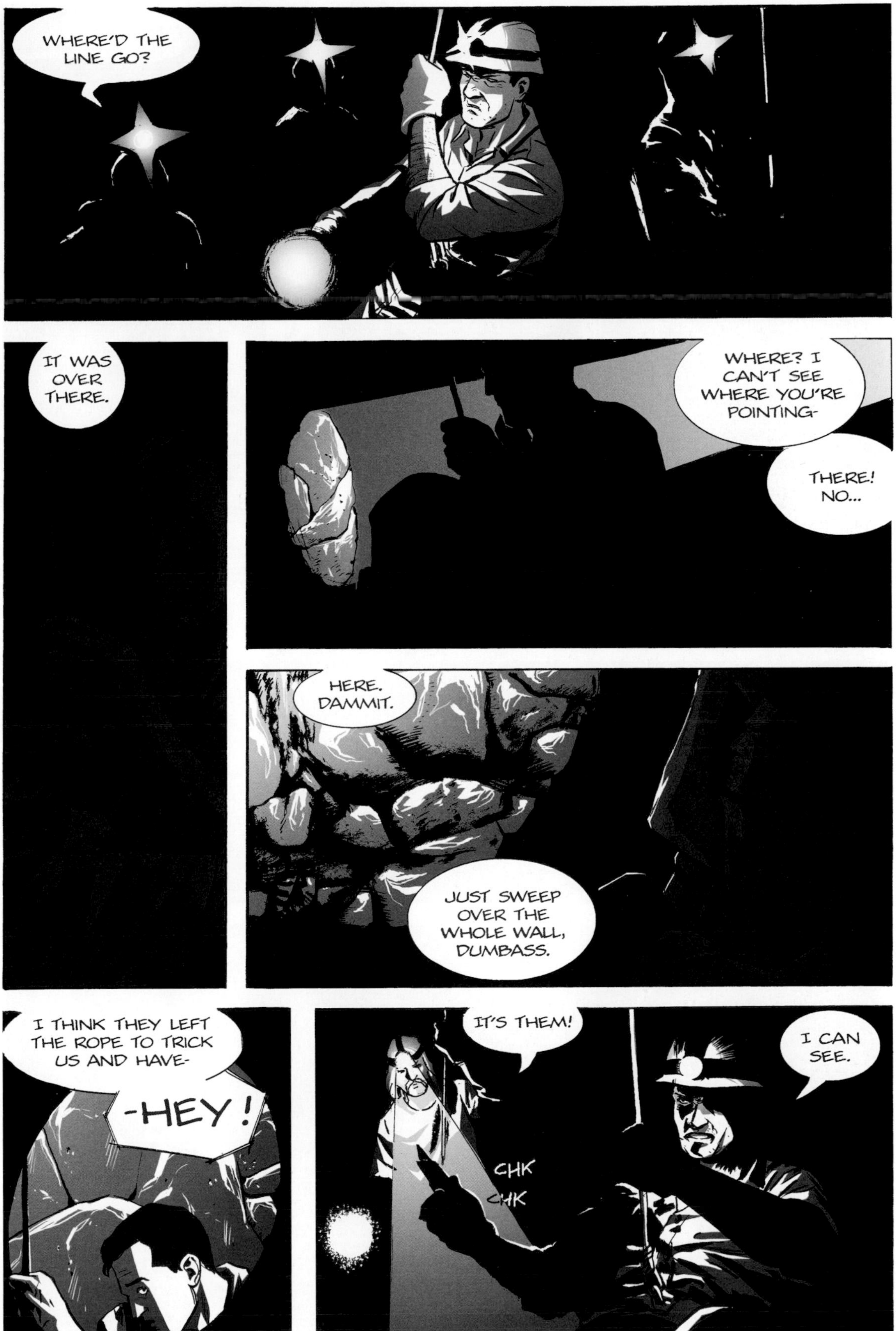
WHERE'D THE LINE GO?
IT WAS OVER THERE.
WHERE? I CAN'T SEE WHERE YOU'RE POINTING-
THERE! NO...
HERE. DAMMIT.
JUST SWEEP OVER THE WHOLE WALL, DUMBASS.
I THINK THEY LEFT THE ROPE TO TRICK US AND HAVE-
-HEY!
IT'S THEM!
I CAN SEE.
CHK
CHK

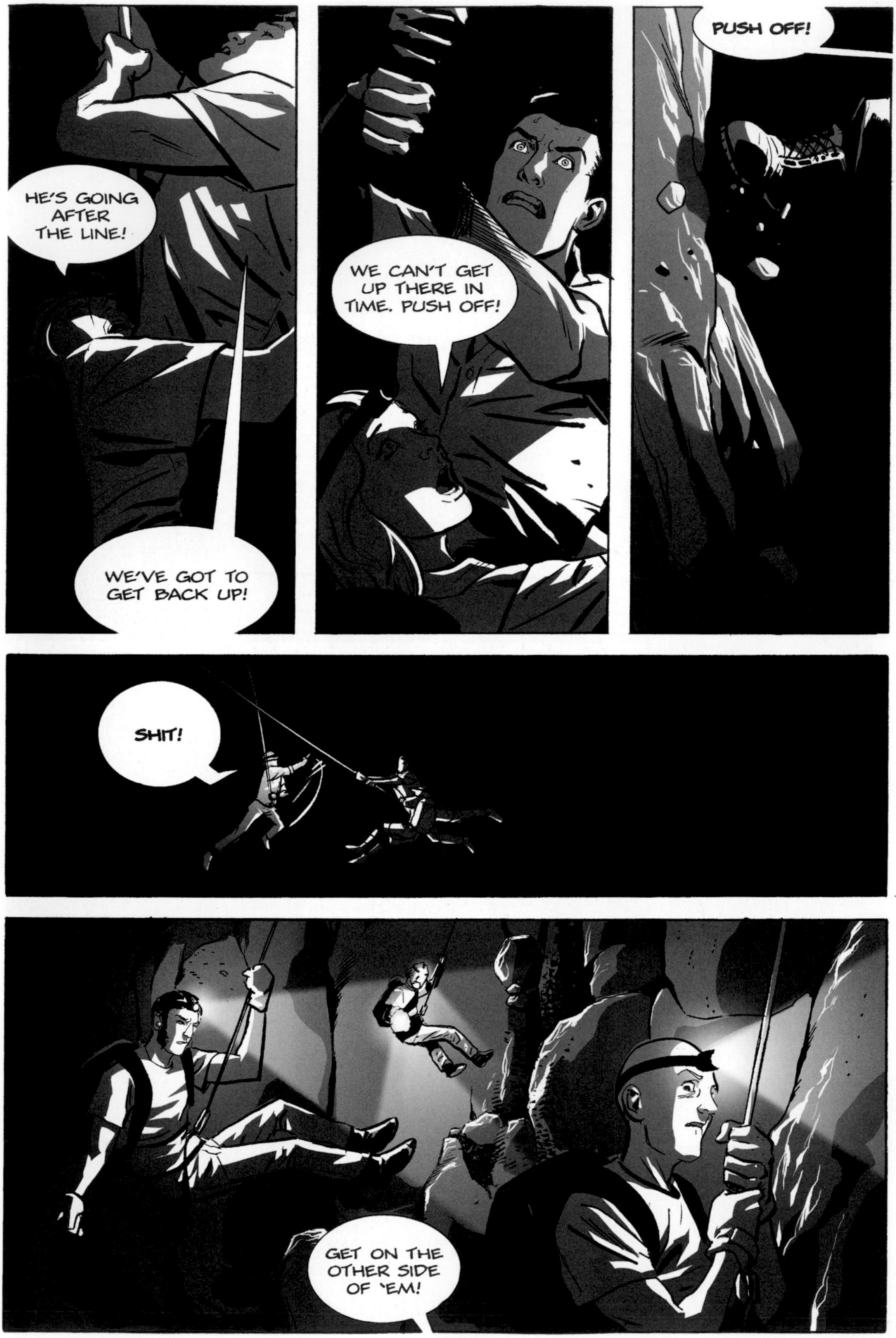
HE'S GOING AFTER THE LINE!
WE'VE GOT TO GET BACK UP!
WE CAN'T GET UP THERE IN TIME. PUSH OFF!
PUSH OFF!
SHIT!
GET ON THE OTHER SIDE OF 'EM!

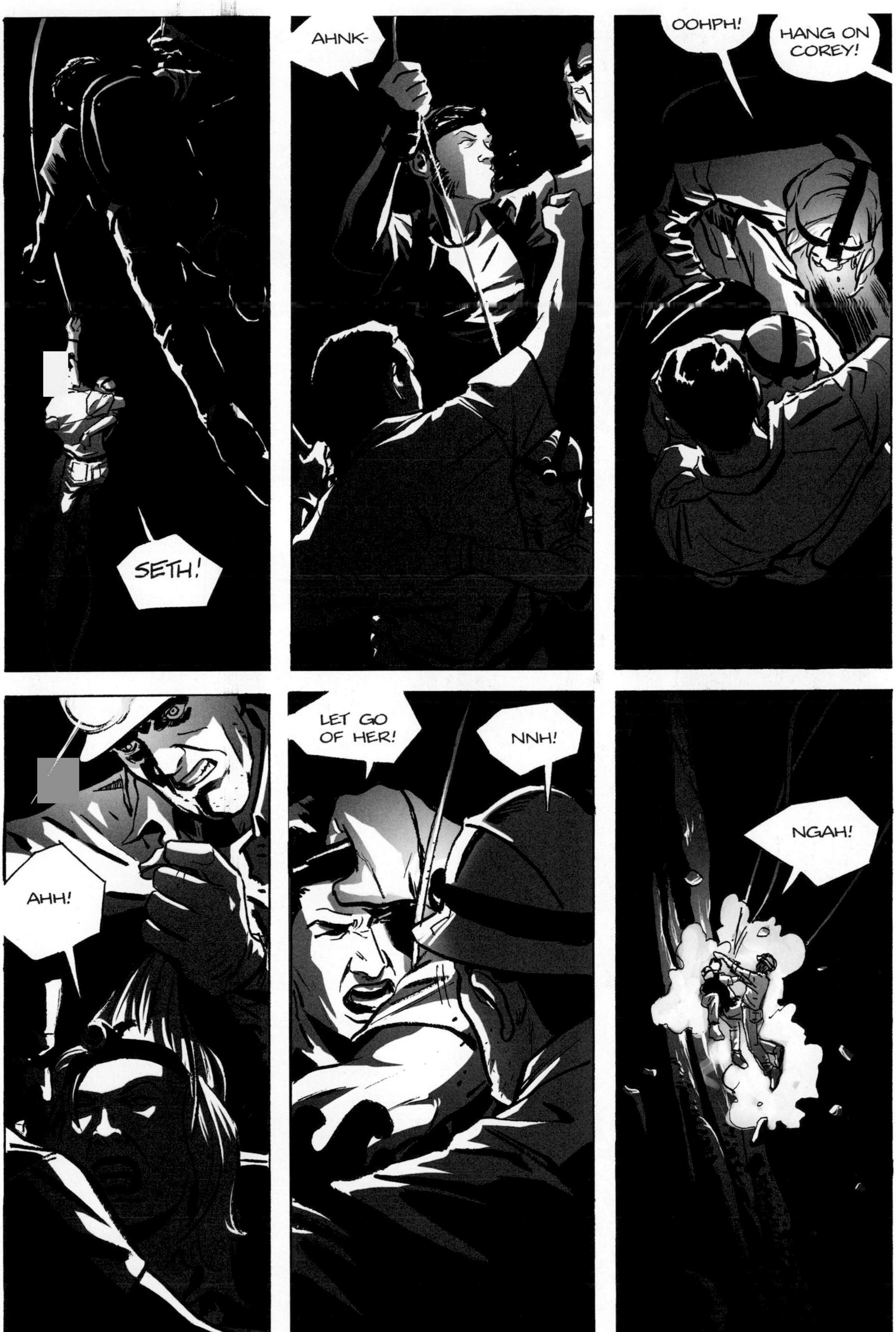
SETH!
AHNK-
OOHPH!
HANG ON COREY!
AHH!
LET GO OF HER!
NNH!
NGAH!

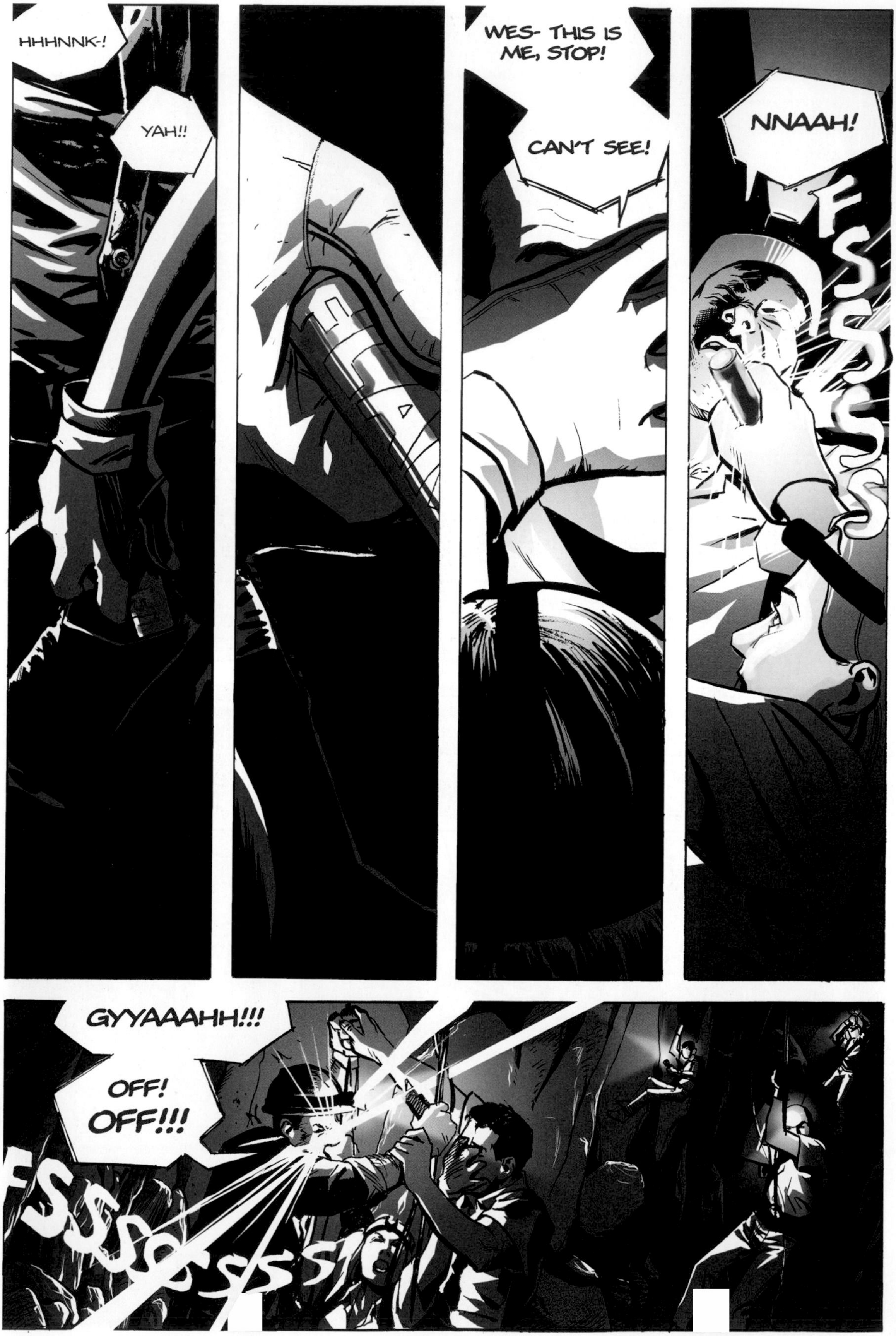
HHHNNK-!
YAH!!
WES- THIS IS ME, STOP!
CAN'T SEE!
NNAAH!
FSSSS
GYYAAAHH!!!
OFF! OFF!!!
FSSSSSSS

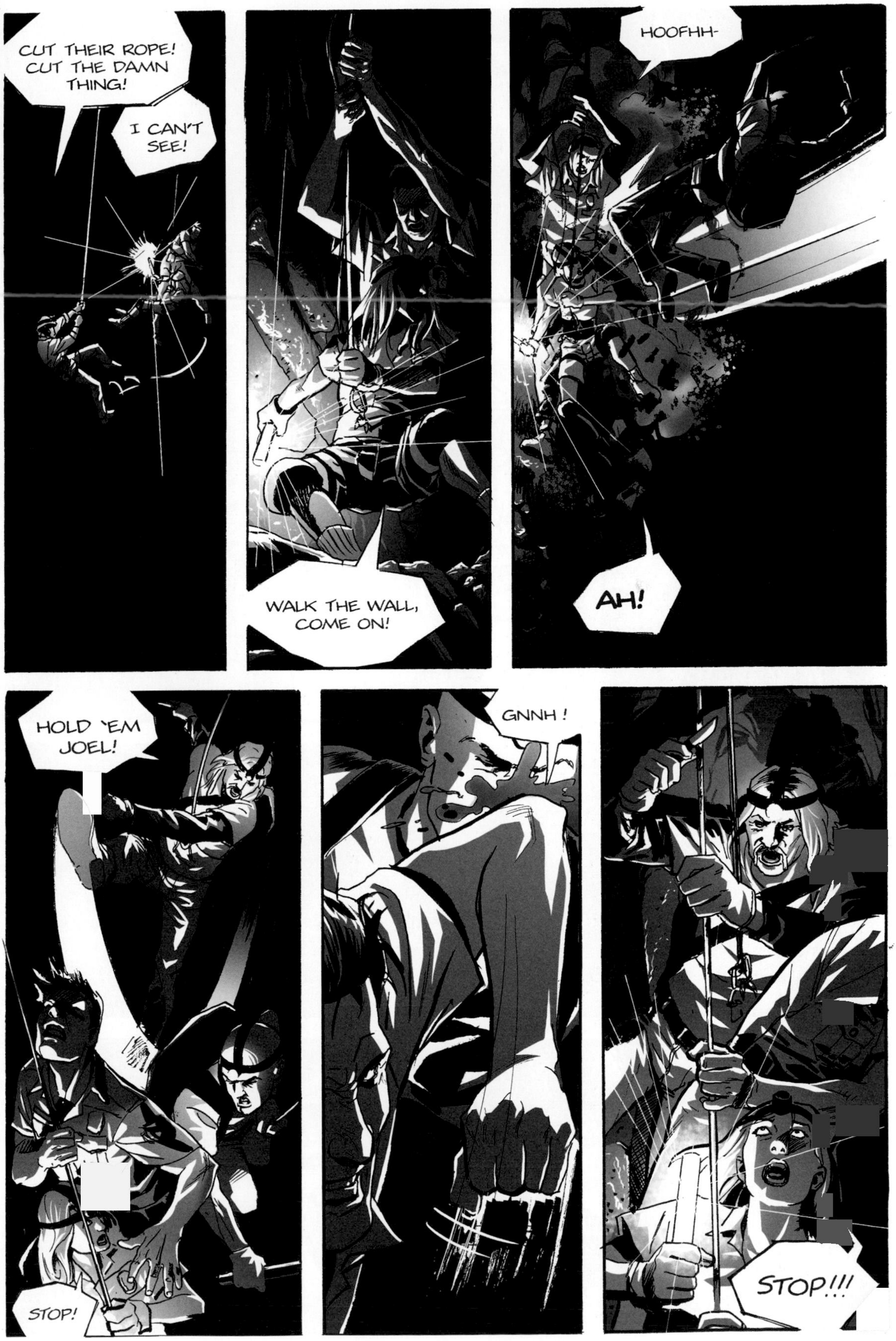
CUT THEIR ROPE! CUT THE DAMN THING!
I CAN'T SEE!
WALK THE WALL, COME ON!
HOOFHH-
AH!
HOLD 'EM JOEL!
STOP!
GNNH !
STOP!!!

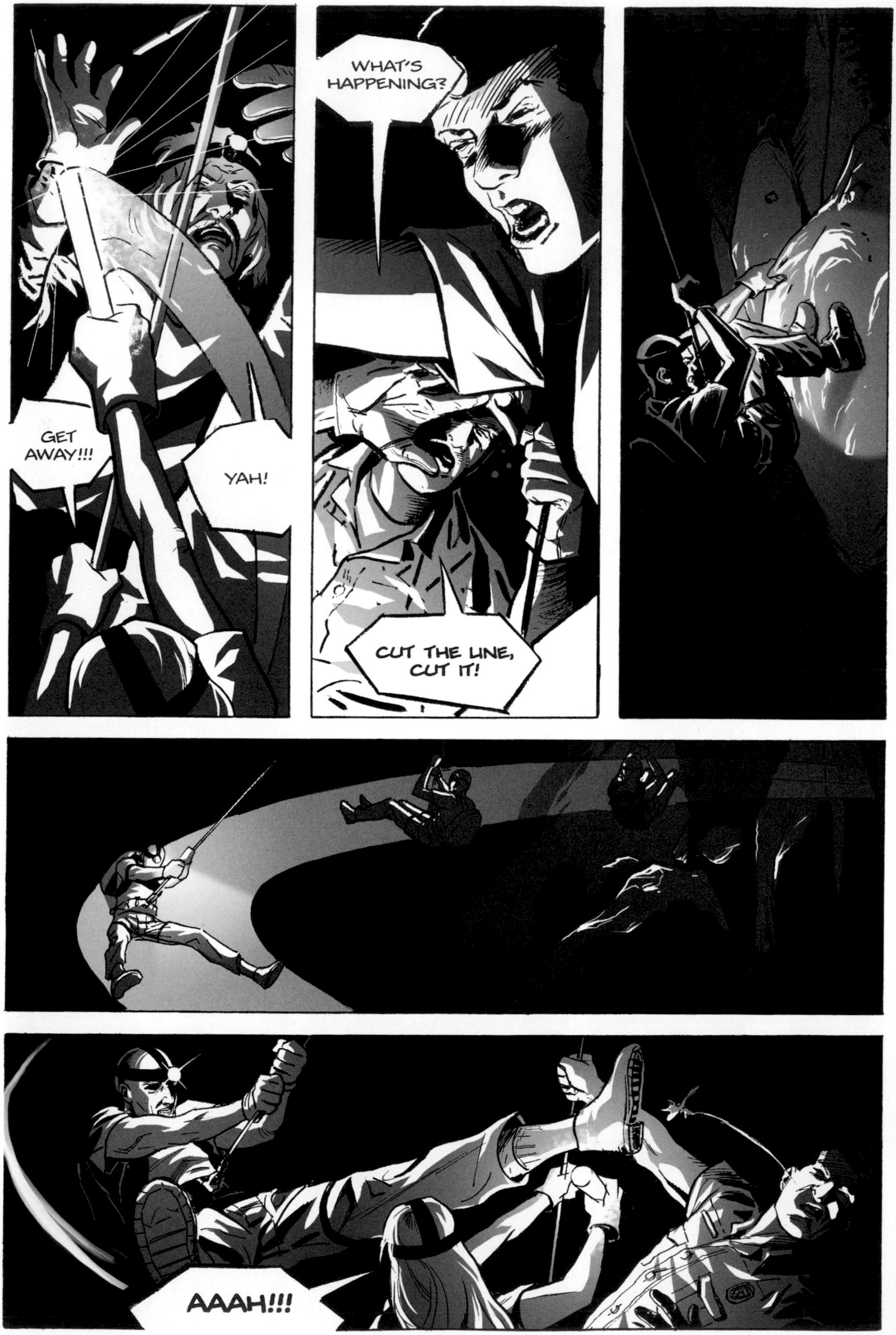
GET AWAY!!!
YAH!
WHAT'S HAPPENING?
CUT THE LINE, CUT IT!
AAAH!!!

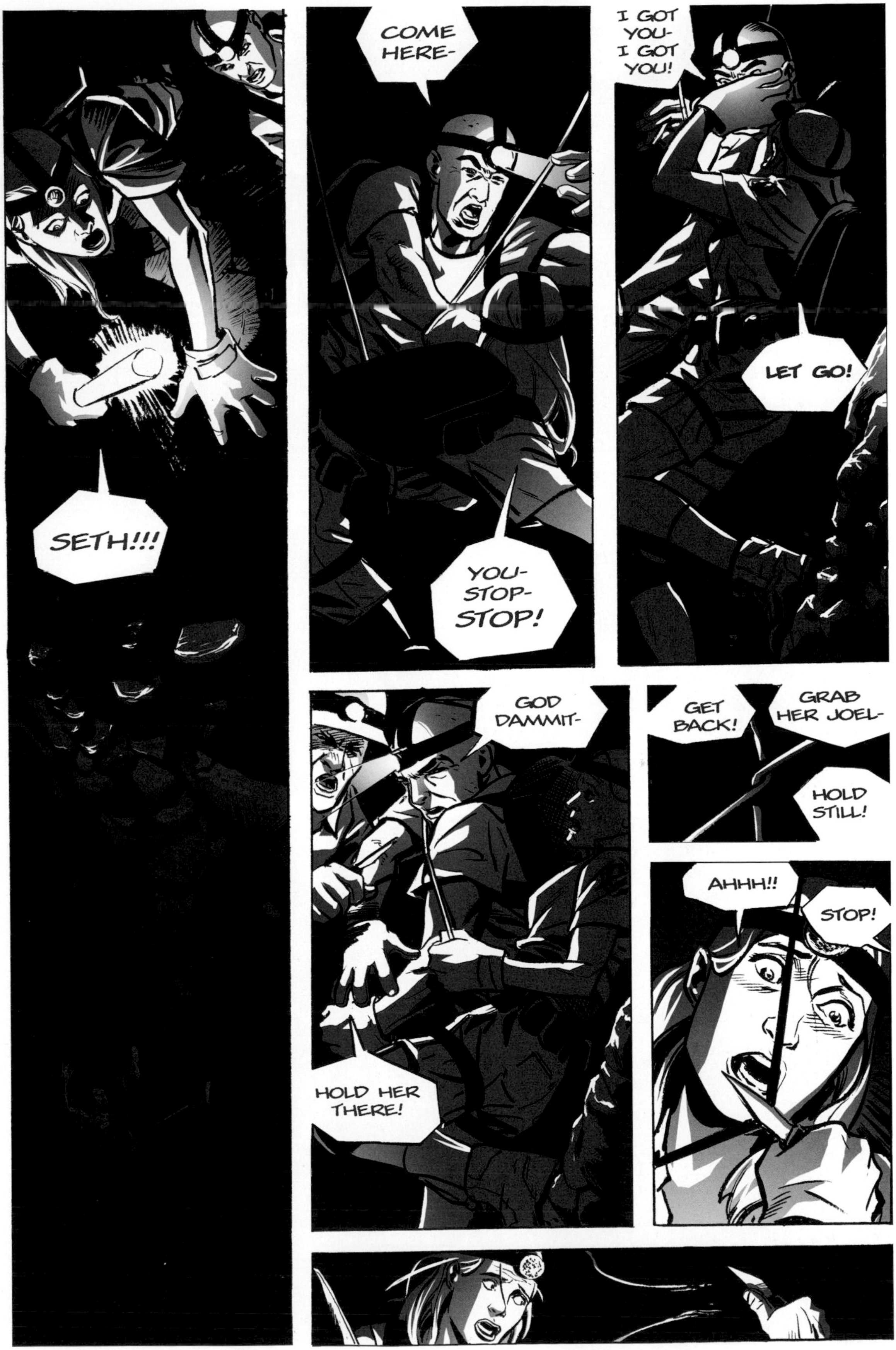
SETH!!!
COME HERE-
YOU- STOP- STOP!
I GOT YOU- I GOT YOU!
LET GO!
GOD DAMMIT-
HOLD HER THERE!
GET BACK!
GRAB HER JOEL-
HOLD STILL!
AHHH!!
STOP!

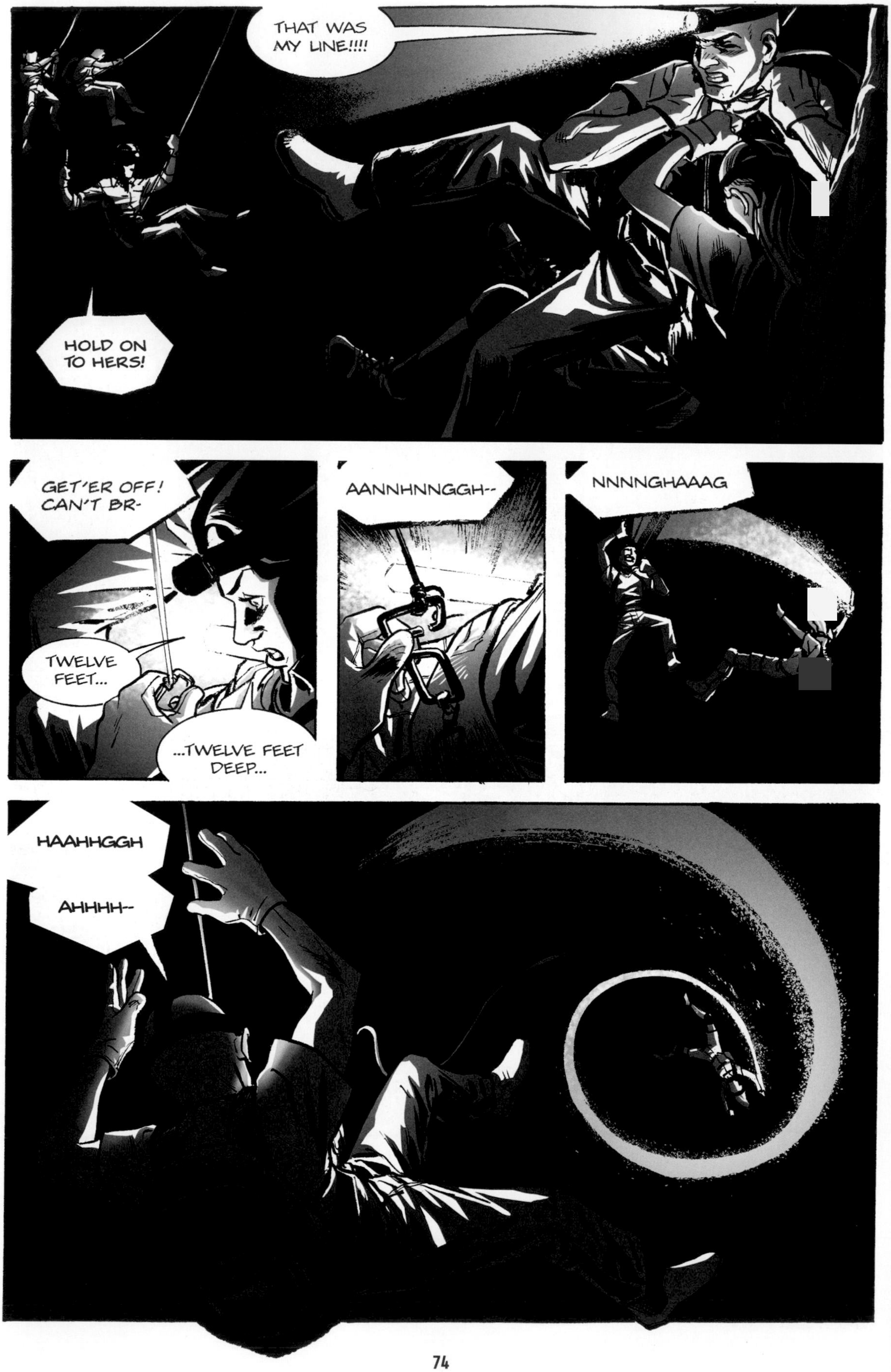
THAT WAS MY LINE!!!!
HOLD ON TO HERS!
GET'ER OFF! CAN'T BR-
TWELVE FEET...
...TWELVE FEET DEEP...
AANNHNNGGH--
NNNNGHAAAG
HAAHHGGH
AHHHH--

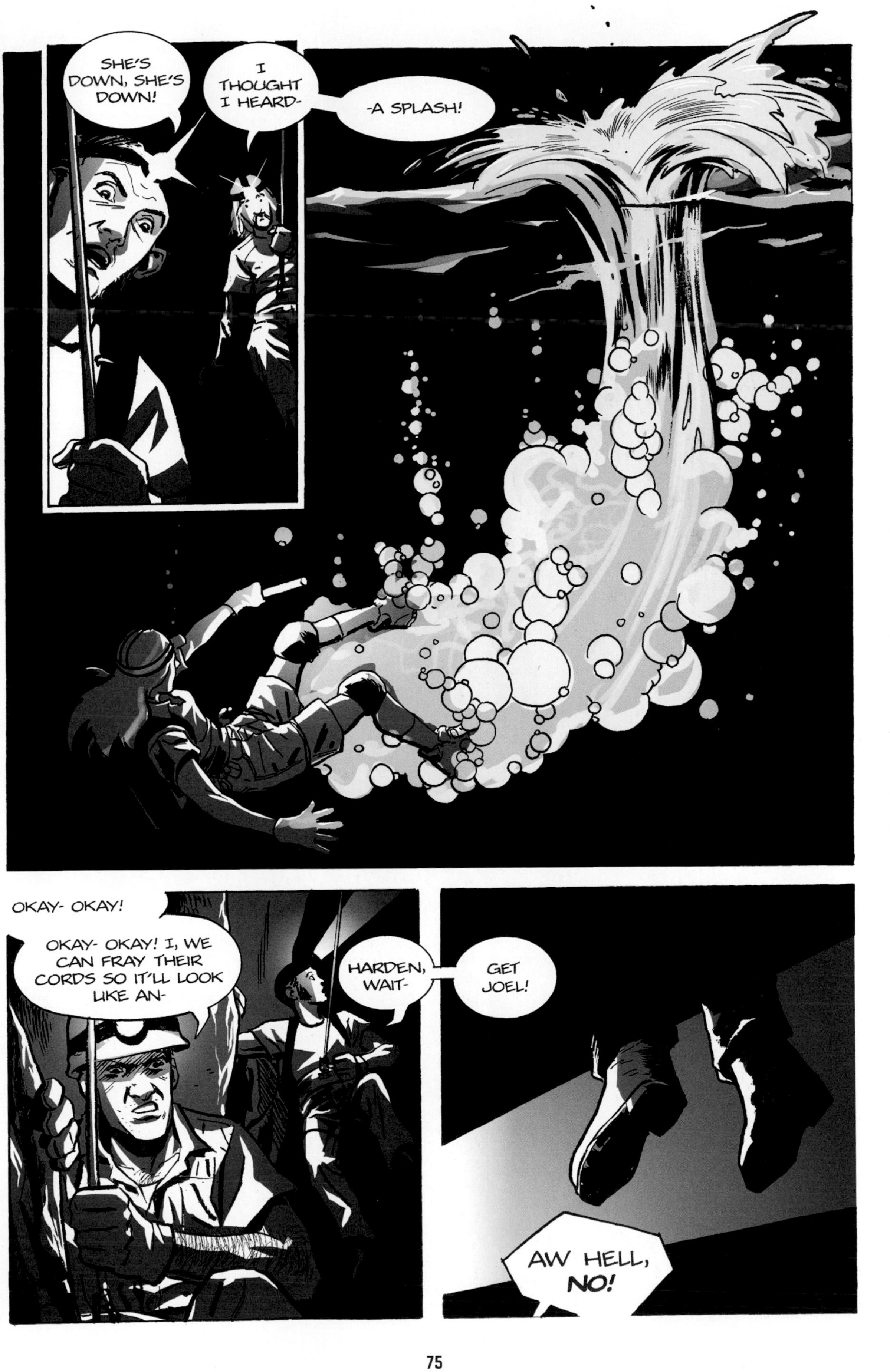
SHE'S DOWN, SHE'S DOWN!
I THOUGHT I HEARD-
-A SPLASH!
OKAY- OKAY!
OKAY- OKAY! I, WE CAN FRAY THEIR CORDS SO IT'LL LOOK LIKE AN-
HARDEN, WAIT-
GET JOEL!
AW HELL, NO!

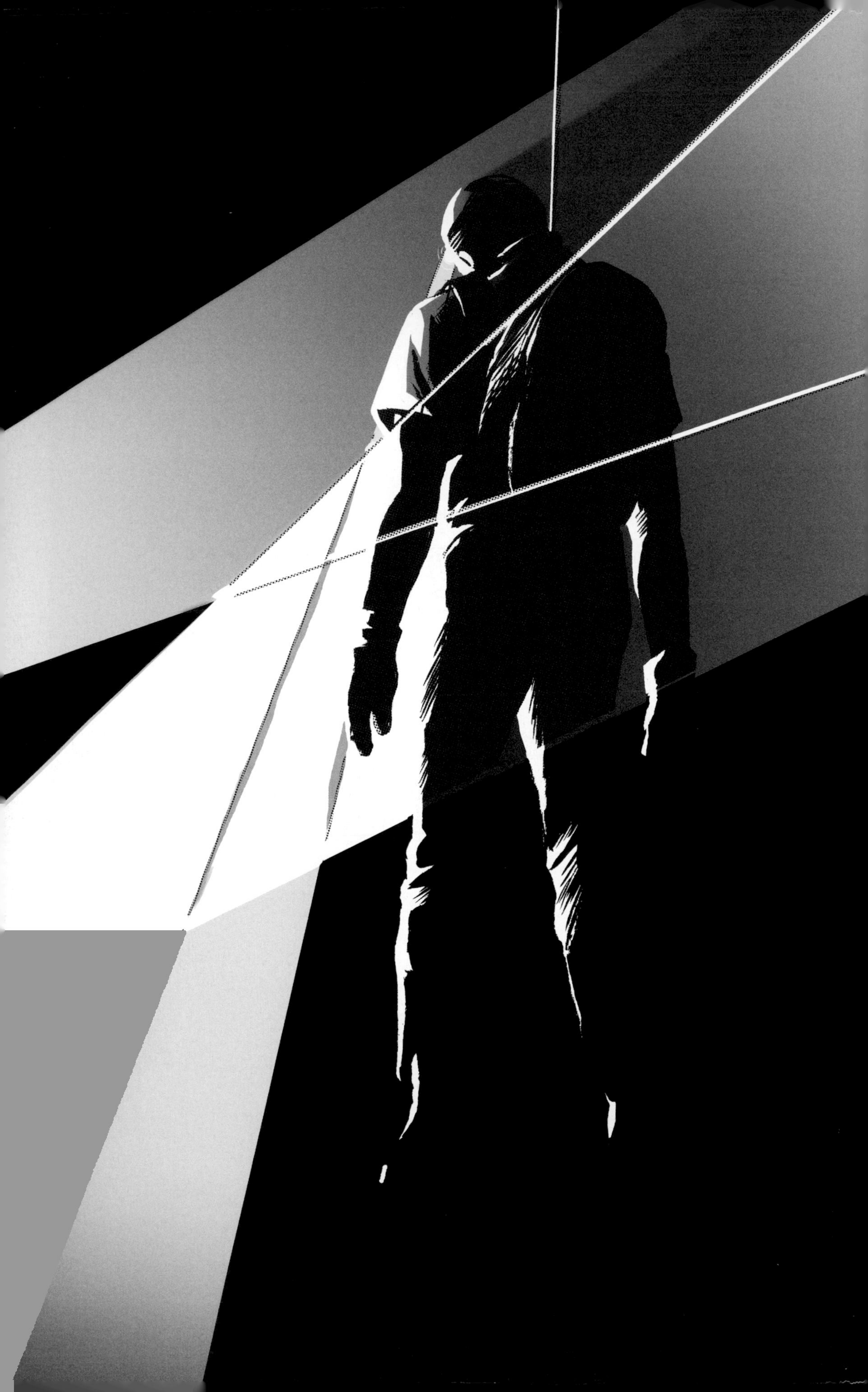

CHAPTER FOUR

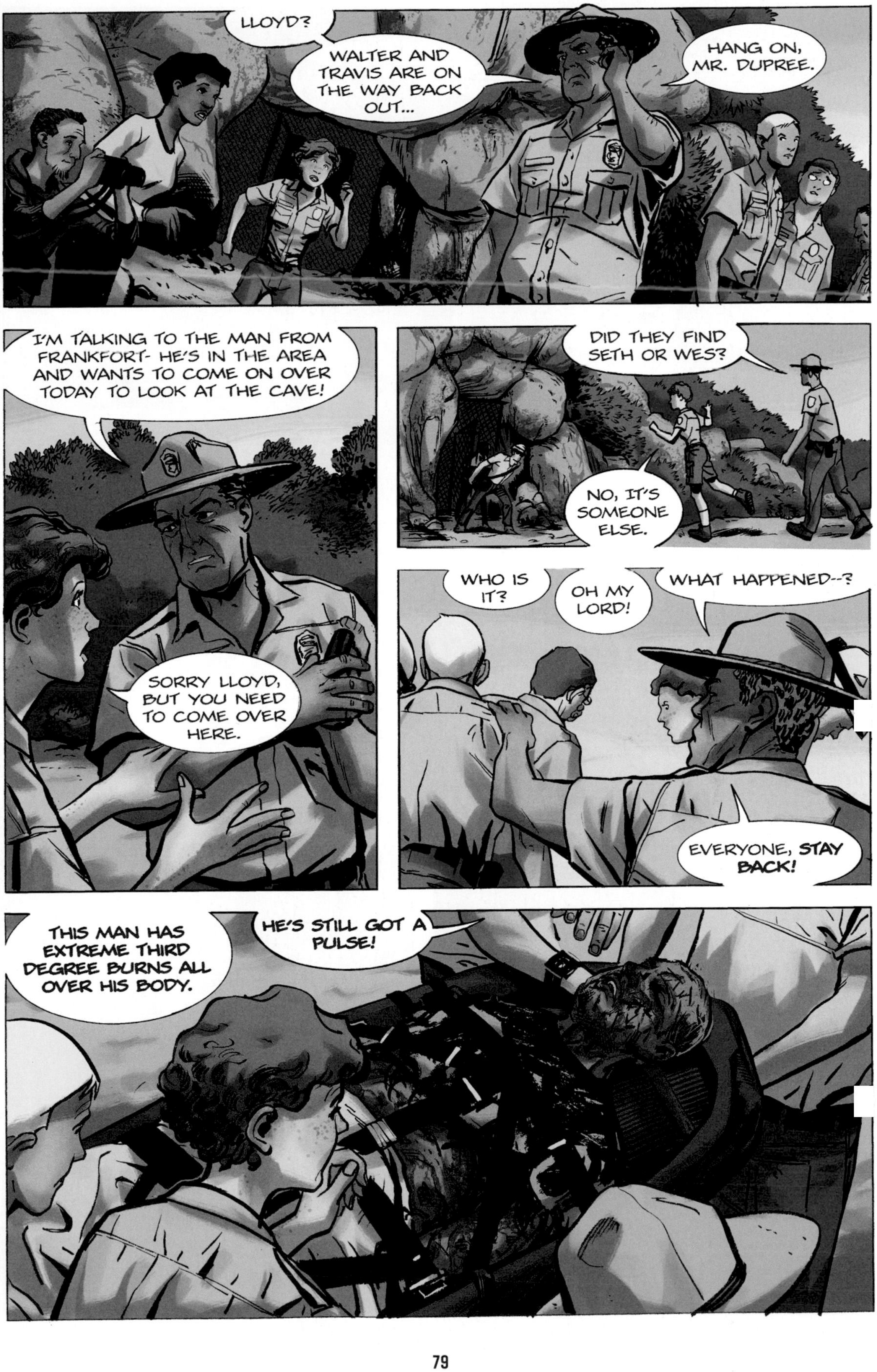

LLOYD?
WALTER AND TRAVIS ARE ON THE WAY BACK OUT...
HANG ON, MR. DUPREE.
I'M TALKING TO THE MAN FROM FRANKFORT- HE'S IN THE AREA AND WANTS TO COME ON OVER TODAY TO LOOK AT THE CAVE!
SORRY LLOYD, BUT YOU NEED TO COME OVER HERE.
DID THEY FIND SETH OR WES?
NO, IT'S SOMEONE ELSE.
WHO IS IT?
OH MY LORD!
WHAT HAPPENED--?
EVERYONE, STAY BACK!
THIS MAN HAS EXTREME THIRD DEGREE BURNS ALL OVER HIS BODY.
HE'S STILL GOT A PULSE!

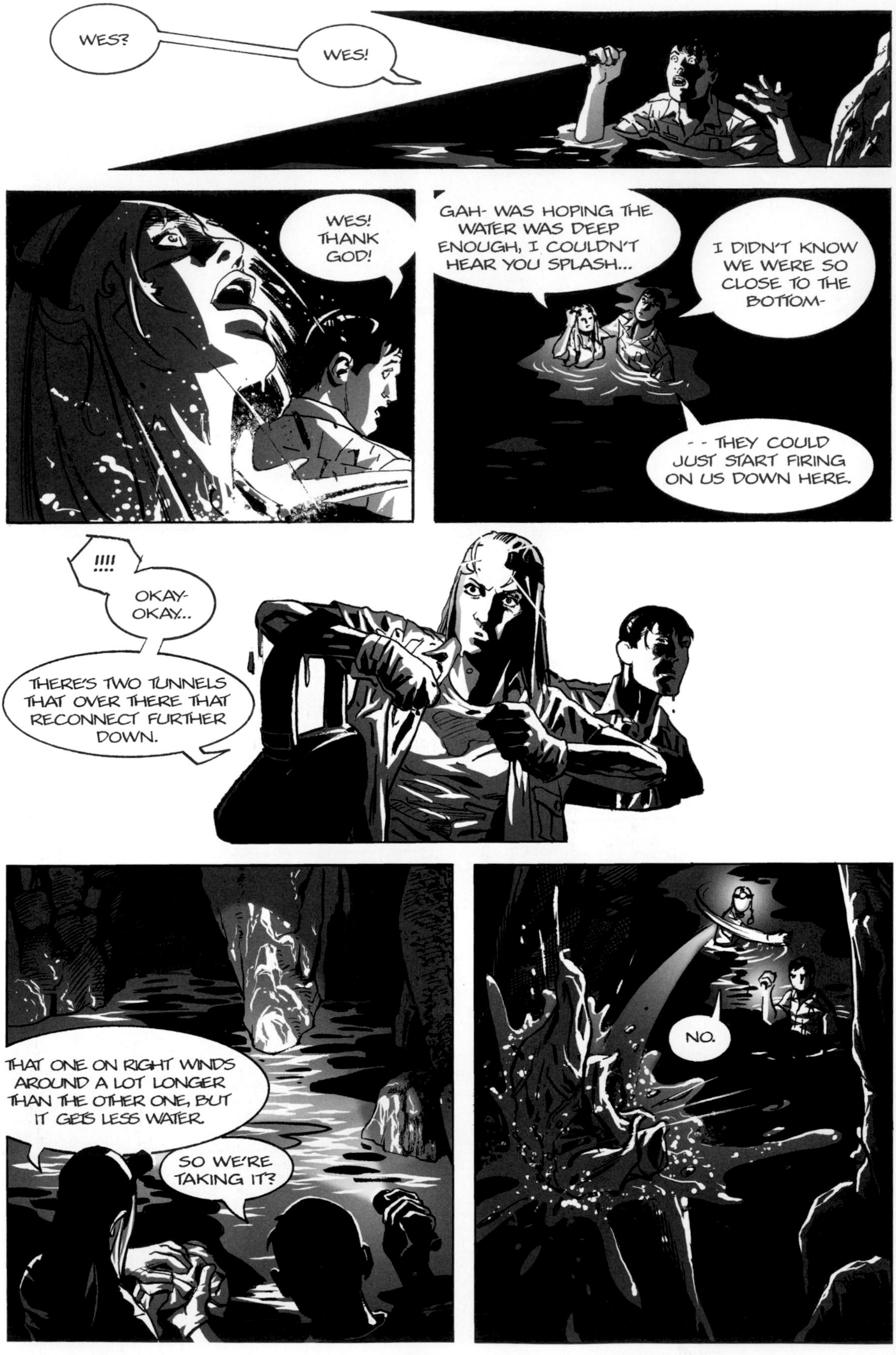
WES?
WES!
WES! THANK GOD!
GAH- WAS HOPING THE WATER WAS DEEP ENOUGH, I COULDN'T HEAR YOU SPLASH...
I DIDN'T KNOW WE WERE SO CLOSE TO THE BOTTOM-
- - THEY COULD JUST START FIRING ON US DOWN HERE.
!!!!
OKAY-OKAY...
THERE'S TWO TUNNELS THAT OVER THERE THAT RECONNECT FURTHER DOWN.
THAT ONE ON RIGHT WINDS AROUND A LOT LONGER THAN THE OTHER ONE, BUT IT GETS LESS WATER.
SO WE'RE TAKING IT?
NO.

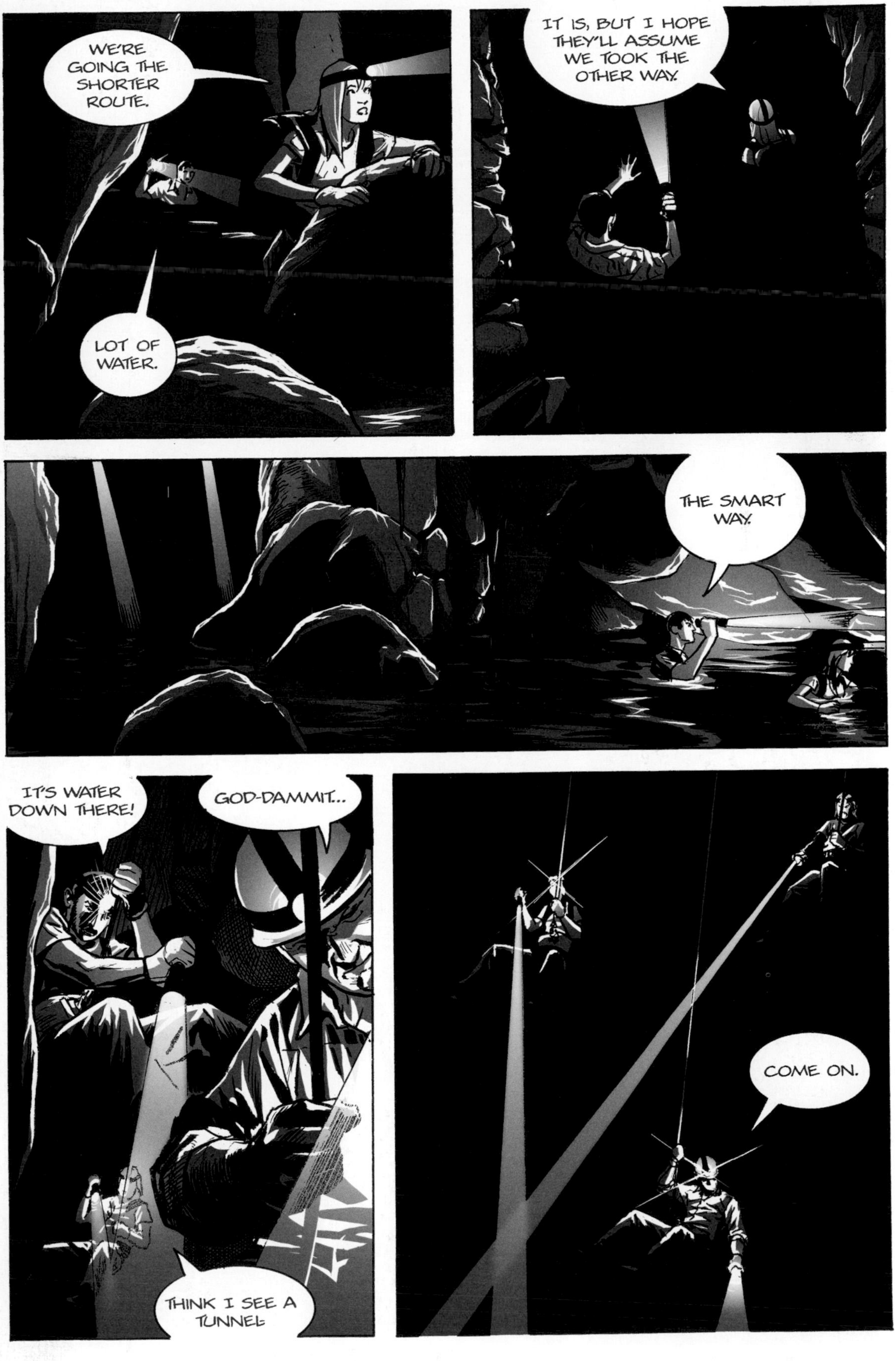
WE'RE GOING THE SHORTER ROUTE.
LOT OF WATER.
IT IS, BUT I HOPE THEY'LL ASSUME WE TOOK THE OTHER WAY.
THE SMART WAY.
IT'S WATER DOWN THERE!
GOD-DAMMIT...
THINK I SEE A TUNNEL
COME ON.

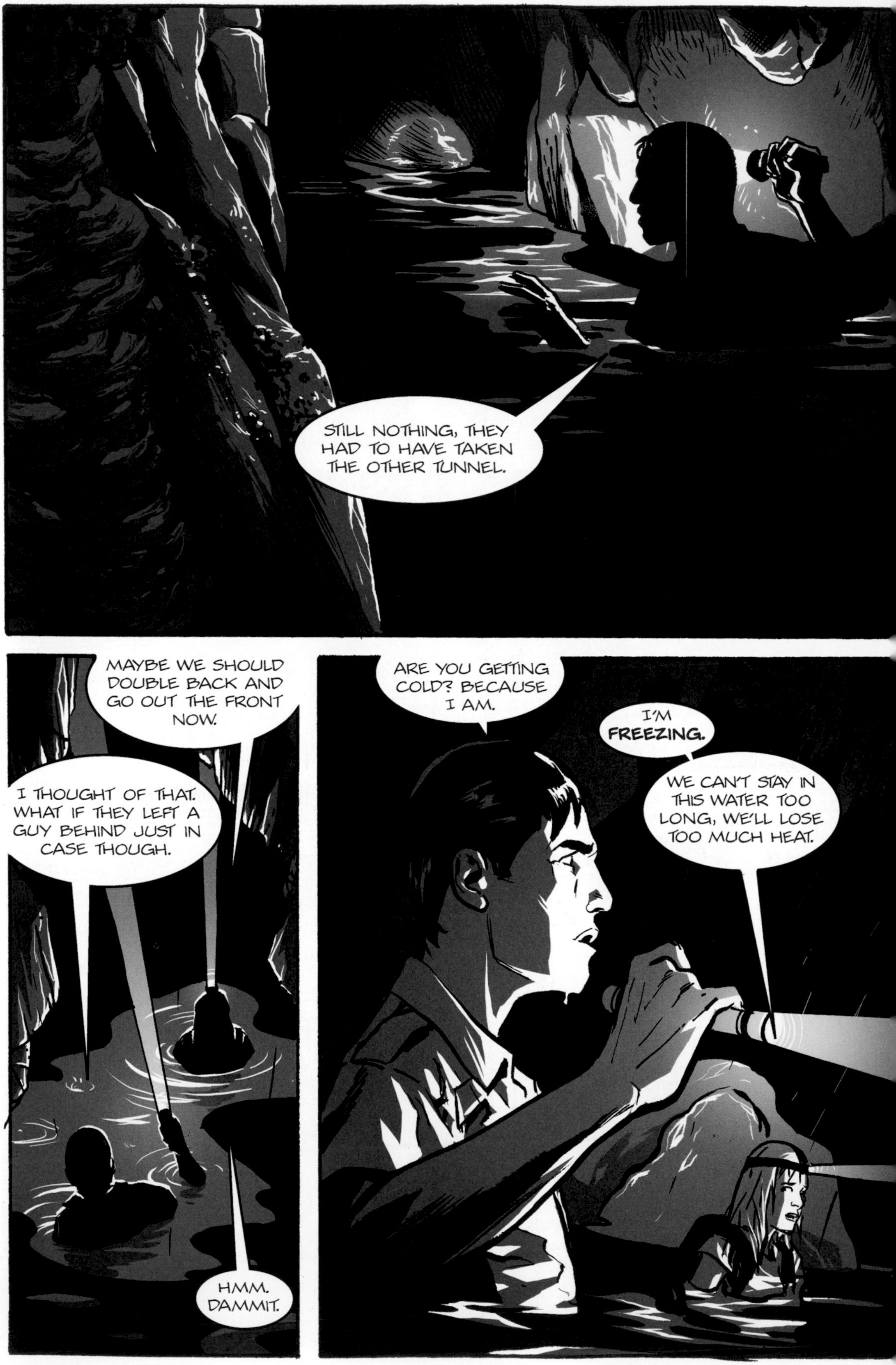
STILL NOTHING, THEY HAD TO HAVE TAKEN THE OTHER TUNNEL.
MAYBE WE SHOULD DOUBLE BACK AND GO OUT THE FRONT NOW.
I THOUGHT OF THAT. WHAT IF THEY LEFT A GUY BEHIND JUST IN CASE THOUGH.
HMM. DAMMIT.
ARE YOU GETTING COLD? BECAUSE I AM.
I'M FREEZING.
WE CAN'T STAY IN THIS WATER TOO LONG, WE'LL LOSE TOO MUCH HEAT.

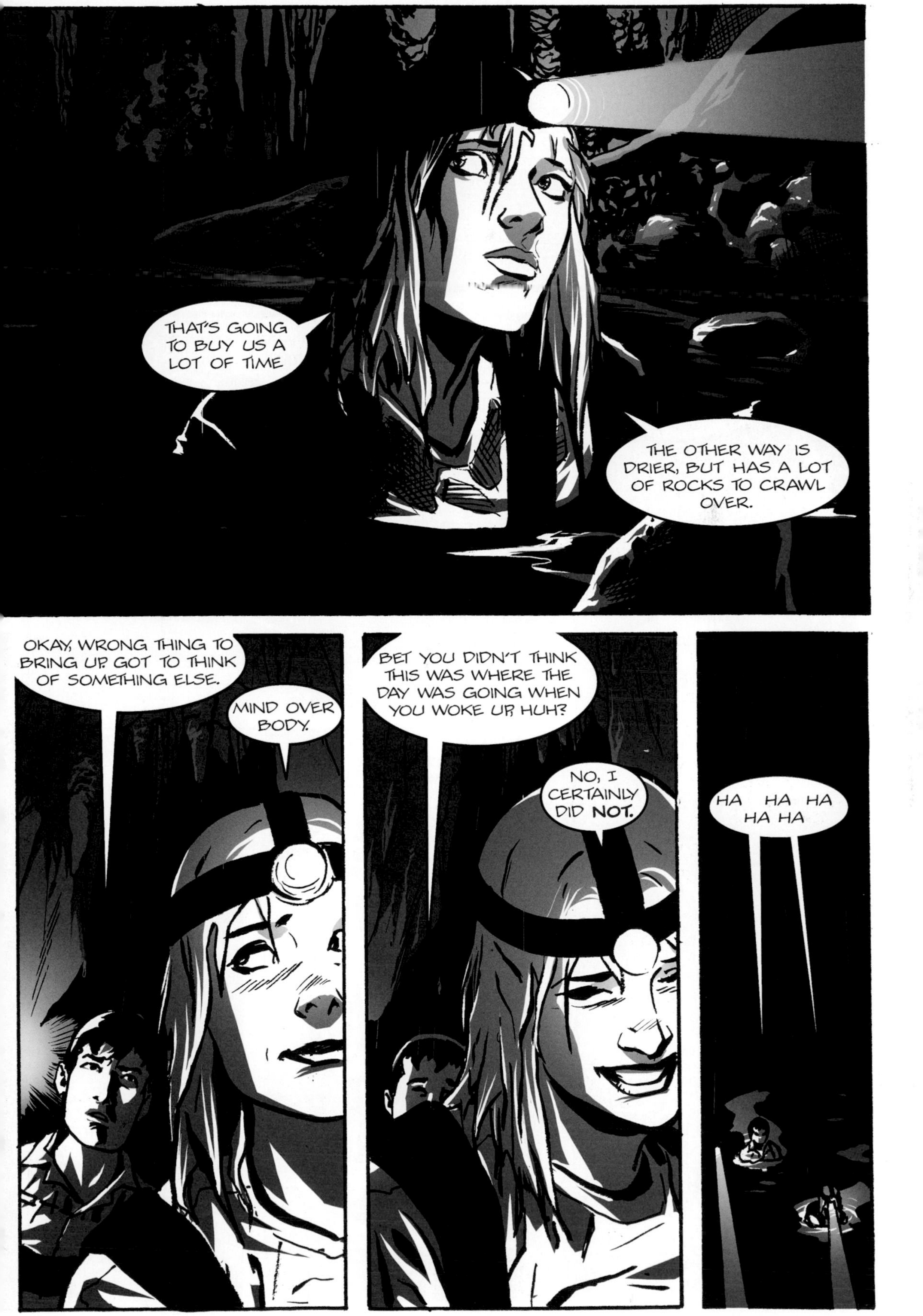
THAT'S GOING TO BUY US A LOT OF TIME
THE OTHER WAY IS DRIER, BUT HAS A LOT OF ROCKS TO CRAWL OVER.
OKAY, WRONG THING TO BRING UP. GOT TO THINK OF SOMETHING ELSE.
MIND OVER BODY.
BET YOU DIDN'T THINK THIS WAS WHERE THE DAY WAS GOING WHEN YOU WOKE UP, HUH?
NO, I CERTAINLY DID **NOT.**
HA HA HA HA HA

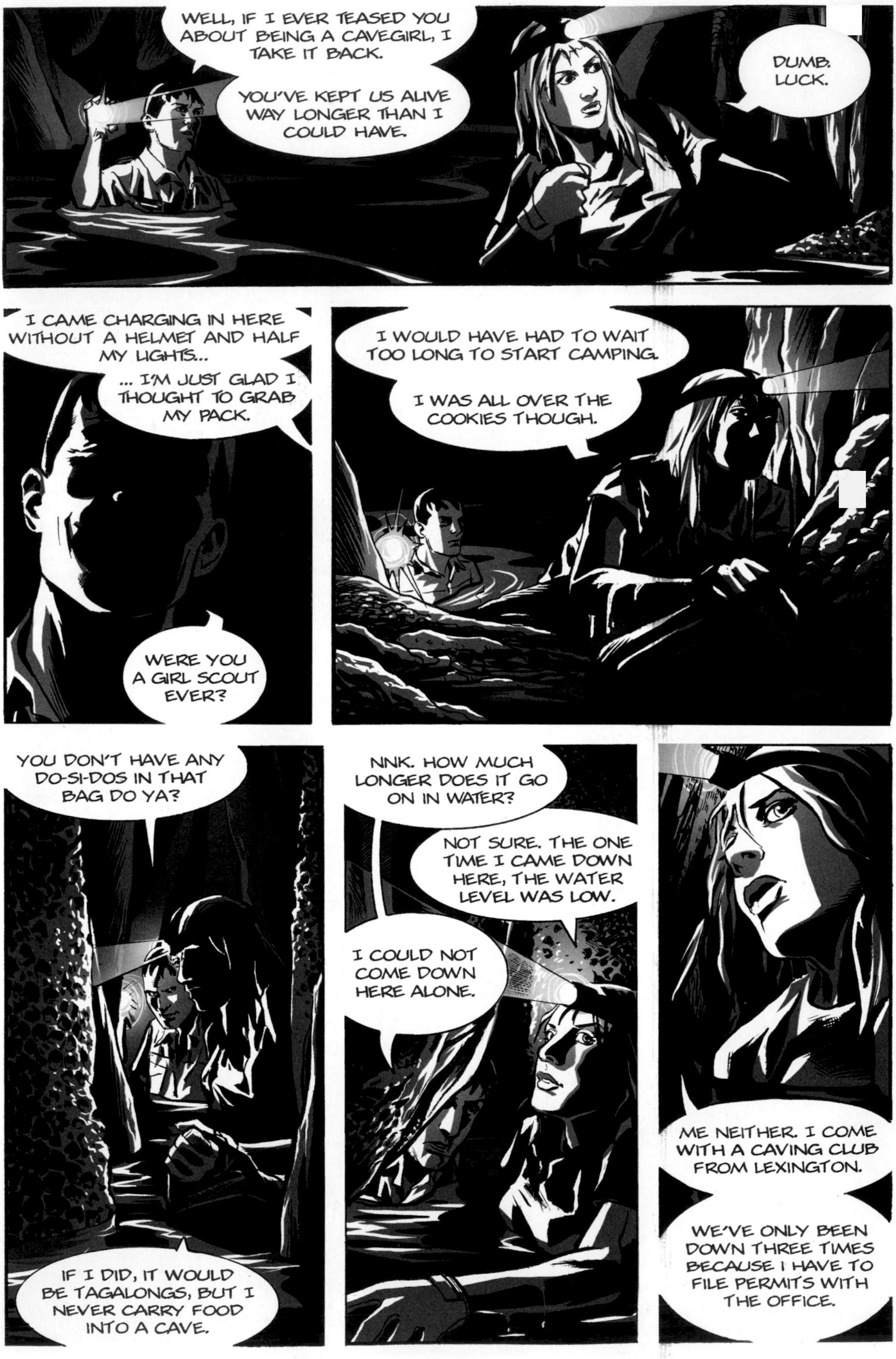
WELL, IF I EVER TEASED YOU ABOUT BEING A CAVEGIRL, I TAKE IT BACK.
YOU'VE KEPT US ALIVE WAY LONGER THAN I COULD HAVE.
DUMB. LUCK.
I CAME CHARGING IN HERE WITHOUT A HELMET AND HALF MY LIGHTS...
... I'M JUST GLAD I THOUGHT TO GRAB MY PACK.
WERE YOU A GIRL SCOUT EVER?
I WOULD HAVE HAD TO WAIT TOO LONG TO START CAMPING.
I WAS ALL OVER THE COOKIES THOUGH.
YOU DON'T HAVE ANY DO-SI-DOS IN THAT BAG DO YA?
IF I DID, IT WOULD BE TAGALONGS, BUT I NEVER CARRY FOOD INTO A CAVE.
NNK. HOW MUCH LONGER DOES IT GO ON IN WATER?
NOT SURE. THE ONE TIME I CAME DOWN HERE, THE WATER LEVEL WAS LOW.
I COULD NOT COME DOWN HERE ALONE.
ME NEITHER. I COME WITH A CAVING CLUB FROM LEXINGTON.
WE'VE ONLY BEEN DOWN THREE TIMES BECAUSE I HAVE TO FILE PERMITS WITH THE OFFICE.

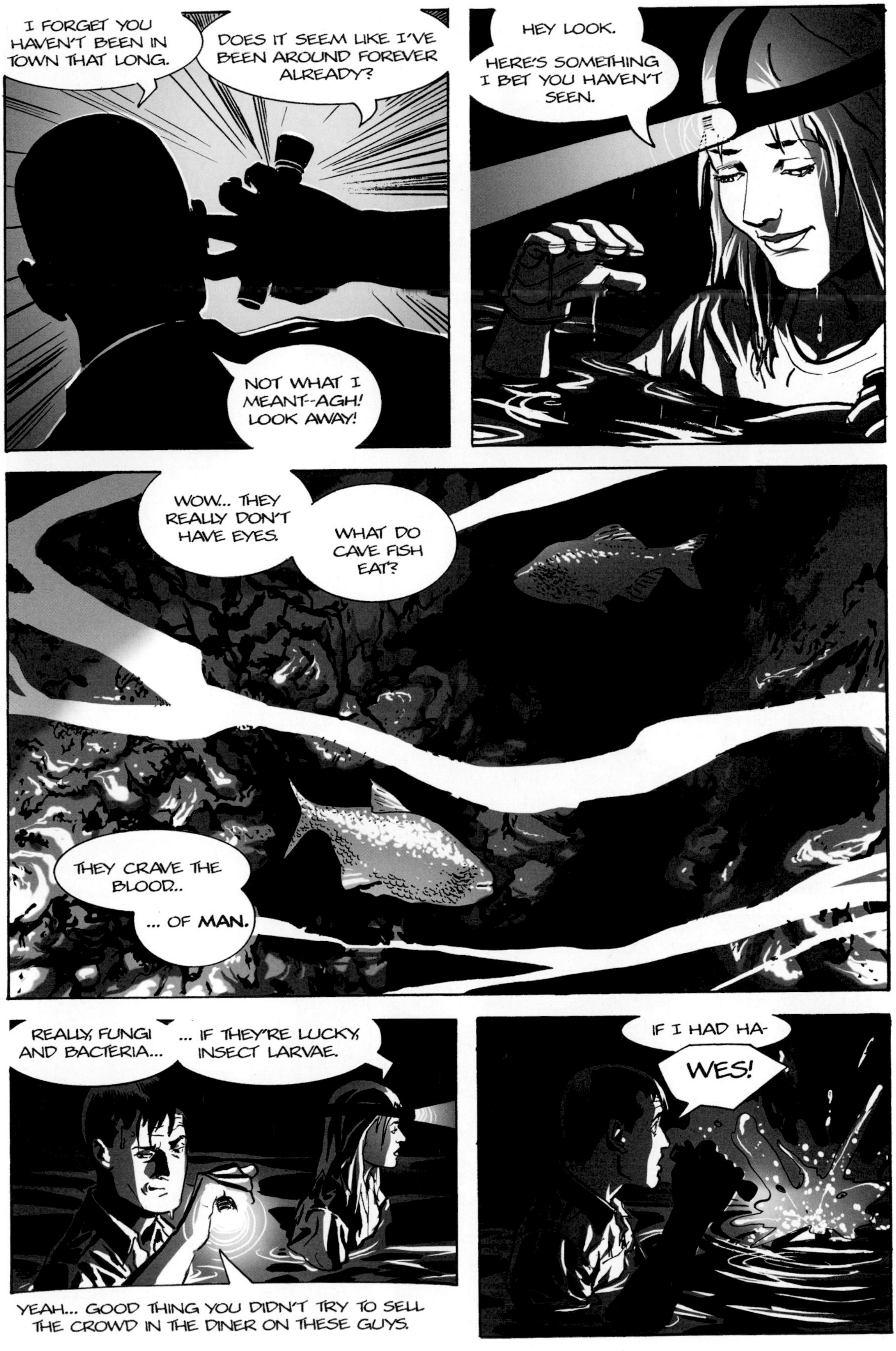
I FORGET YOU HAVEN'T BEEN IN TOWN THAT LONG.
DOES IT SEEM LIKE I'VE BEEN AROUND FOREVER ALREADY?
NOT WHAT I MEANT--AGH! LOOK AWAY!
HEY LOOK.
HERE'S SOMETHING I BET YOU HAVEN'T SEEN.
WOW... THEY REALLY DON'T HAVE EYES.
WHAT DO CAVE FISH EAT?
THEY CRAVE THE BLOOD..
... OF MAN.
REALLY, FUNGI AND BACTERIA...
... IF THEY'RE LUCKY, INSECT LARVAE.
YEAH... GOOD THING YOU DIDN'T TRY TO SELL THE CROWD IN THE DINER ON THESE GUYS.
IF I HAD HA-
WES!

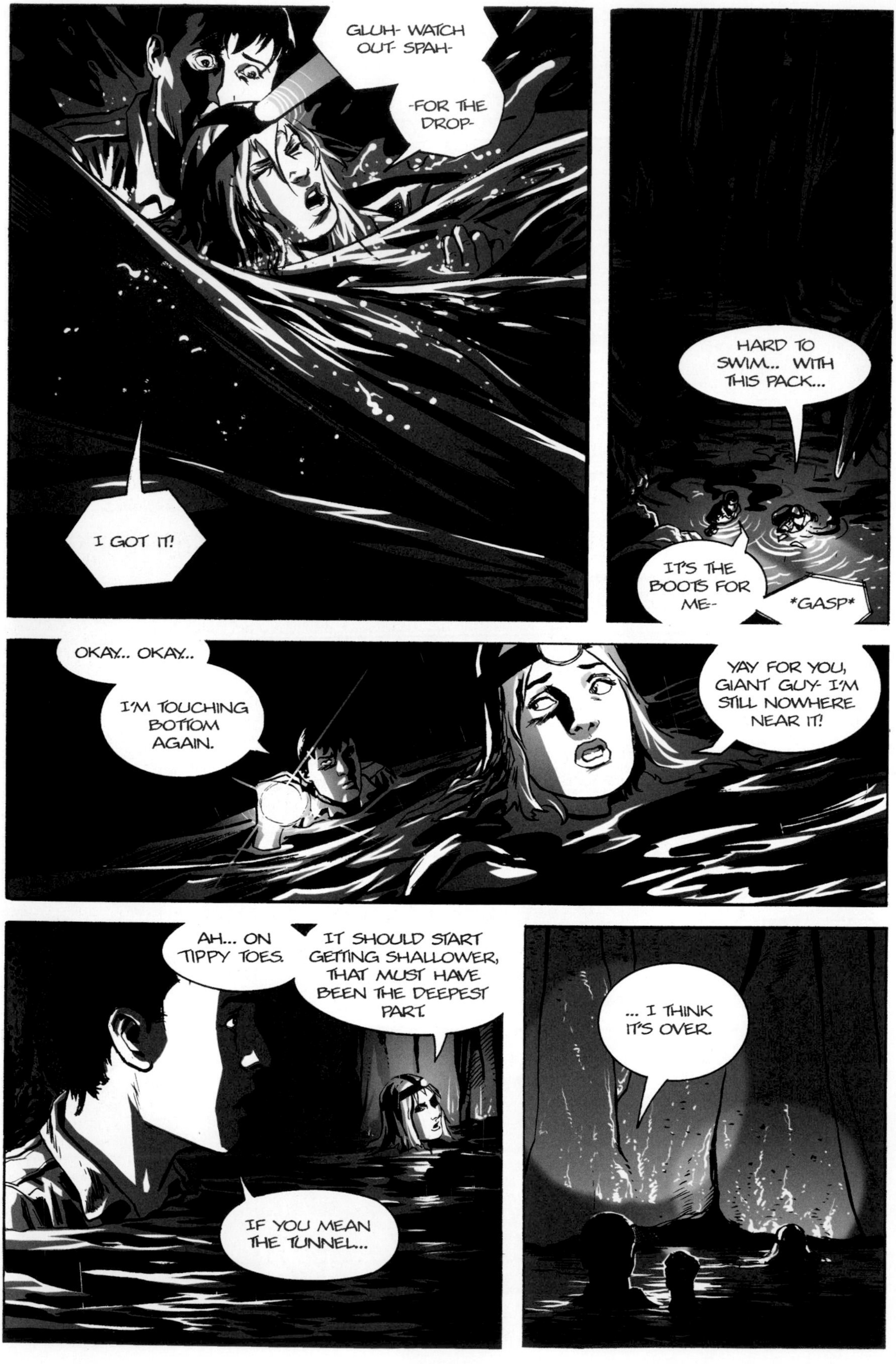
GLUH- WATCH OUT- SPAH-
-FOR THE DROP-
I GOT IT!
HARD TO SWIM... WITH THIS PACK...
IT'S THE BOOTS FOR ME-
GASP
OKAY... OKAY...
I'M TOUCHING BOTTOM AGAIN.
YAY FOR YOU, GIANT GUY- I'M STILL NOWHERE NEAR IT!
AH... ON TIPPY TOES.
IT SHOULD START GETTING SHALLOWER, THAT MUST HAVE BEEN THE DEEPEST PART.
IF YOU MEAN THE TUNNEL...
... I THINK IT'S OVER.

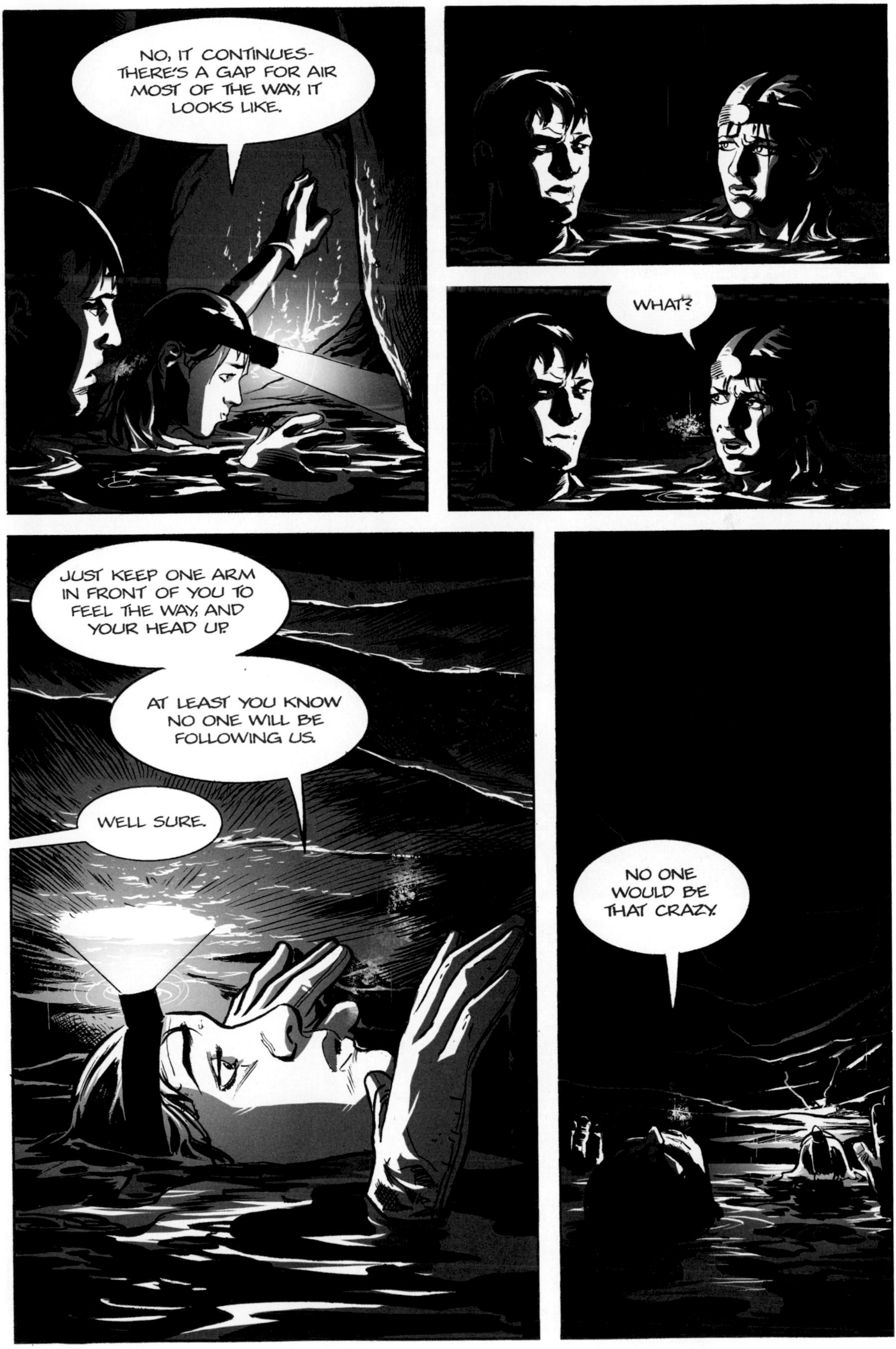
NO, IT CONTINUES- THERE'S A GAP FOR AIR MOST OF THE WAY, IT LOOKS LIKE.
WHAT?
JUST KEEP ONE ARM IN FRONT OF YOU TO FEEL THE WAY, AND YOUR HEAD UP.
AT LEAST YOU KNOW NO ONE WILL BE FOLLOWING US.
WELL SURE.
NO ONE WOULD BE THAT CRAZY.

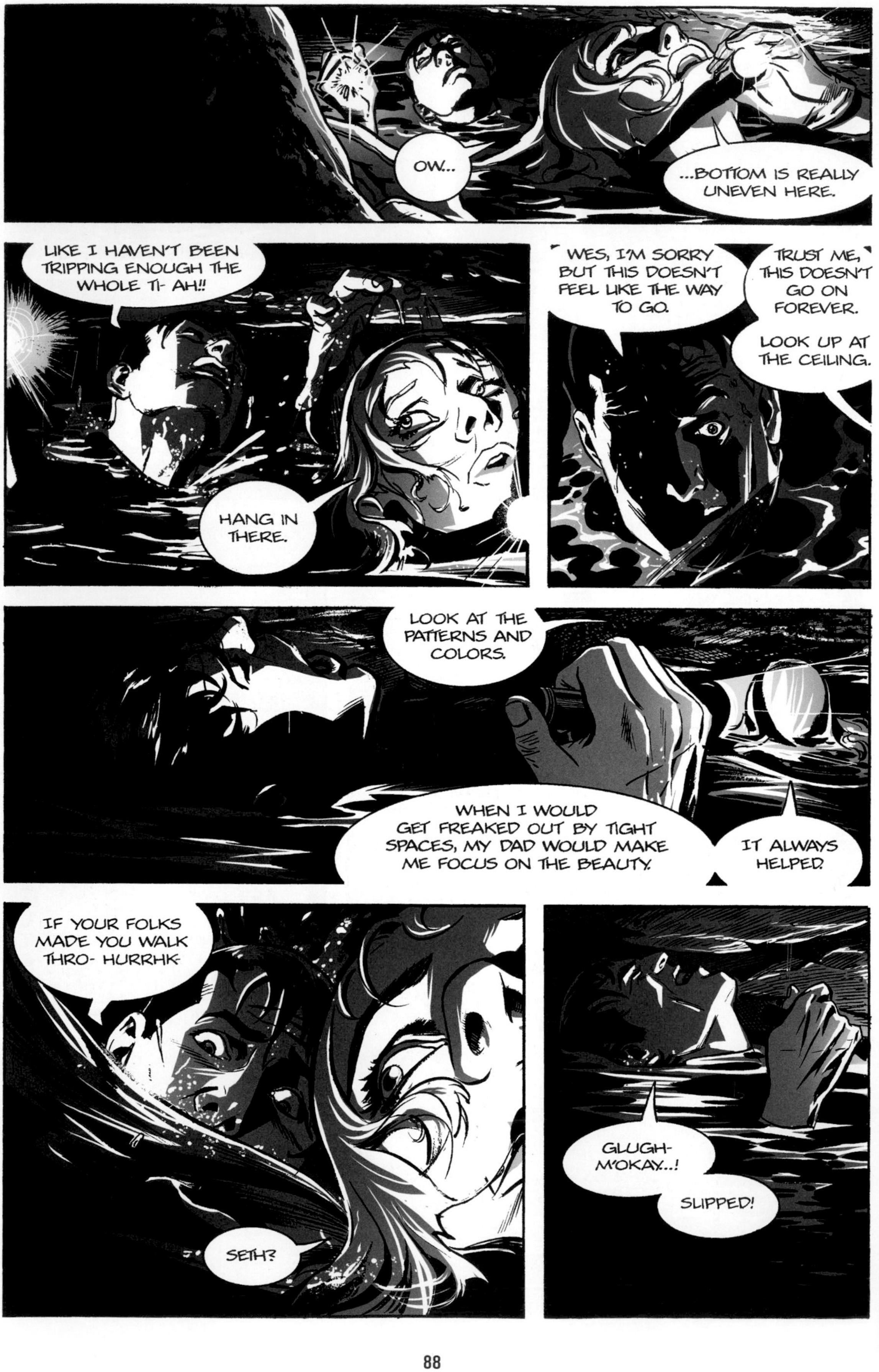
OW...
...BOTTOM IS REALLY UNEVEN HERE.
LIKE I HAVEN'T BEEN TRIPPING ENOUGH THE WHOLE TI- AH!!
HANG IN THERE.
WES, I'M SORRY BUT THIS DOESN'T FEEL LIKE THE WAY TO GO.
TRUST ME, THIS DOESN'T GO ON FOREVER.
LOOK UP AT THE CEILING.
LOOK AT THE PATTERNS AND COLORS.
WHEN I WOULD GET FREAKED OUT BY TIGHT SPACES, MY DAD WOULD MAKE ME FOCUS ON THE BEAUTY.
IT ALWAYS HELPED.
IF YOUR FOLKS MADE YOU WALK THRO- HURRHK-
SETH?
GLUGH- M'OKAY...!
SLIPPED!

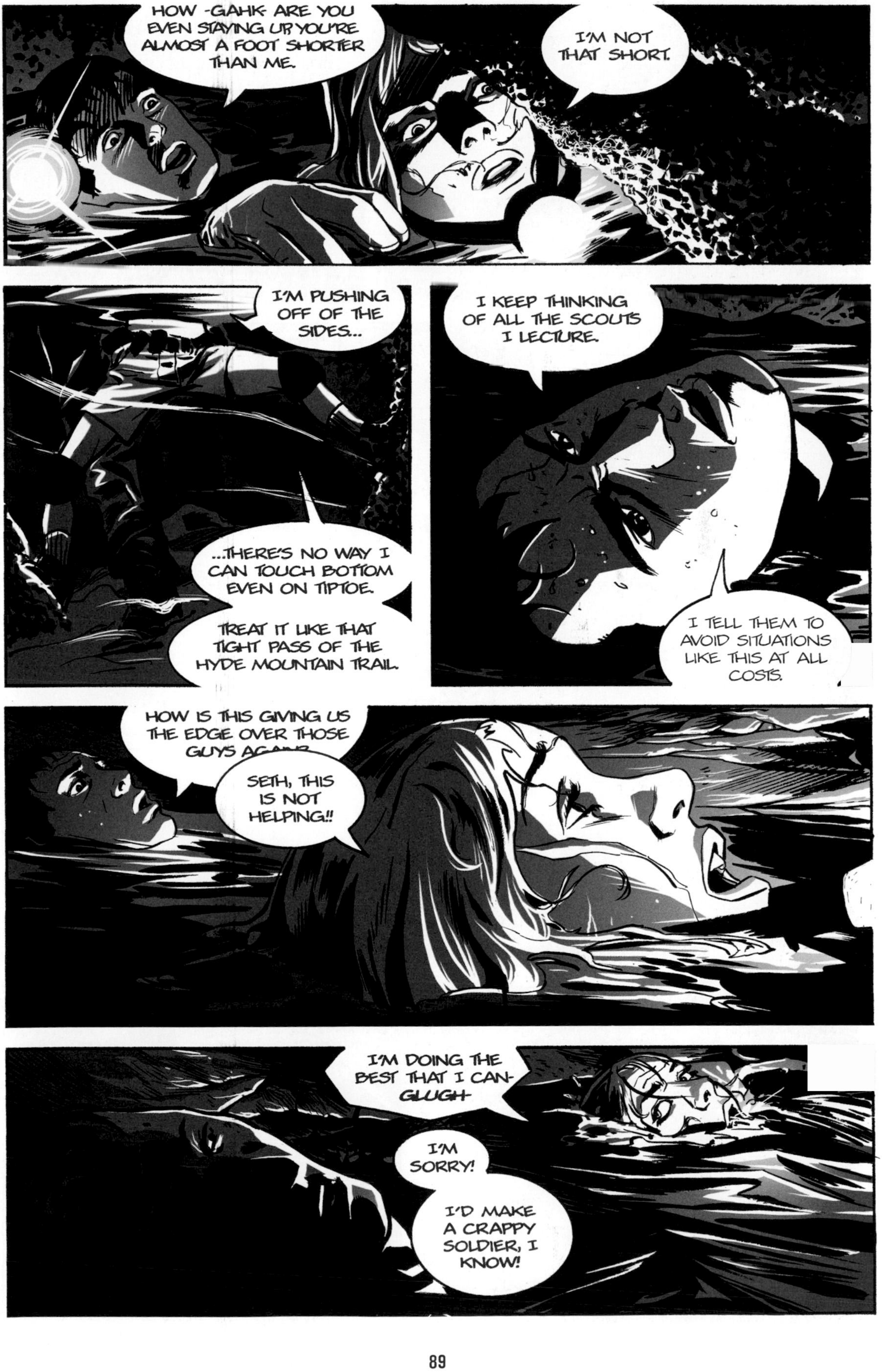
HOW -GAHK- ARE YOU EVEN STAYING UP, YOU'RE ALMOST A FOOT SHORTER THAN ME.
I'M NOT THAT SHORT.
I'M PUSHING OFF OF THE SIDES...
...THERE'S NO WAY I CAN TOUCH BOTTOM EVEN ON TIPTOE.
TREAT IT LIKE THAT TIGHT PASS OF THE HYDE MOUNTAIN TRAIL.
I KEEP THINKING OF ALL THE SCOUTS I LECTURE.
I TELL THEM TO AVOID SITUATIONS LIKE THIS AT ALL COSTS.
HOW IS THIS GIVING US THE EDGE OVER THOSE GUYS
SETH, THIS IS NOT HELPING!!
I'M DOING THE BEST THAT I CAN-
GLUGH
I'M SORRY!
I'D MAKE A CRAPPY SOLDIER, I KNOW!

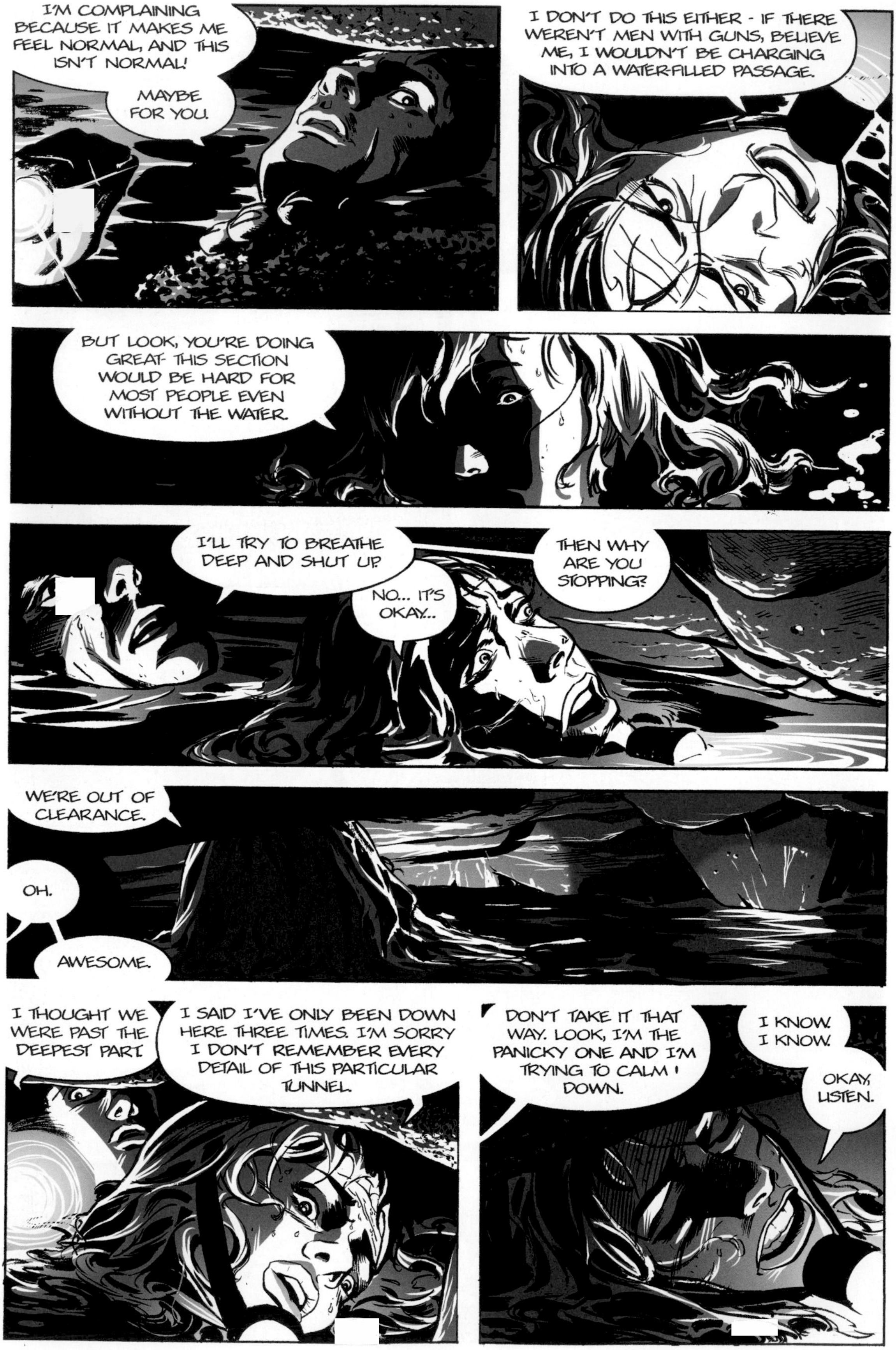
I'M COMPLAINING BECAUSE IT MAKES ME FEEL NORMAL, AND THIS ISN'T NORMAL!
MAYBE FOR YOU.
I DON'T DO THIS EITHER - IF THERE WEREN'T MEN WITH GUNS, BELIEVE ME, I WOULDN'T BE CHARGING INTO A WATER-FILLED PASSAGE.
BUT LOOK, YOU'RE DOING GREAT- THIS SECTION WOULD BE HARD FOR MOST PEOPLE EVEN WITHOUT THE WATER.
I'LL TRY TO BREATHE DEEP AND SHUT UP.
NO... IT'S OKAY...
THEN WHY ARE YOU STOPPING?
WE'RE OUT OF CLEARANCE.
OH.
AWESOME.
I THOUGHT WE WERE PAST THE DEEPEST PART.
I SAID I'VE ONLY BEEN DOWN HERE THREE TIMES. I'M SORRY I DON'T REMEMBER EVERY DETAIL OF THIS PARTICULAR TUNNEL.
DON'T TAKE IT THAT WAY. LOOK, I'M THE PANICKY ONE AND I'M TRYING TO CALM DOWN.
I KNOW. I KNOW.
OKAY, LISTEN.

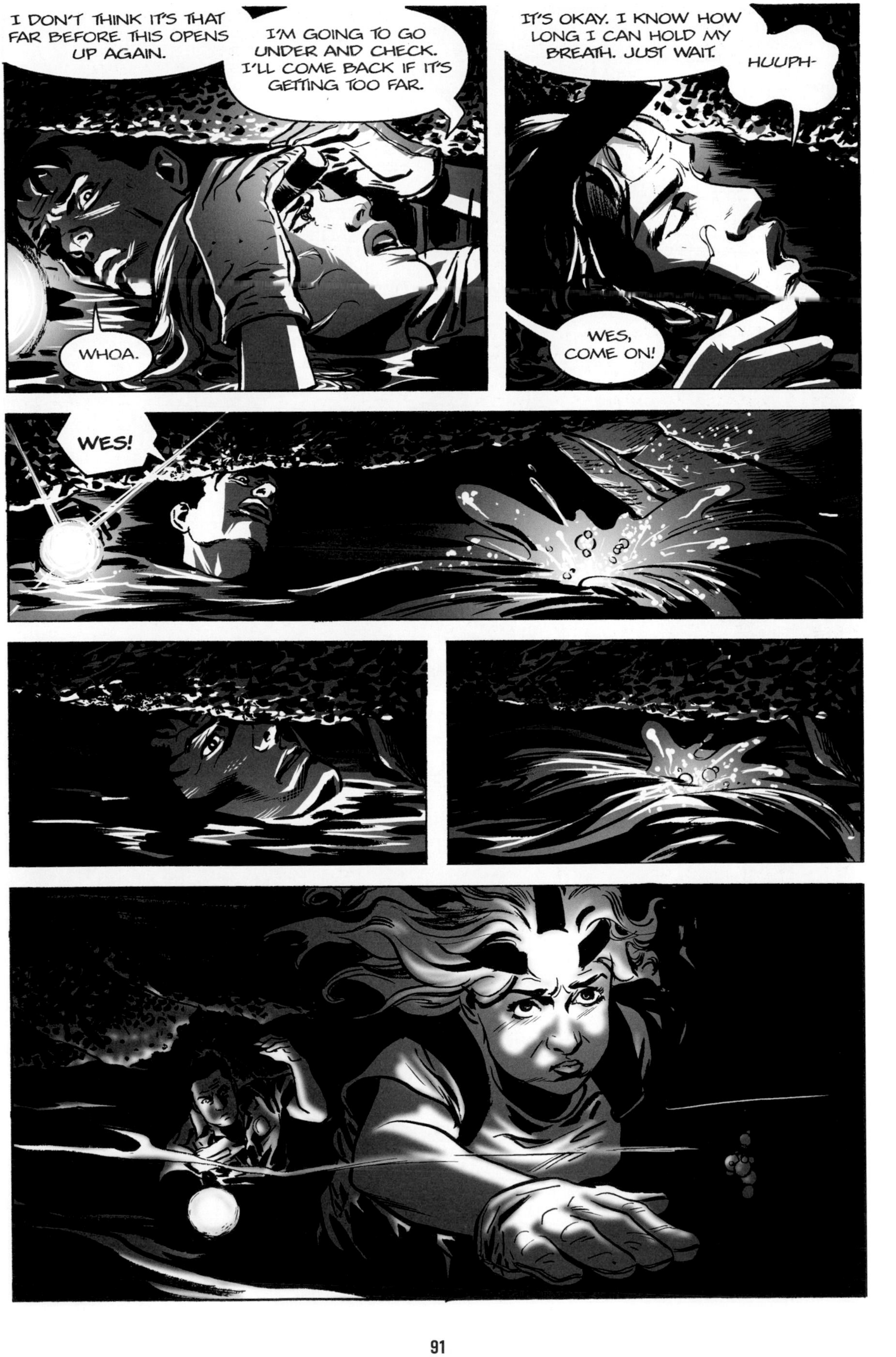
I DON'T THINK IT'S THAT FAR BEFORE THIS OPENS UP AGAIN.
I'M GOING TO GO UNDER AND CHECK. I'LL COME BACK IF IT'S GETTING TOO FAR.
WHOA.
IT'S OKAY. I KNOW HOW LONG I CAN HOLD MY BREATH. JUST WAIT.
HUUPH-
WES, COME ON!
WES!

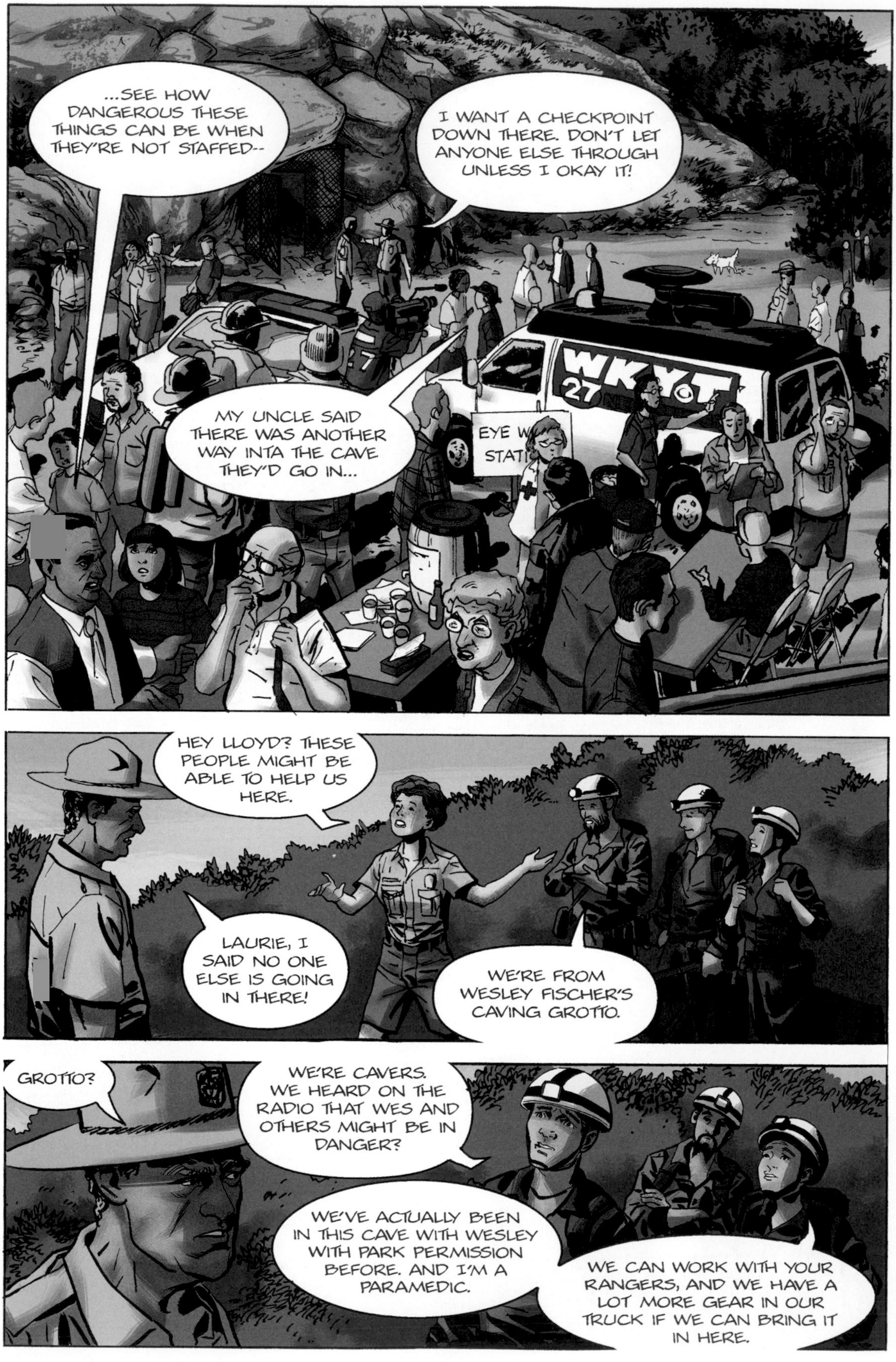
...SEE HOW DANGEROUS THESE THINGS CAN BE WHEN THEY'RE NOT STAFFED--
I WANT A CHECKPOINT DOWN THERE. DON'T LET ANYONE ELSE THROUGH UNLESS I OKAY IT!
WKYT 27
MY UNCLE SAID THERE WAS ANOTHER WAY INTA THE CAVE THEY'D GO IN...
HEY LLOYD? THESE PEOPLE MIGHT BE ABLE TO HELP US HERE.
LAURIE, I SAID NO ONE ELSE IS GOING IN THERE!
WE'RE FROM WESLEY FISCHER'S CAVING GROTTO.
GROTTO?
WE'RE CAVERS. WE HEARD ON THE RADIO THAT WES AND OTHERS MIGHT BE IN DANGER?
WE'VE ACTUALLY BEEN IN THIS CAVE WITH WESLEY WITH PARK PERMISSION BEFORE. AND I'M A PARAMEDIC.
WE CAN WORK WITH YOUR RANGERS, AND WE HAVE A LOT MORE GEAR IN OUR TRUCK IF WE CAN BRING IT IN HERE.

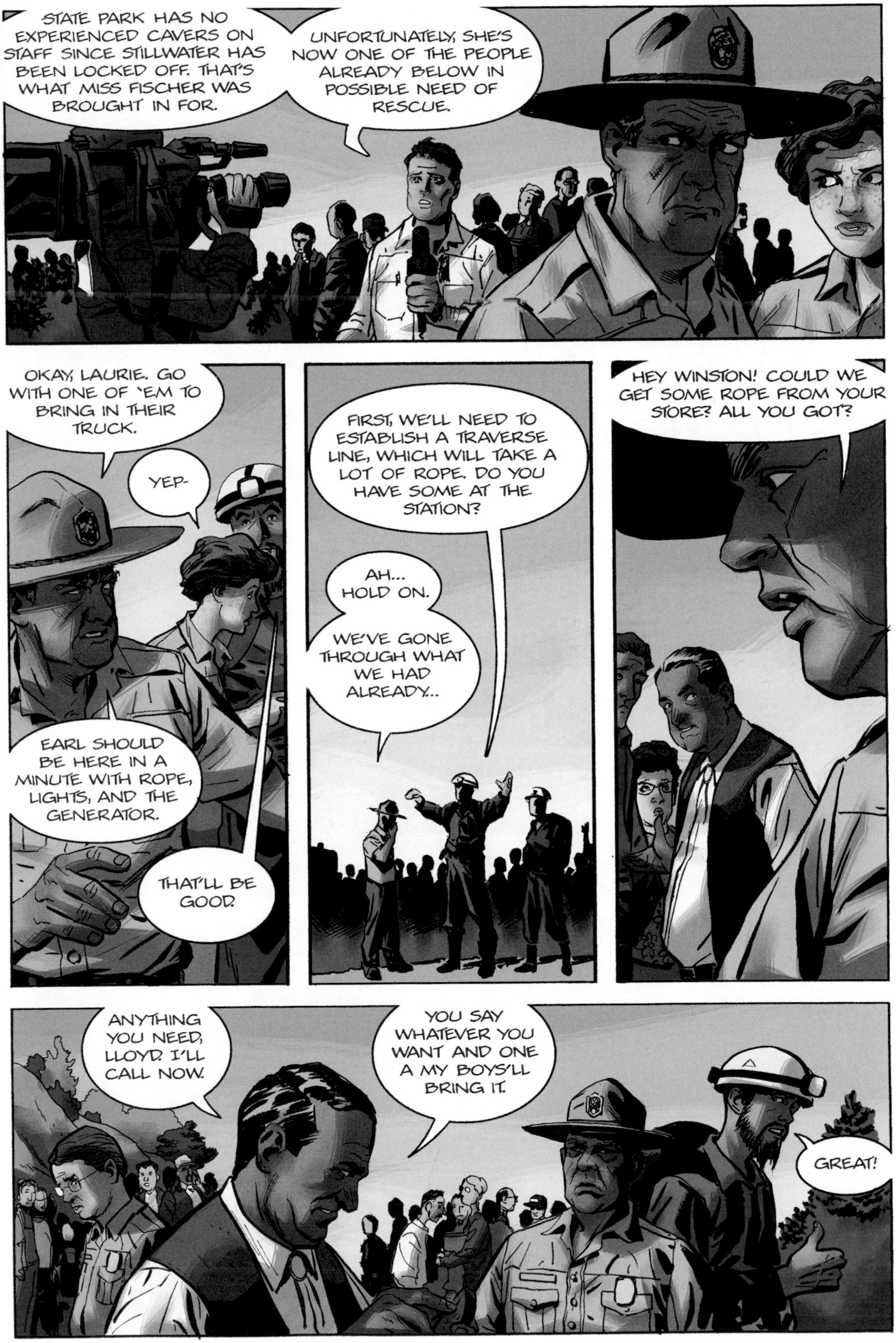
STATE PARK HAS NO EXPERIENCED CAVERS ON STAFF SINCE STILLWATER HAS BEEN LOCKED OFF. THAT'S WHAT MISS FISCHER WAS BROUGHT IN FOR.
UNFORTUNATELY, SHE'S NOW ONE OF THE PEOPLE ALREADY BELOW IN POSSIBLE NEED OF RESCUE.
OKAY, LAURIE. GO WITH ONE OF 'EM TO BRING IN THEIR TRUCK.
YEP-
EARL SHOULD BE HERE IN A MINUTE WITH ROPE, LIGHTS, AND THE GENERATOR.
THAT'LL BE GOOD.
FIRST, WE'LL NEED TO ESTABLISH A TRAVERSE LINE, WHICH WILL TAKE A LOT OF ROPE. DO YOU HAVE SOME AT THE STATION?
AH... HOLD ON.
WE'VE GONE THROUGH WHAT WE HAD ALREADY...
HEY WINSTON! COULD WE GET SOME ROPE FROM YOUR STORE? ALL YOU GOT?
ANYTHING YOU NEED, LLOYD. I'LL CALL NOW.
YOU SAY WHATEVER YOU WANT AND ONE A MY BOYS'LL BRING IT.
GREAT!

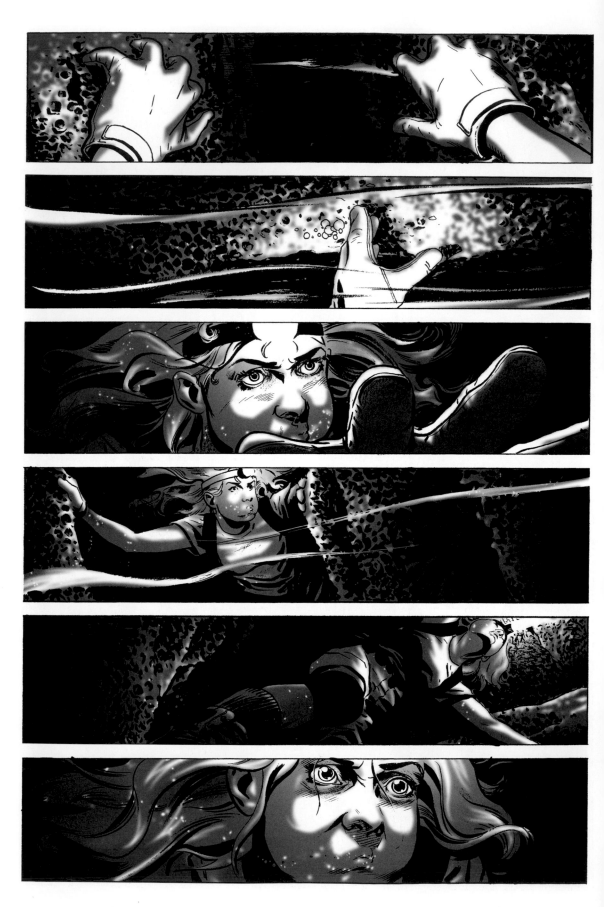

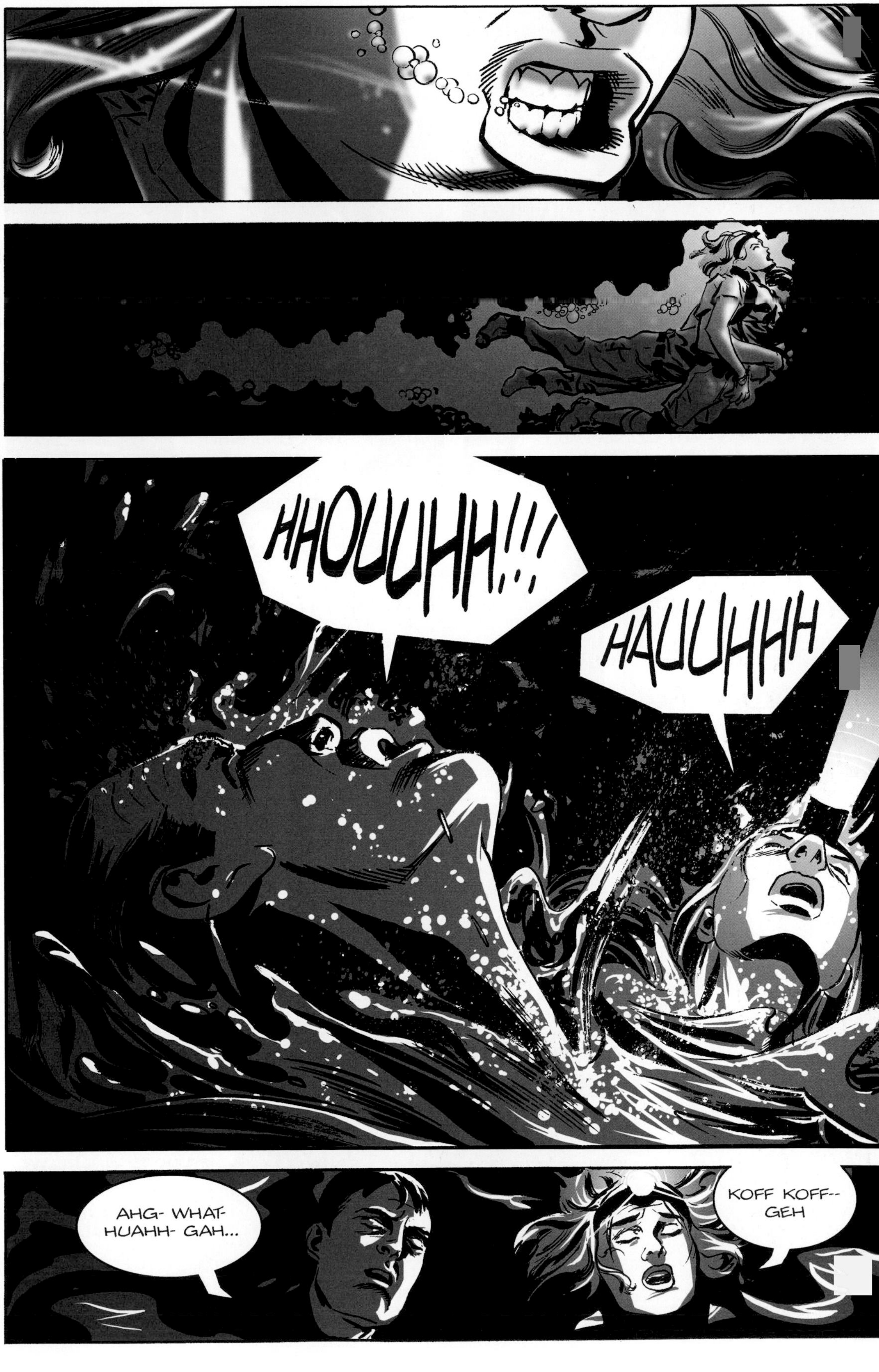
HHOUUHH!!!
HAUUHHH
AHG- WHAT-
HUAHH- GAH...
KOFF KOFF--
GEH

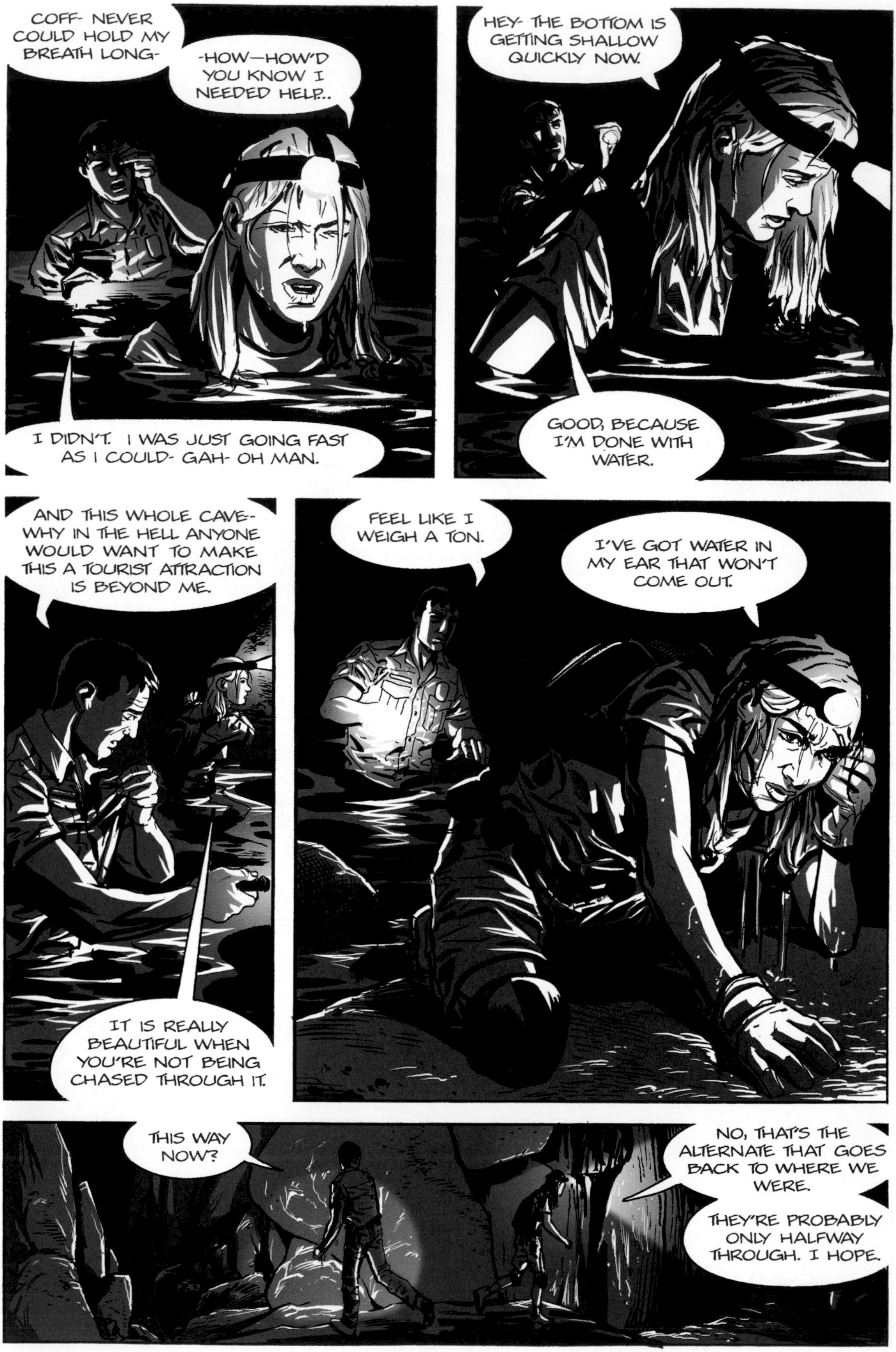
COFF- NEVER COULD HOLD MY BREATH LONG-
-HOW—HOW'D YOU KNOW I NEEDED HELP..
I DIDN'T. I WAS JUST GOING FAST AS I COULD- GAH- OH MAN.
HEY- THE BOTTOM IS GETTING SHALLOW QUICKLY NOW.
GOOD, BECAUSE I'M DONE WITH WATER.
AND THIS WHOLE CAVE- WHY IN THE HELL ANYONE WOULD WANT TO MAKE THIS A TOURIST ATTRACTION IS BEYOND ME.
IT IS REALLY BEAUTIFUL WHEN YOU'RE NOT BEING CHASED THROUGH IT.
FEEL LIKE I WEIGH A TON.
I'VE GOT WATER IN MY EAR THAT WON'T COME OUT.
THIS WAY NOW?
NO, THAT'S THE ALTERNATE THAT GOES BACK TO WHERE WE WERE.
THEY'RE PROBABLY ONLY HALFWAY THROUGH. I HOPE.

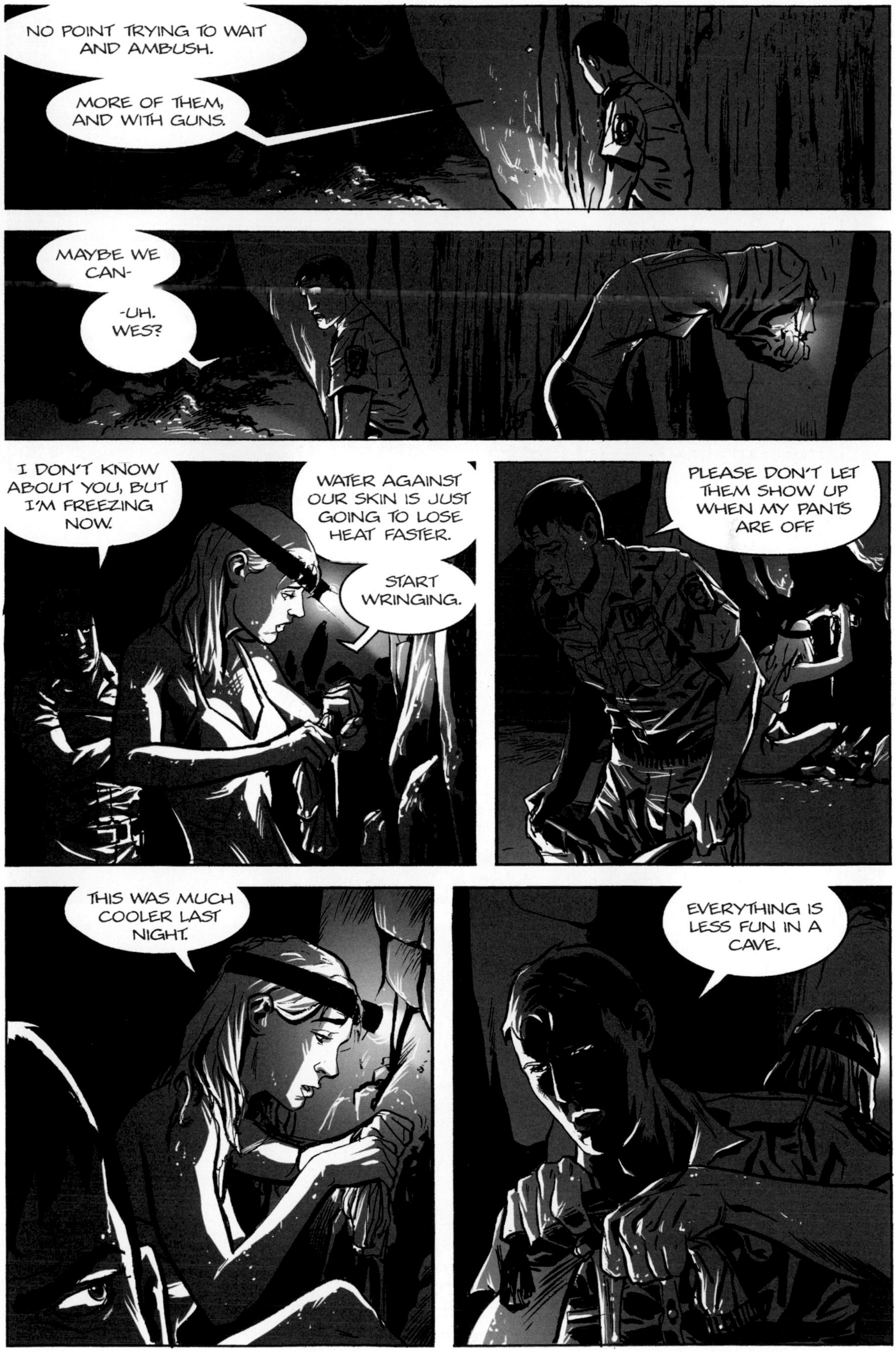
NO POINT TRYING TO WAIT AND AMBUSH.
MORE OF THEM, AND WITH GUNS.
MAYBE WE CAN-
-UH. WES?
I DON'T KNOW ABOUT YOU, BUT I'M FREEZING NOW.
WATER AGAINST OUR SKIN IS JUST GOING TO LOSE HEAT FASTER.
START WRINGING.
PLEASE DON'T LET THEM SHOW UP WHEN MY PANTS ARE OFF.
THIS WAS MUCH COOLER LAST NIGHT.
EVERYTHING IS LESS FUN IN A CAVE.

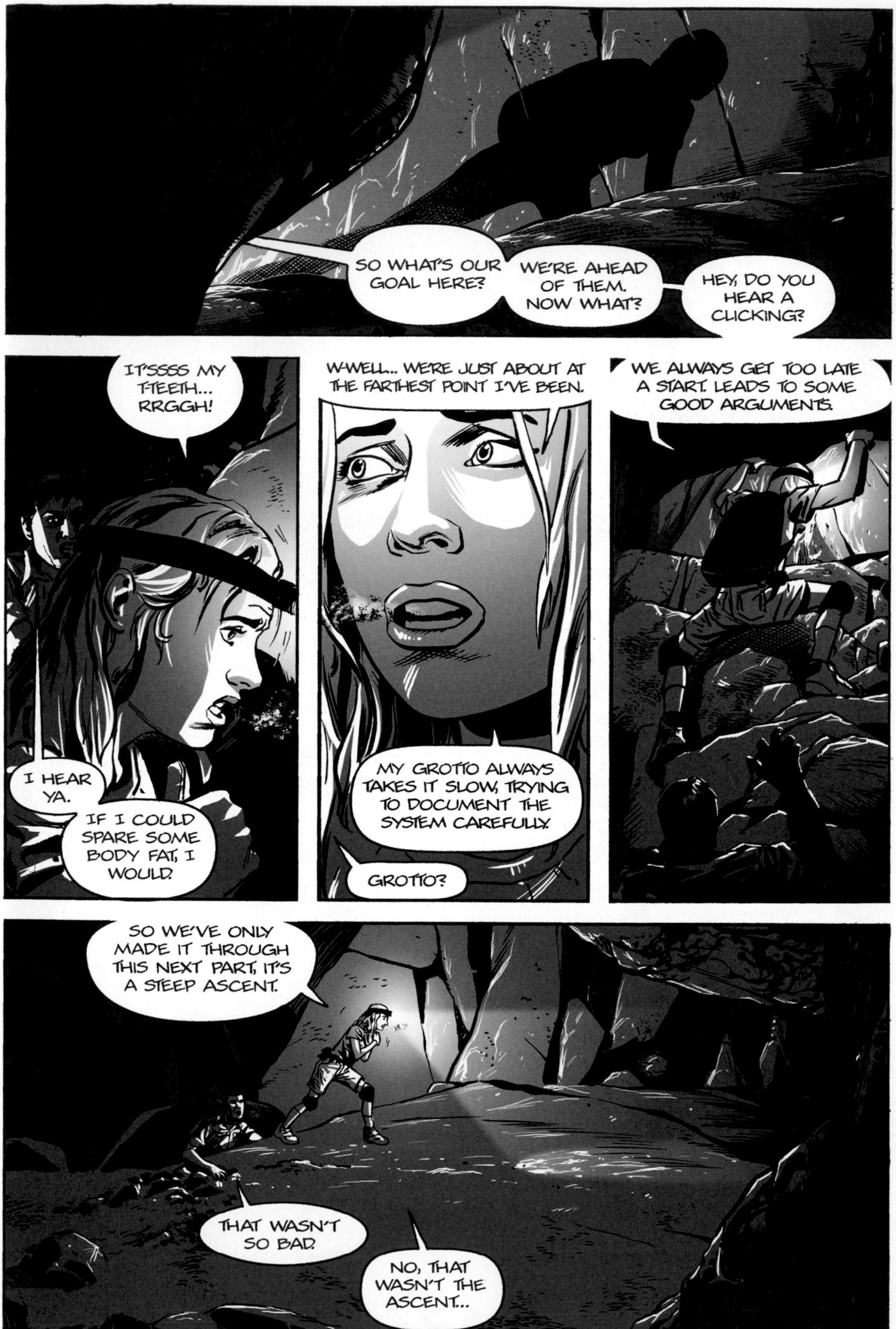

SO WHAT'S OUR GOAL HERE?
WE'RE AHEAD OF THEM. NOW WHAT?
HEY, DO YOU HEAR A CLICKING?
IT'SSSS MY T-TEETH... RRGGH!
I HEAR YA.
IF I COULD SPARE SOME BODY FAT, I WOULD.
W-WELL... WE'RE JUST ABOUT AT THE FARTHEST POINT I'VE BEEN.
MY GROTTO ALWAYS TAKES IT SLOW, TRYING TO DOCUMENT THE SYSTEM CAREFULLY.
GROTTO?
WE ALWAYS GET TOO LATE A START. LEADS TO SOME GOOD ARGUMENTS.
SO WE'VE ONLY MADE IT THROUGH THIS NEXT PART, IT'S A STEEP ASCENT.
THAT WASN'T SO BAD.
NO, THAT WASN'T THE ASCENT...

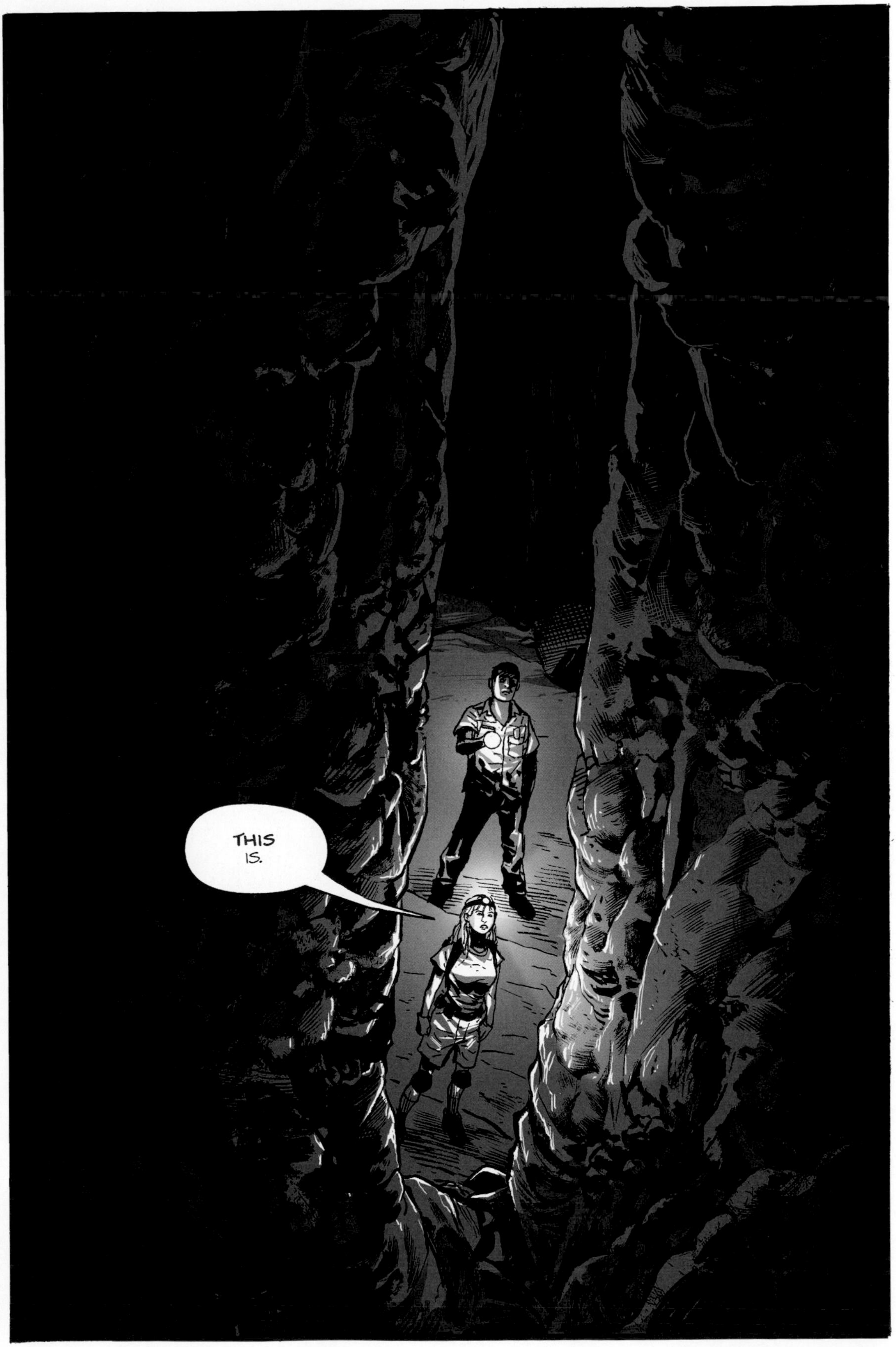
THIS IS.

CHAPTER FIVE

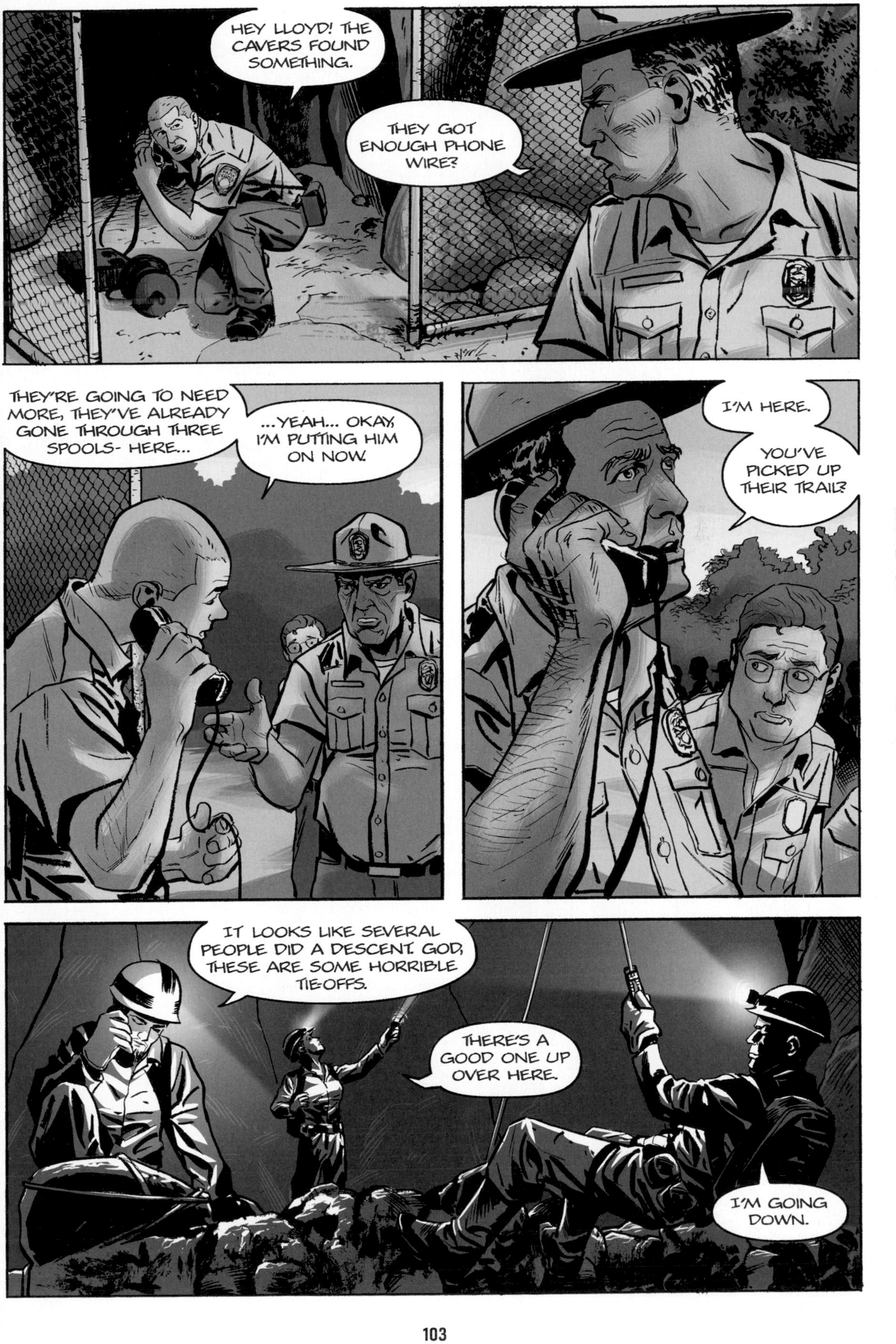
HEY LLOYD! THE CAVERS FOUND SOMETHING.
THEY GOT ENOUGH PHONE WIRE?
THEY'RE GOING TO NEED MORE, THEY'VE ALREADY GONE THROUGH THREE SPOOLS- HERE...
...YEAH... OKAY, I'M PUTTING HIM ON NOW.
I'M HERE.
YOU'VE PICKED UP THEIR TRAIL?
IT LOOKS LIKE SEVERAL PEOPLE DID A DESCENT. GOD, THESE ARE SOME HORRIBLE TIE-OFFS.
THERE'S A GOOD ONE UP OVER HERE.
I'M GOING DOWN.

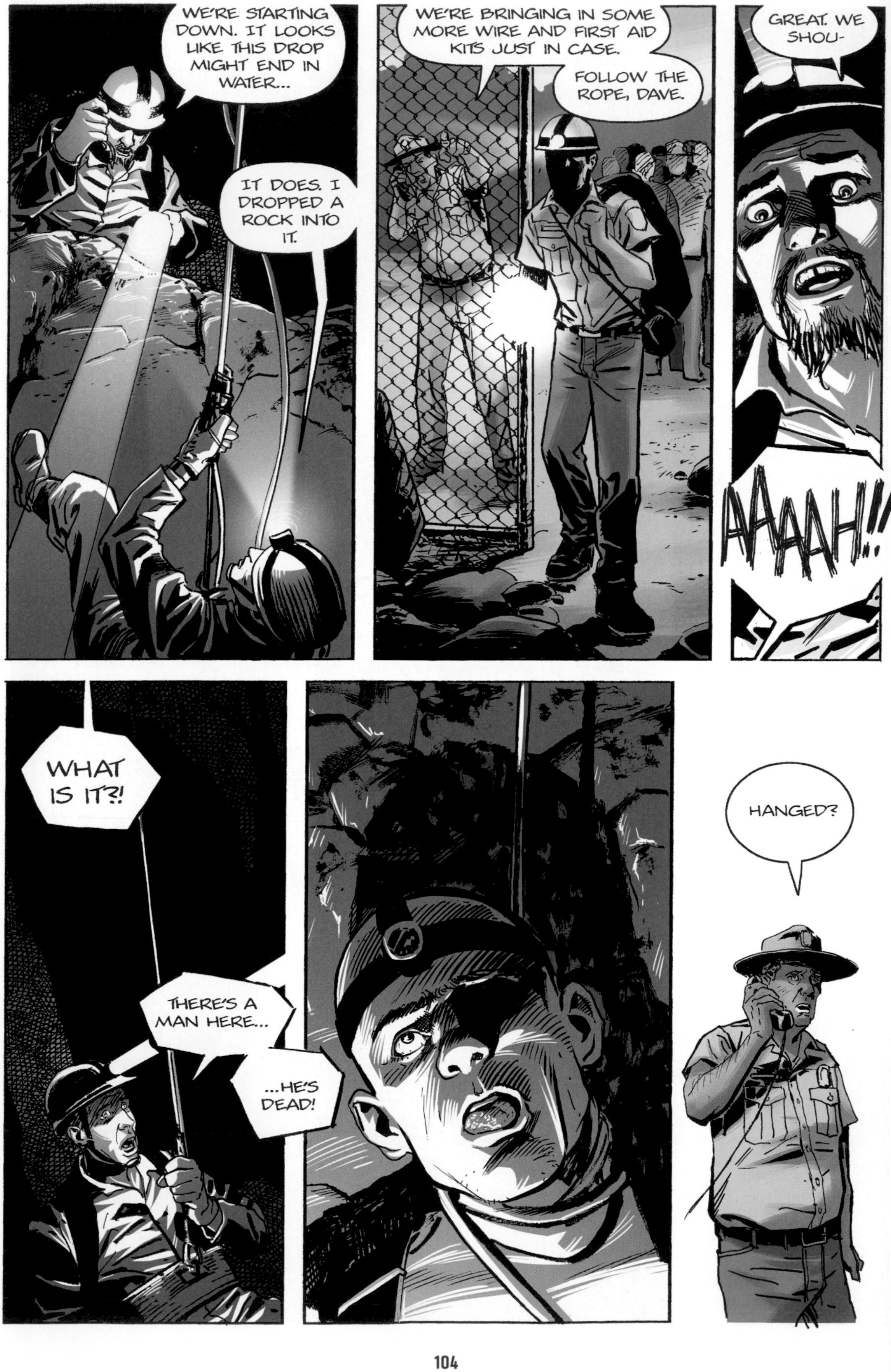

WE'RE STARTING DOWN. IT LOOKS LIKE THIS DROP MIGHT END IN WATER...
IT DOES. I DROPPED A ROCK INTO IT.
WE'RE BRINGING IN SOME MORE WIRE AND FIRST AID KITS JUST IN CASE.
FOLLOW THE ROPE, DAVE.
GREAT. WE SHOU-
AAAAH!!
WHAT IS IT?!
THERE'S A MAN HERE...
...HE'S DEAD!
HANGED?

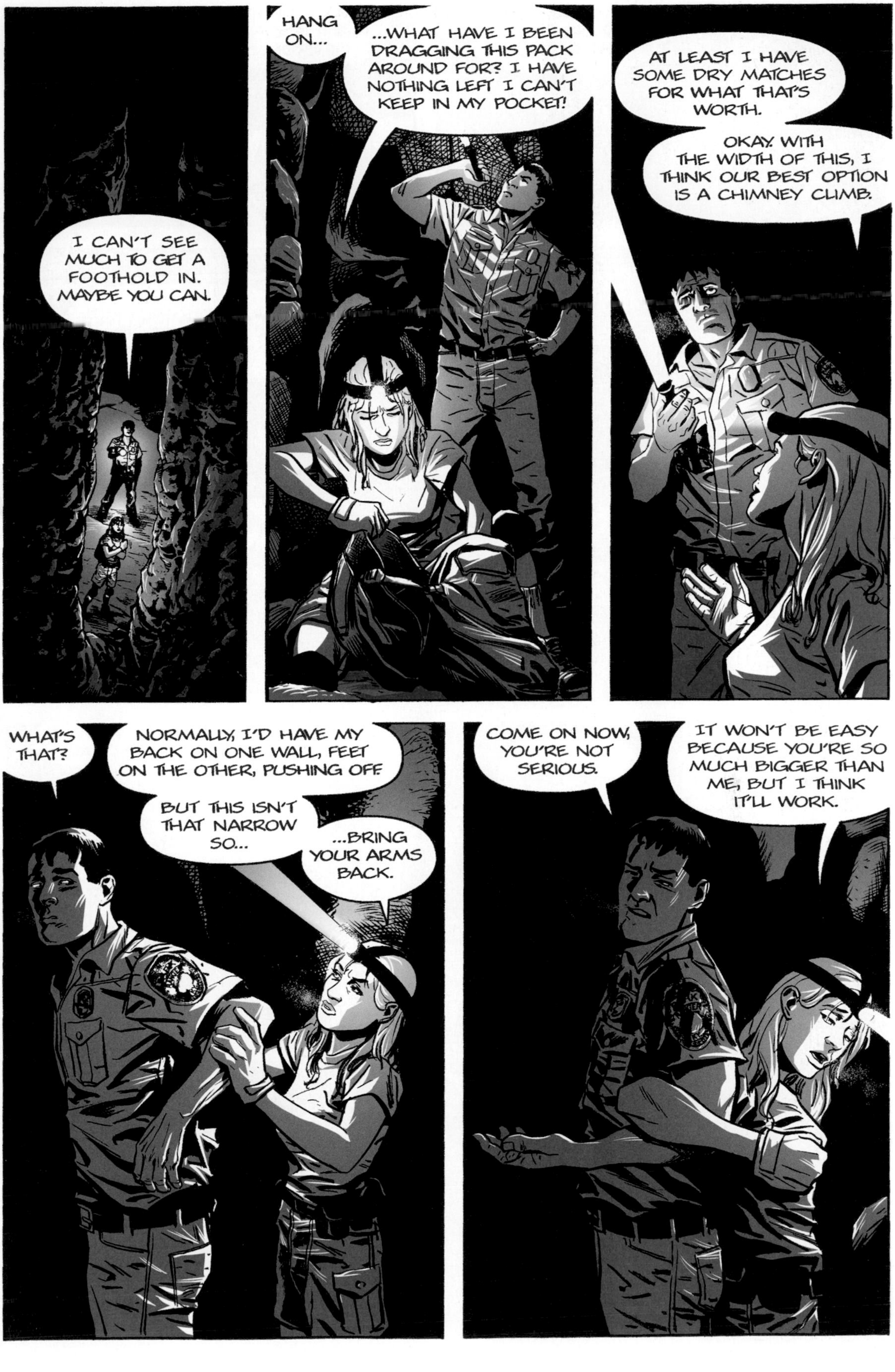
I CAN'T SEE MUCH TO GET A FOOTHOLD IN. MAYBE YOU CAN.
HANG ON...
...WHAT HAVE I BEEN DRAGGING THIS PACK AROUND FOR? I HAVE NOTHING LEFT I CAN'T KEEP IN MY POCKET!
AT LEAST I HAVE SOME DRY MATCHES FOR WHAT THAT'S WORTH.
OKAY. WITH THE WIDTH OF THIS, I THINK OUR BEST OPTION IS A CHIMNEY CLIMB.
WHAT'S THAT?
NORMALLY, I'D HAVE MY BACK ON ONE WALL, FEET ON THE OTHER, PUSHING OFF.
BUT THIS ISN'T THAT NARROW SO...
...BRING YOUR ARMS BACK.
COME ON NOW, YOU'RE NOT SERIOUS.
IT WON'T BE EASY BECAUSE YOU'RE SO MUCH BIGGER THAN ME, BUT I THINK IT'LL WORK.

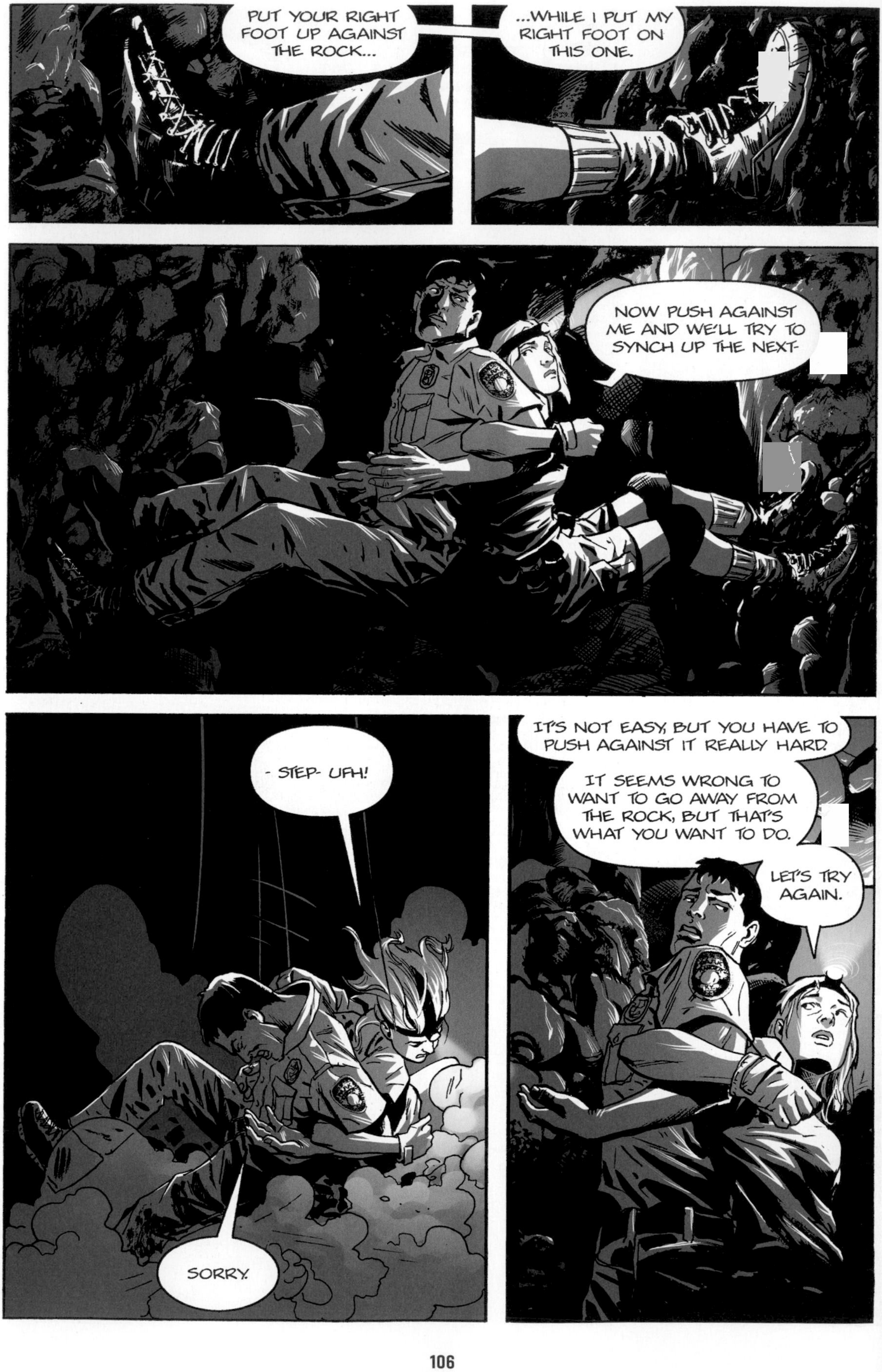
PUT YOUR RIGHT FOOT UP AGAINST THE ROCK...
...WHILE I PUT MY RIGHT FOOT ON THIS ONE.
NOW PUSH AGAINST ME AND WE'LL TRY TO SYNCH UP THE NEXT-
- STEP- UFH!
SORRY.
IT'S NOT EASY, BUT YOU HAVE TO PUSH AGAINST IT REALLY HARD.
IT SEEMS WRONG TO WANT TO GO AWAY FROM THE ROCK, BUT THAT'S WHAT YOU WANT TO DO.
LET'S TRY AGAIN.

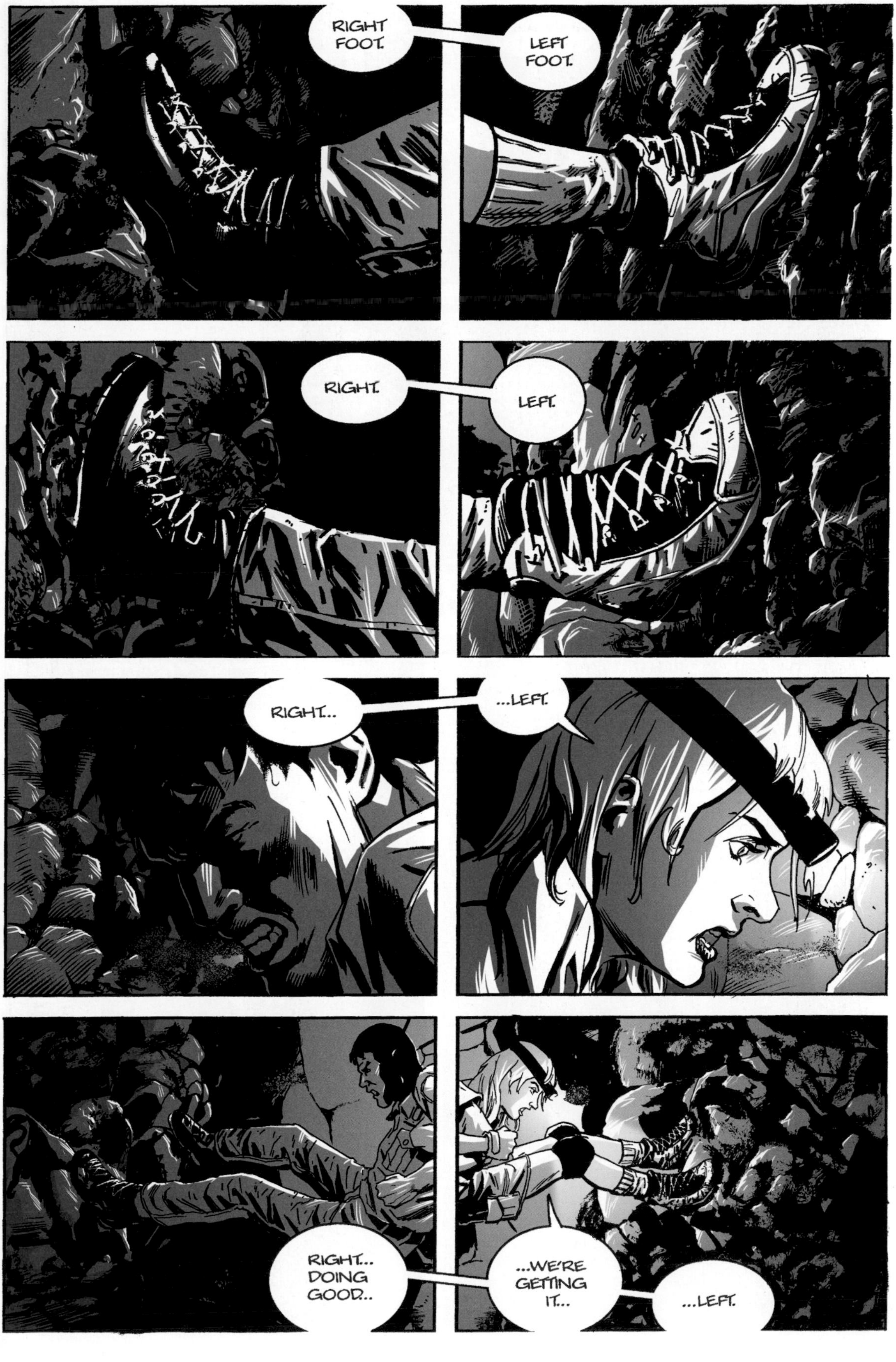
RIGHT FOOT.
LEFT FOOT.
RIGHT.
LEFT.
RIGHT...
...LEFT.
RIGHT... DOING GOOD..
...WE'RE GETTING IT...
...LEFT.

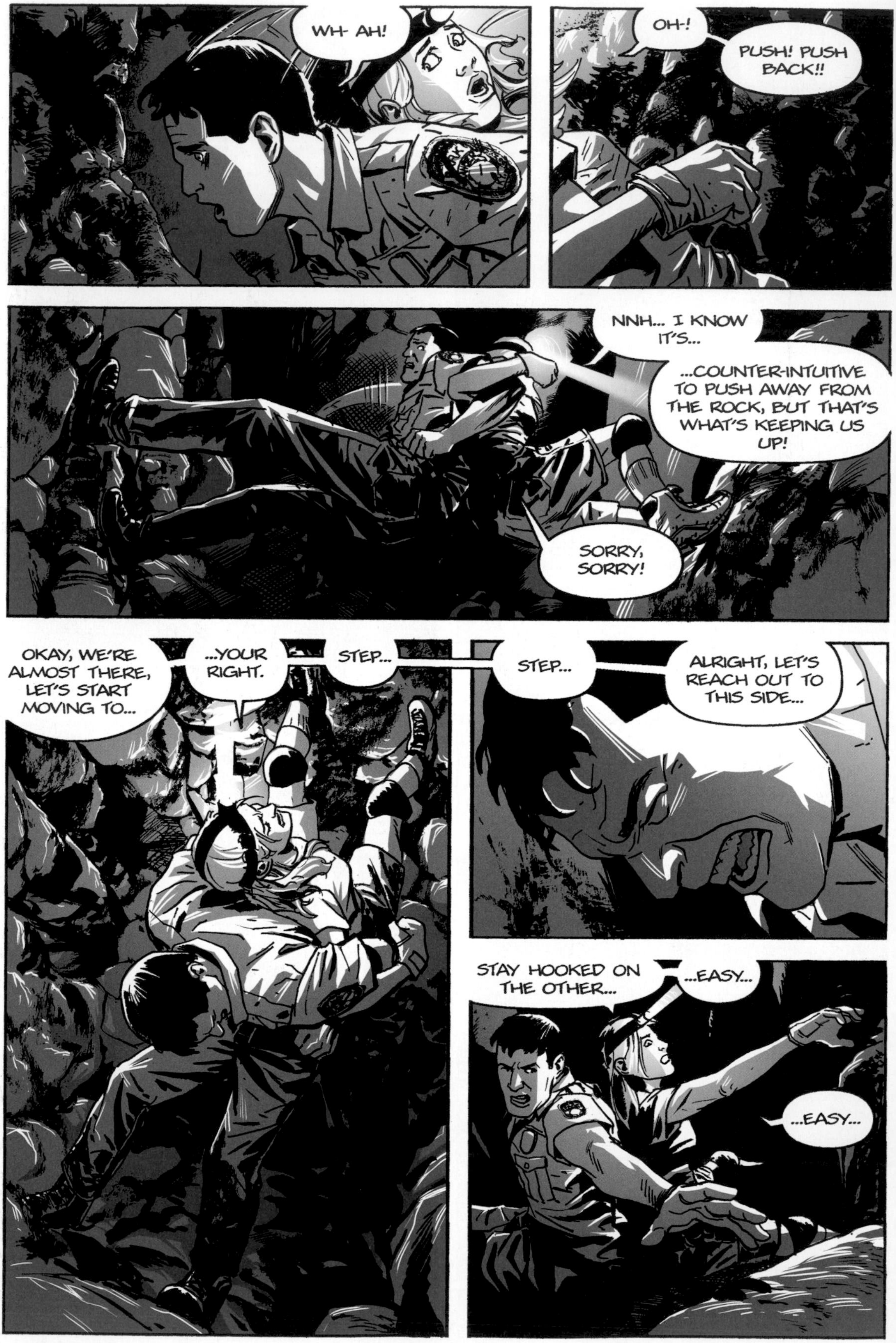
WH- AH!
OH-!
PUSH! PUSH BACK!!
NNH... I KNOW IT'S...
...COUNTER-INTUITIVE TO PUSH AWAY FROM THE ROCK, BUT THAT'S WHAT'S KEEPING US UP!
SORRY, SORRY!
OKAY, WE'RE ALMOST THERE, LET'S START MOVING TO...
...YOUR RIGHT.
STEP...
STEP...
ALRIGHT, LET'S REACH OUT TO THIS SIDE...
STAY HOOKED ON THE OTHER...
...EASY...
...EASY...

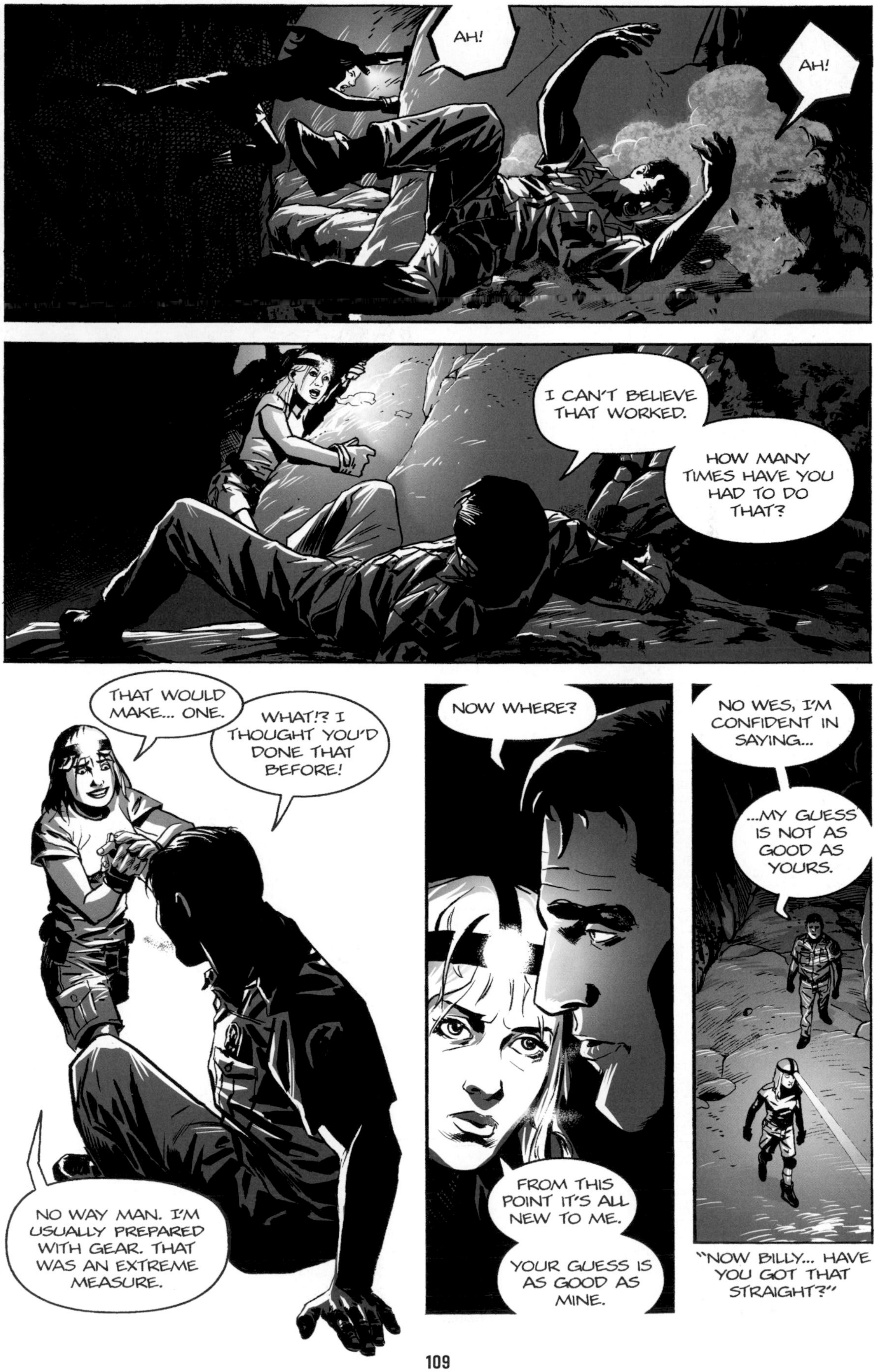
AH!
AH!
I CAN'T BELIEVE THAT WORKED.
HOW MANY TIMES HAVE YOU HAD TO DO THAT?
THAT WOULD MAKE... ONE.
WHAT!? I THOUGHT YOU'D DONE THAT BEFORE!
NO WAY MAN. I'M USUALLY PREPARED WITH GEAR. THAT WAS AN EXTREME MEASURE.
NOW WHERE?
FROM THIS POINT IT'S ALL NEW TO ME.
YOUR GUESS IS AS GOOD AS MINE.
NO WES, I'M CONFIDENT IN SAYING...
...MY GUESS IS NOT AS GOOD AS YOURS.
"NOW BILLY... HAVE YOU GOT THAT STRAIGHT?"

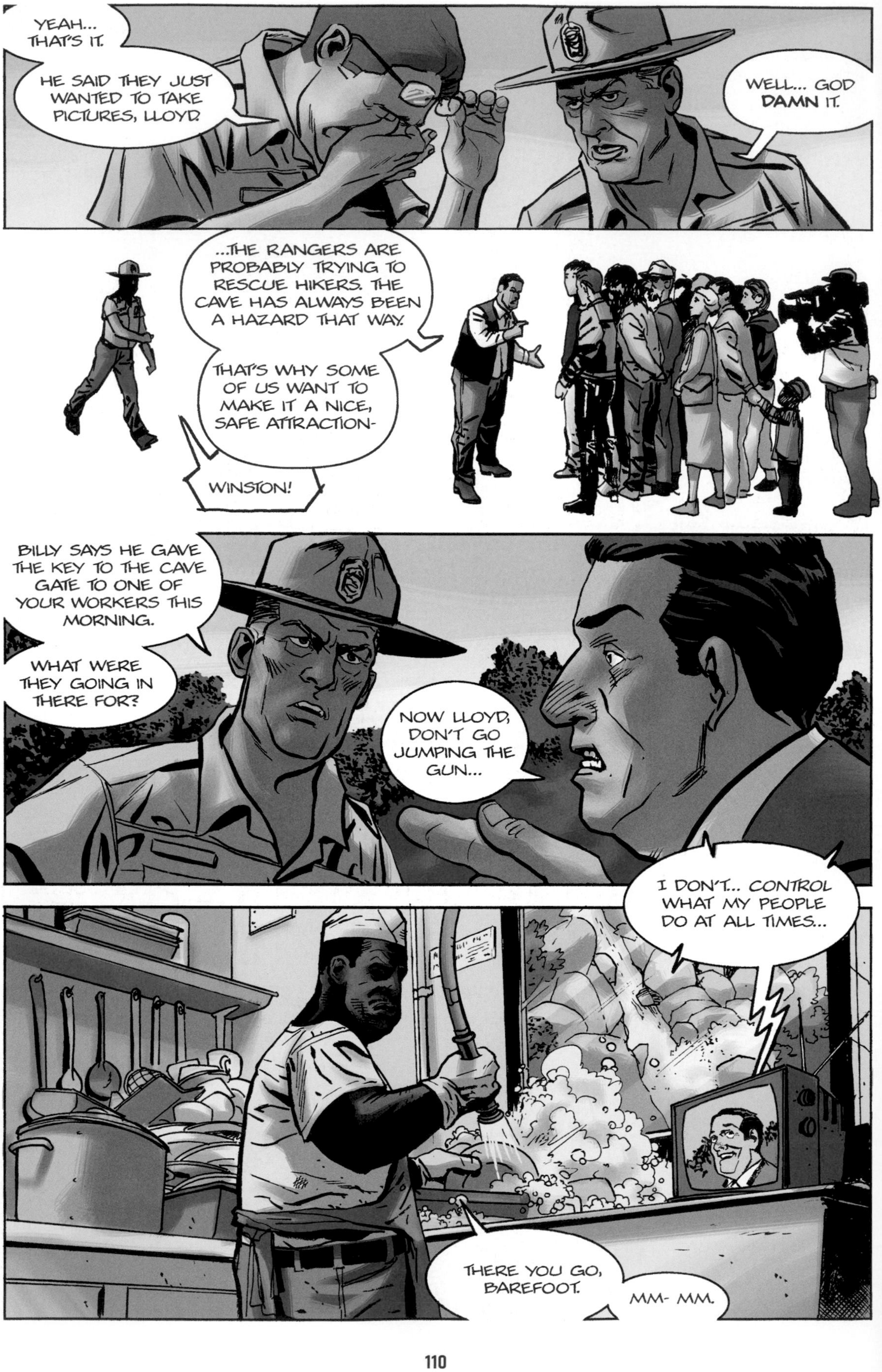
YEAH... THAT'S IT.
HE SAID THEY JUST WANTED TO TAKE PICTURES, LLOYD.
WELL... GOD **DAMN** IT.
...THE RANGERS ARE PROBABLY TRYING TO RESCUE HIKERS. THE CAVE HAS ALWAYS BEEN A HAZARD THAT WAY.
THAT'S WHY SOME OF US WANT TO MAKE IT A NICE, SAFE ATTRACTION-
WINSTON!
BILLY SAYS HE GAVE THE KEY TO THE CAVE GATE TO ONE OF YOUR WORKERS THIS MORNING.
WHAT WERE THEY GOING IN THERE FOR?
NOW LLOYD, DON'T GO JUMPING THE GUN...
I DON'T... CONTROL WHAT MY PEOPLE DO AT ALL TIMES...
THERE YOU GO, BAREFOOT.
MM- MM.

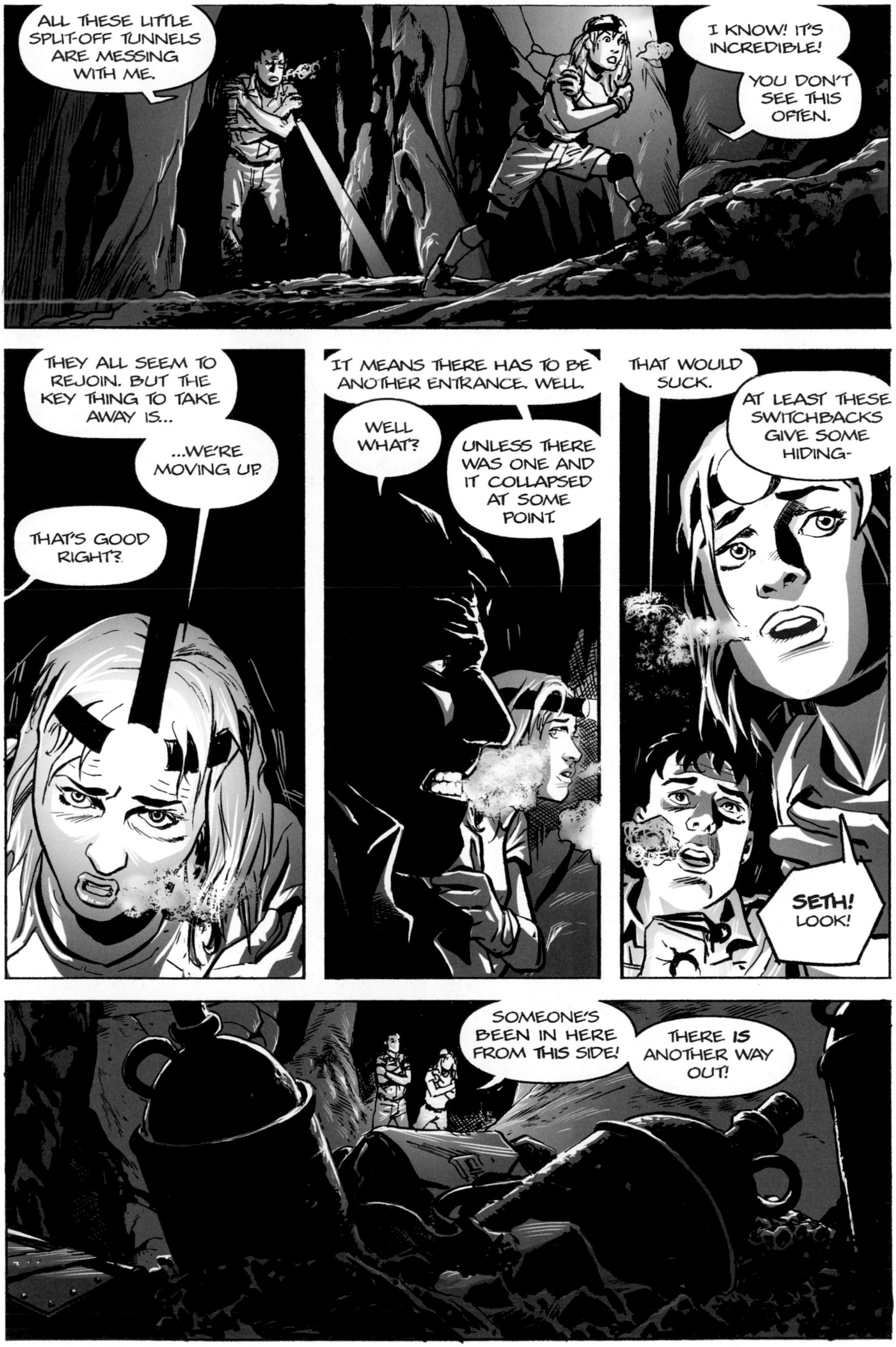
ALL THESE LITTLE SPLIT-OFF TUNNELS ARE MESSING WITH ME.
I KNOW! IT'S INCREDIBLE!
YOU DON'T SEE THIS OFTEN.
THEY ALL SEEM TO REJOIN. BUT THE KEY THING TO TAKE AWAY IS...
...WE'RE MOVING UP.
THAT'S GOOD RIGHT?
IT MEANS THERE HAS TO BE ANOTHER ENTRANCE. WELL.
WELL WHAT?
UNLESS THERE WAS ONE AND IT COLLAPSED AT SOME POINT.
THAT WOULD SUCK.
AT LEAST THESE SWITCHBACKS GIVE SOME HIDING-
SETH! LOOK!
SOMEONE'S BEEN IN HERE FROM THIS SIDE!
THERE IS ANOTHER WAY OUT!

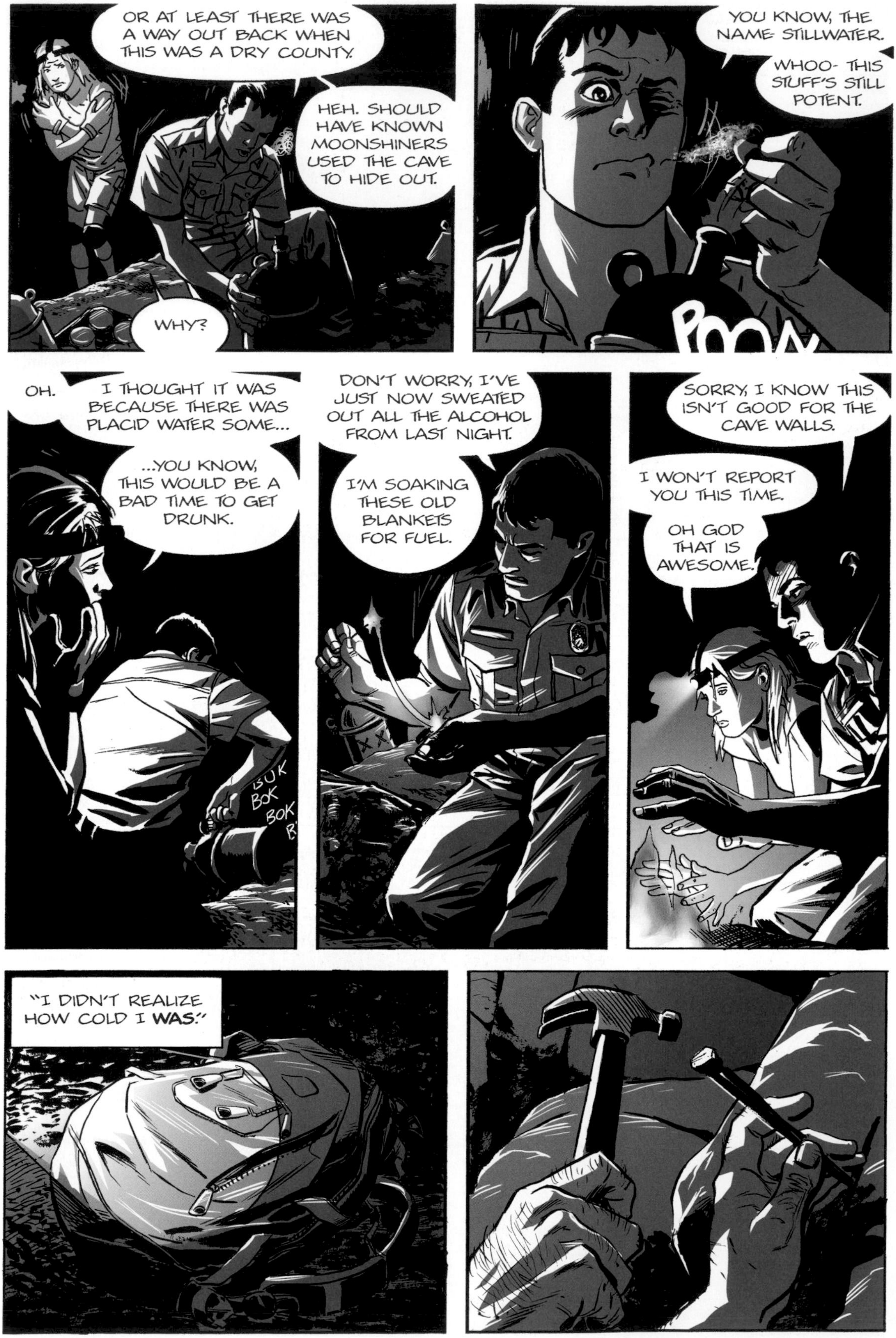

OR AT LEAST THERE WAS A WAY OUT BACK WHEN THIS WAS A DRY COUNTY.
HEH. SHOULD HAVE KNOWN MOONSHINERS USED THE CAVE TO HIDE OUT.
WHY?
YOU KNOW, THE NAME STILLWATER.
WHOO- THIS STUFF'S STILL POTENT.
POOM
OH.
I THOUGHT IT WAS BECAUSE THERE WAS PLACID WATER SOME...
...YOU KNOW, THIS WOULD BE A BAD TIME TO GET DRUNK.
BUK BOK BOK
DON'T WORRY, I'VE JUST NOW SWEATED OUT ALL THE ALCOHOL FROM LAST NIGHT.
I'M SOAKING THESE OLD BLANKETS FOR FUEL.
SORRY, I KNOW THIS ISN'T GOOD FOR THE CAVE WALLS.
I WON'T REPORT YOU THIS TIME.
OH GOD THAT IS AWESOME.
"I DIDN'T REALIZE HOW COLD I WAS."

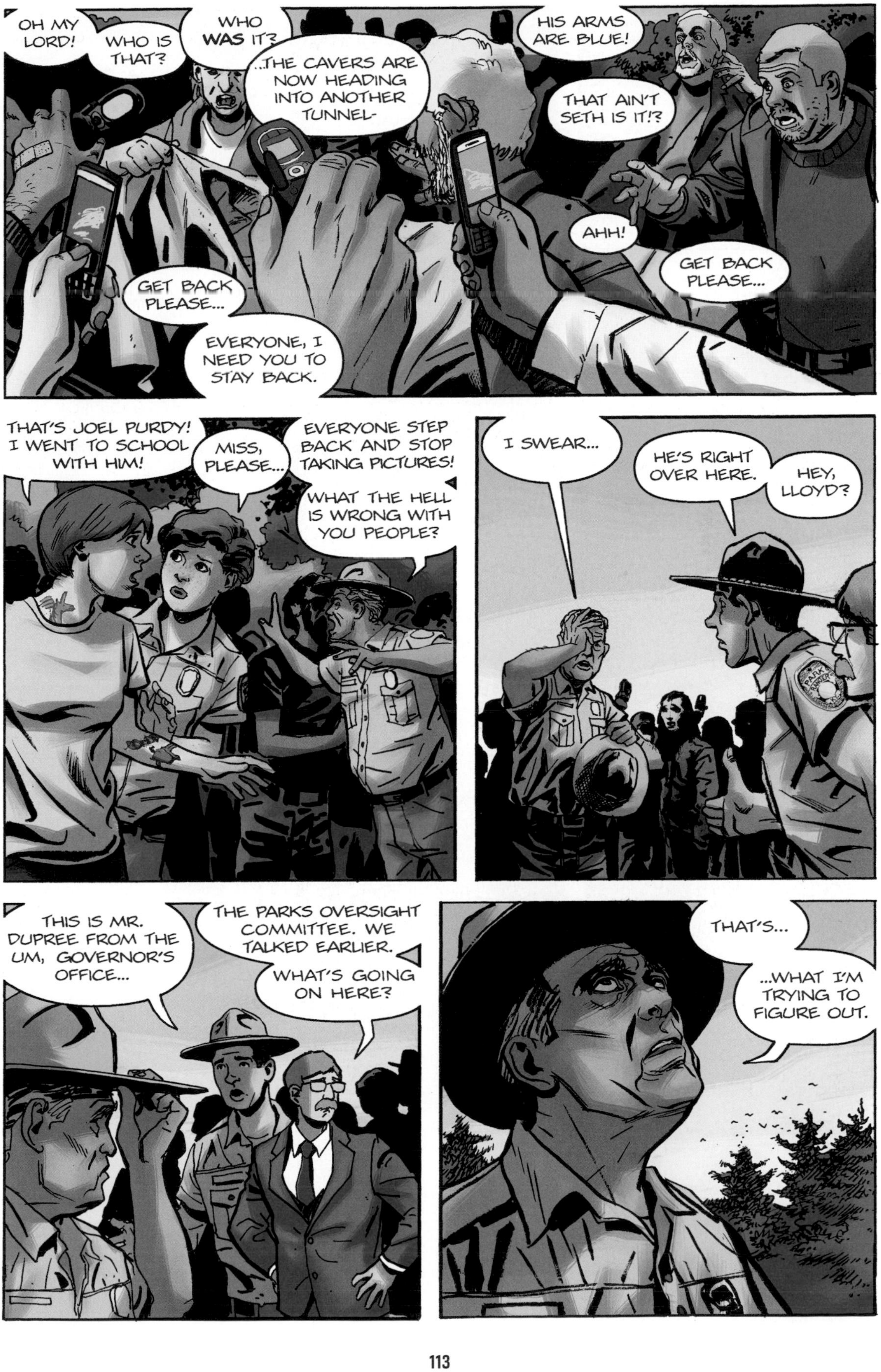
OH MY LORD!
WHO IS THAT?
WHO WAS IT?
...THE CAVERS ARE NOW HEADING INTO ANOTHER TUNNEL-
HIS ARMS ARE BLUE!
THAT AIN'T SETH IS IT!?
AHH!
GET BACK PLEASE...
GET BACK PLEASE...
EVERYONE, I NEED YOU TO STAY BACK.
THAT'S JOEL PURDY! I WENT TO SCHOOL WITH HIM!
MISS, PLEASE...
EVERYONE STEP BACK AND STOP TAKING PICTURES!
WHAT THE HELL IS WRONG WITH YOU PEOPLE?
I SWEAR...
HE'S RIGHT OVER HERE.
HEY, LLOYD?
THIS IS MR. DUPREE FROM THE UM, GOVERNOR'S OFFICE...
THE PARKS OVERSIGHT COMMITTEE. WE TALKED EARLIER.
WHAT'S GOING ON HERE?
THAT'S...
...WHAT I'M TRYING TO FIGURE OUT.

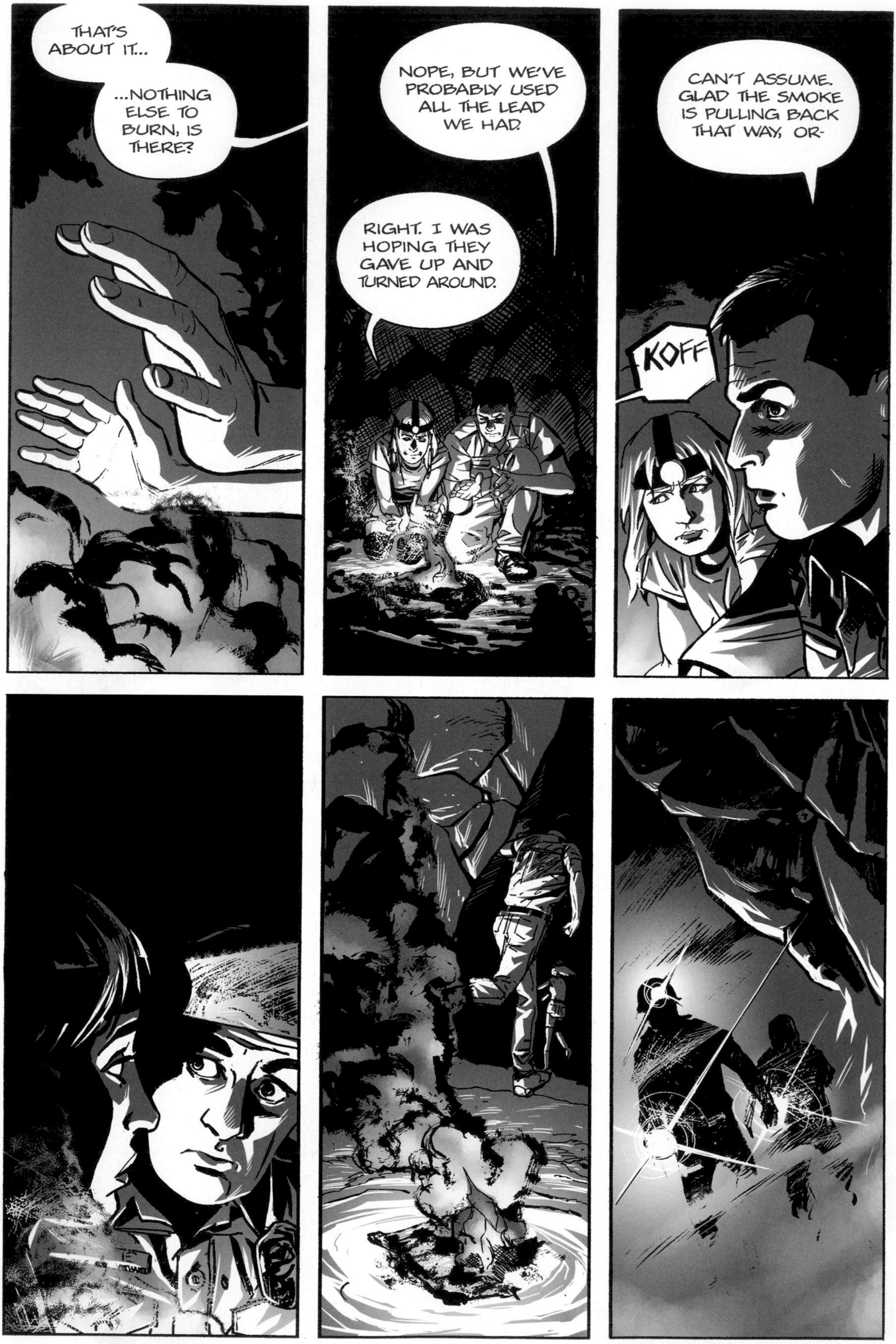
THAT'S ABOUT IT...
...NOTHING ELSE TO BURN, IS THERE?
NOPE, BUT WE'VE PROBABLY USED ALL THE LEAD WE HAD.
RIGHT. I WAS HOPING THEY GAVE UP AND TURNED AROUND.
CAN'T ASSUME. GLAD THE SMOKE IS PULLING BACK THAT WAY, OR-
KOFF

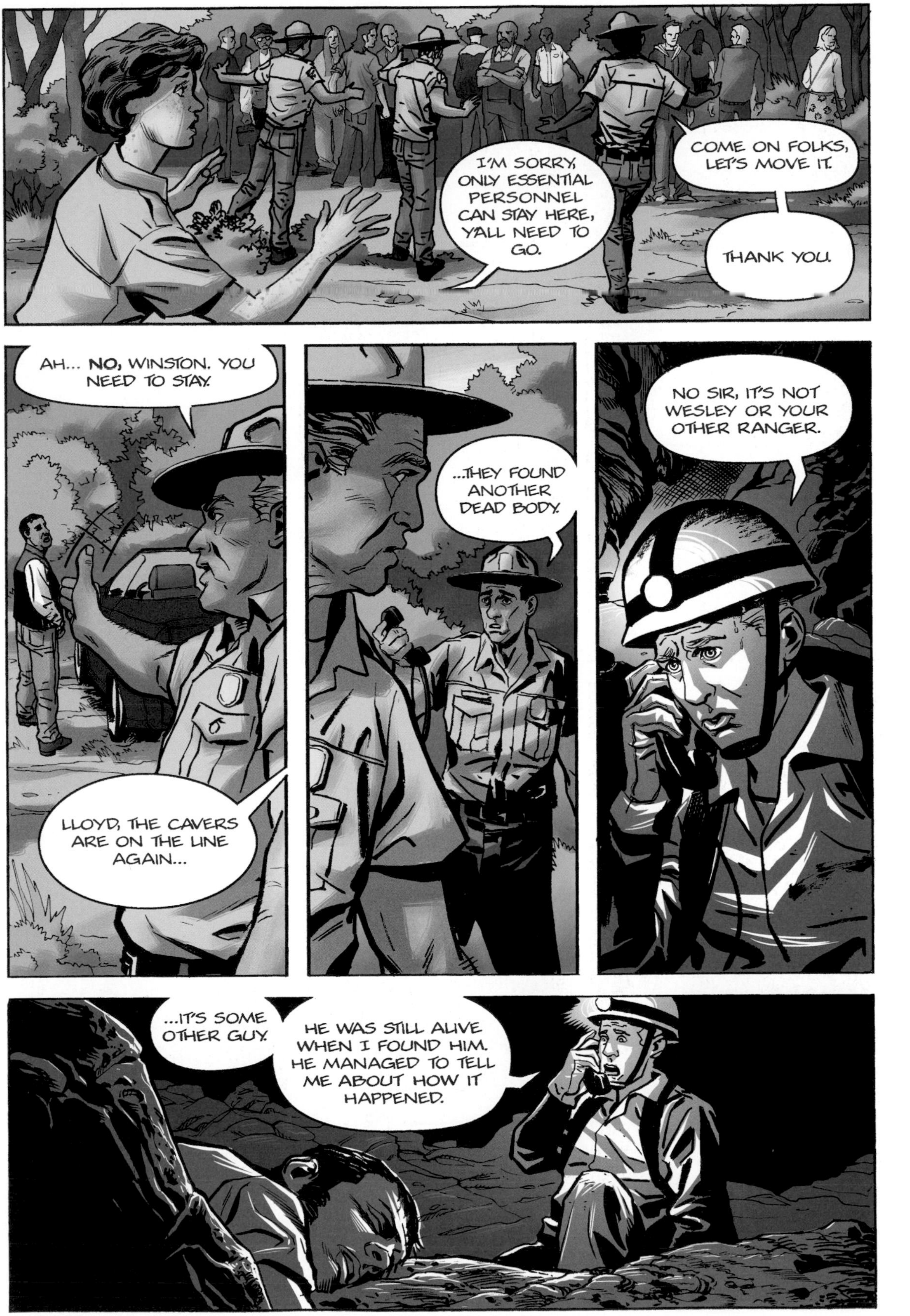
I'M SORRY, ONLY ESSENTIAL PERSONNEL CAN STAY HERE, Y'ALL NEED TO GO.
COME ON FOLKS, LET'S MOVE IT.
THANK YOU.
AH... **NO,** WINSTON. YOU NEED TO STAY.
LLOYD, THE CAVERS ARE ON THE LINE AGAIN...
...THEY FOUND ANOTHER DEAD BODY.
NO SIR, IT'S NOT WESLEY OR YOUR OTHER RANGER.
...IT'S SOME OTHER GUY.
HE WAS STILL ALIVE WHEN I FOUND HIM. HE MANAGED TO TELL ME ABOUT HOW IT HAPPENED.

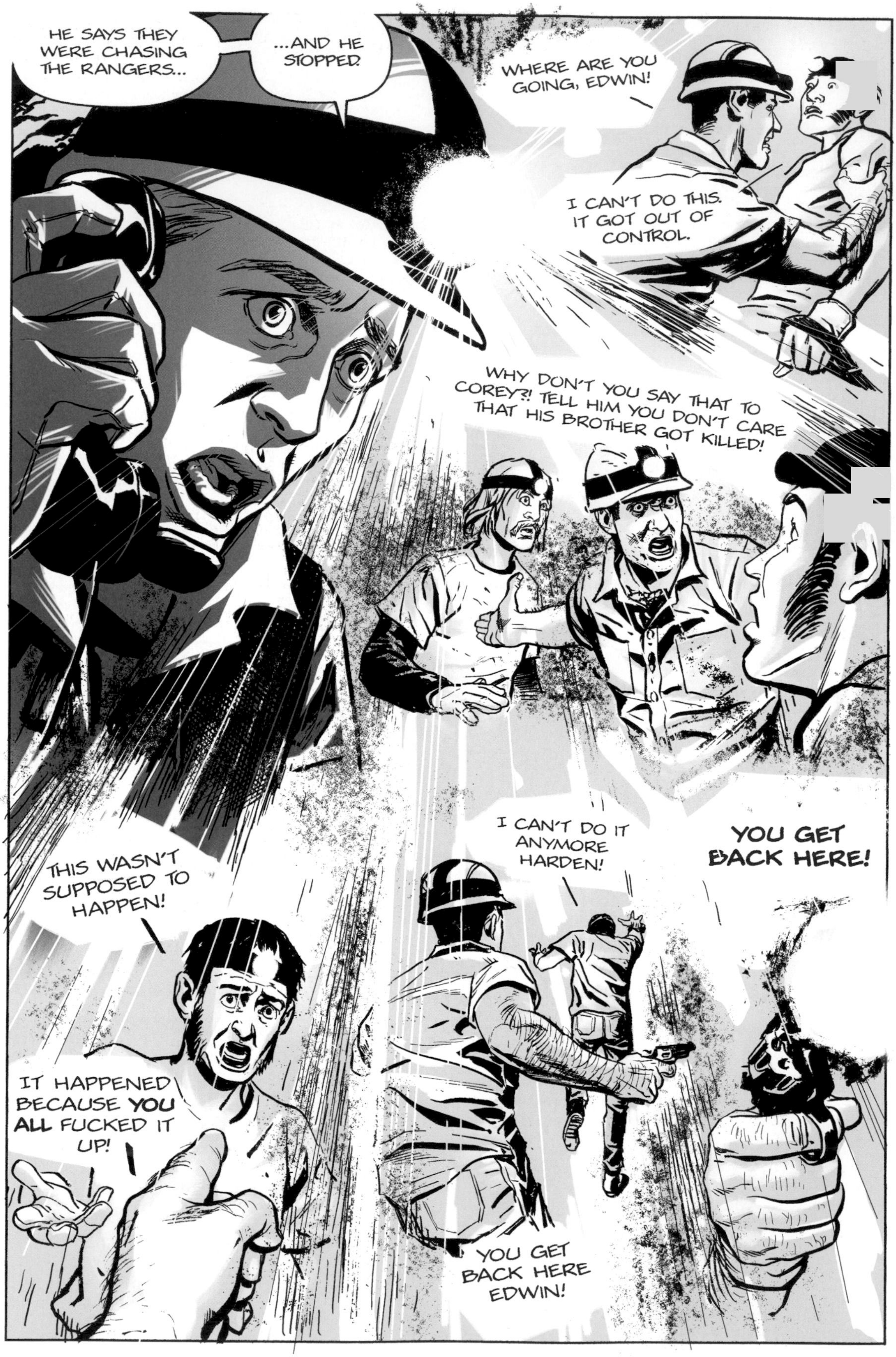
HE SAYS THEY WERE CHASING THE RANGERS...
...AND HE STOPPED.
WHERE ARE YOU GOING, EDWIN!
I CAN'T DO THIS. IT GOT OUT OF CONTROL.
WHY DON'T YOU SAY THAT TO COREY?! TELL HIM YOU DON'T CARE THAT HIS BROTHER GOT KILLED!
THIS WASN'T SUPPOSED TO HAPPEN!
IT HAPPENED BECAUSE **YOU ALL** FUCKED IT UP!
I CAN'T DO IT ANYMORE HARDEN!
YOU GET BACK HERE!
YOU GET BACK HERE EDWIN!

I TRIED CPR, BUT...

...HE WAS GONE.

...I COULD ANSWER THAT, BUT MY LAWYER WOULD GIVE ME THE DICKENS WHAT WITH HOW SERIOUS ALL THIS IS.

SO I BETTER HOLD OFF FOR NOW...

YOU SON OF A BITCH!

THERE'S ANOTHER MAN DEAD DOWN THERE!

THERE'S AN ARMED KILLER CHASING MY RANGERS!

WHO THE HELL IS THIS HARDEN FELLER, WINSTON!?

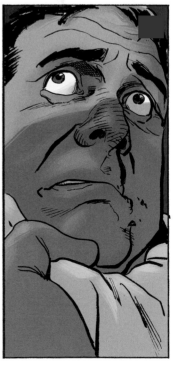

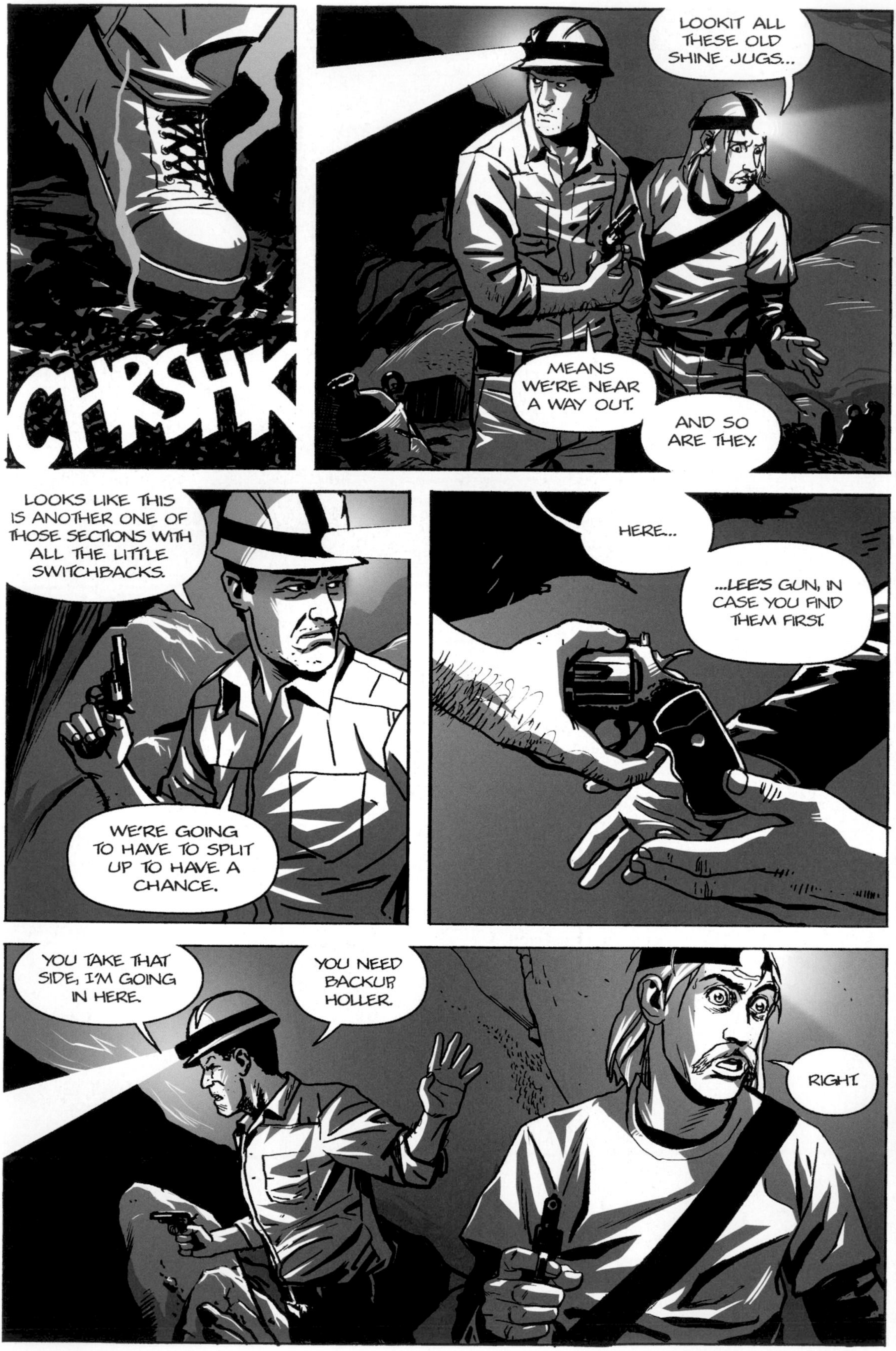
CHRSHK
LOOKIT ALL THESE OLD SHINE JUGS...
MEANS WE'RE NEAR A WAY OUT.
AND SO ARE THEY.
LOOKS LIKE THIS IS ANOTHER ONE OF THOSE SECTIONS WITH ALL THE LITTLE SWITCHBACKS.
WE'RE GOING TO HAVE TO SPLIT UP TO HAVE A CHANCE.
HERE...
...LEE'S GUN, IN CASE YOU FIND THEM FIRST.
YOU TAKE THAT SIDE, I'M GOING IN HERE.
YOU NEED BACKUP, HOLLER.
RIGHT.

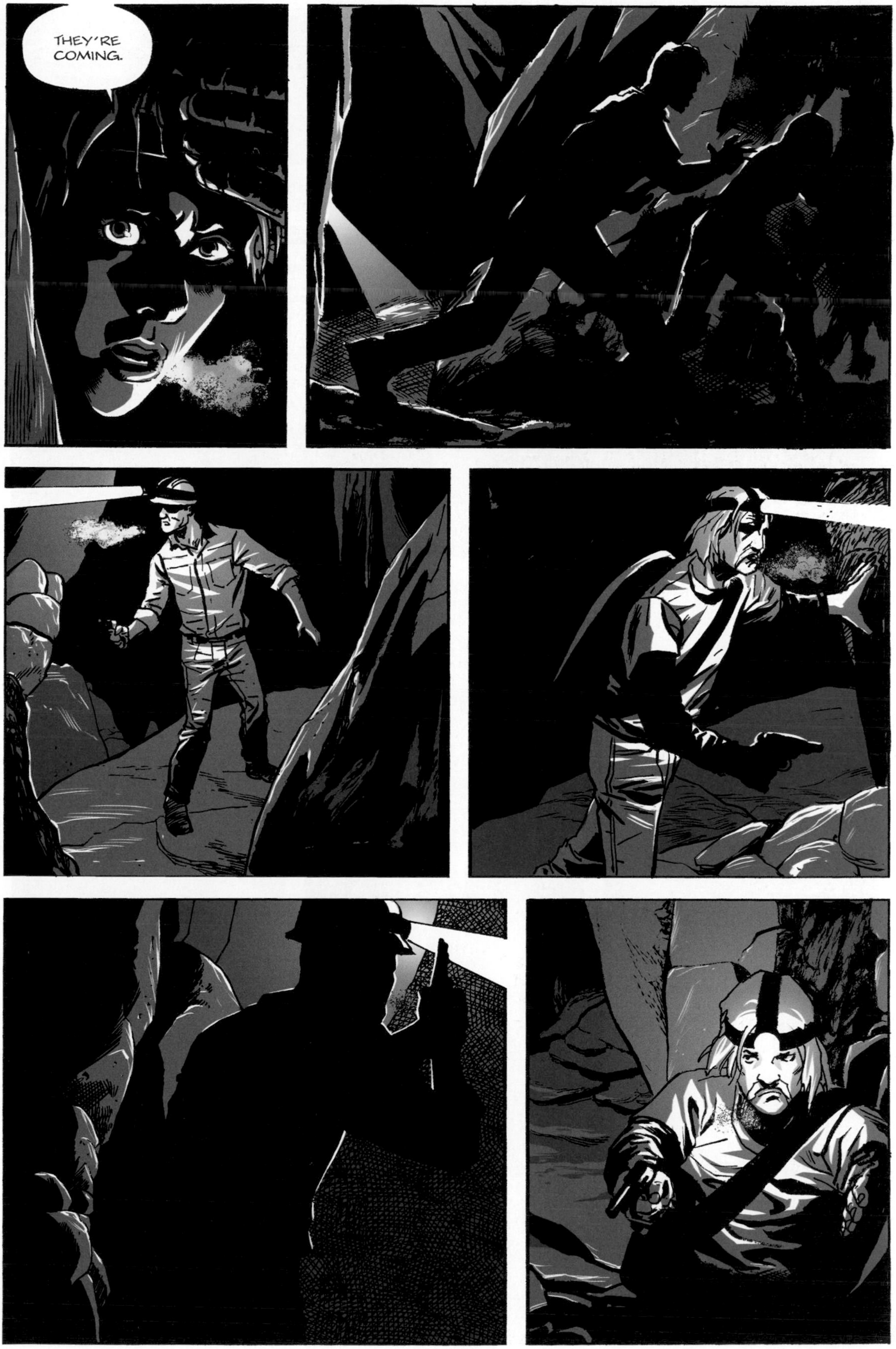
THEY'RE COMING.

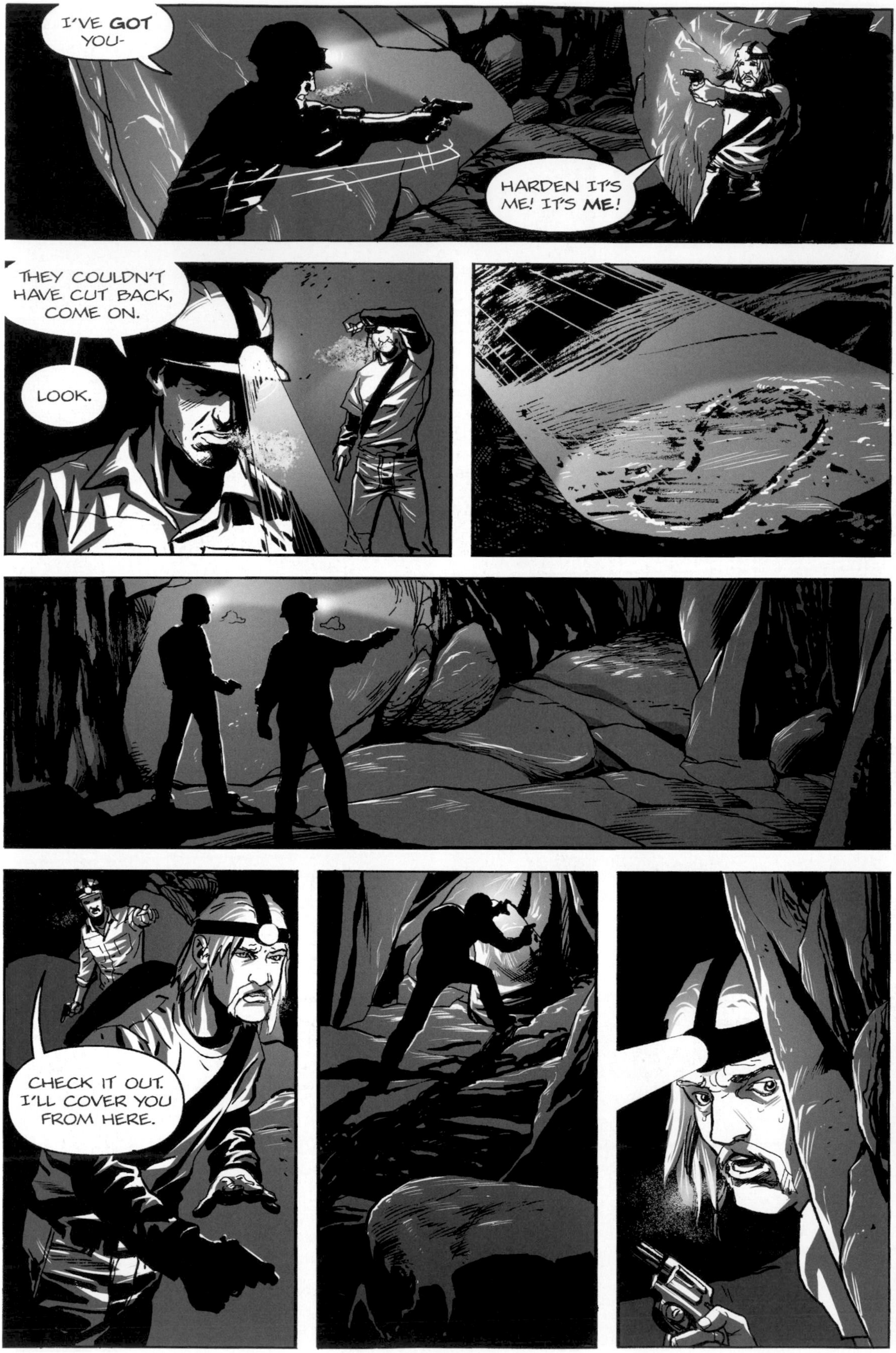
I'VE GOT YOU-
HARDEN IT'S ME! IT'S ME!
THEY COULDN'T HAVE CUT BACK, COME ON.
LOOK.
CHECK IT OUT. I'LL COVER YOU FROM HERE.

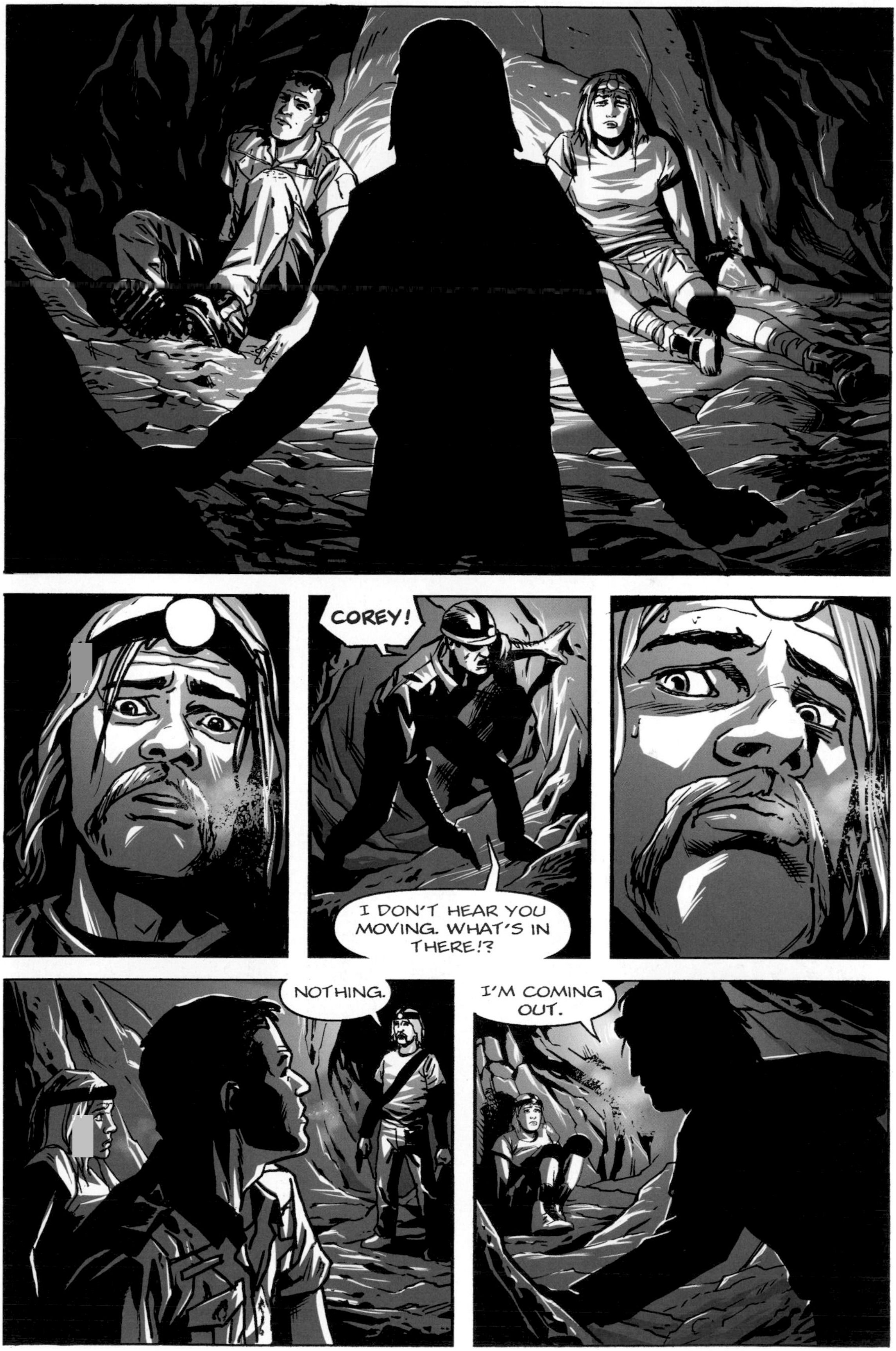
COREY!
I DON'T HEAR YOU MOVING. WHAT'S IN THERE!?
NOTHING.
I'M COMING OUT.

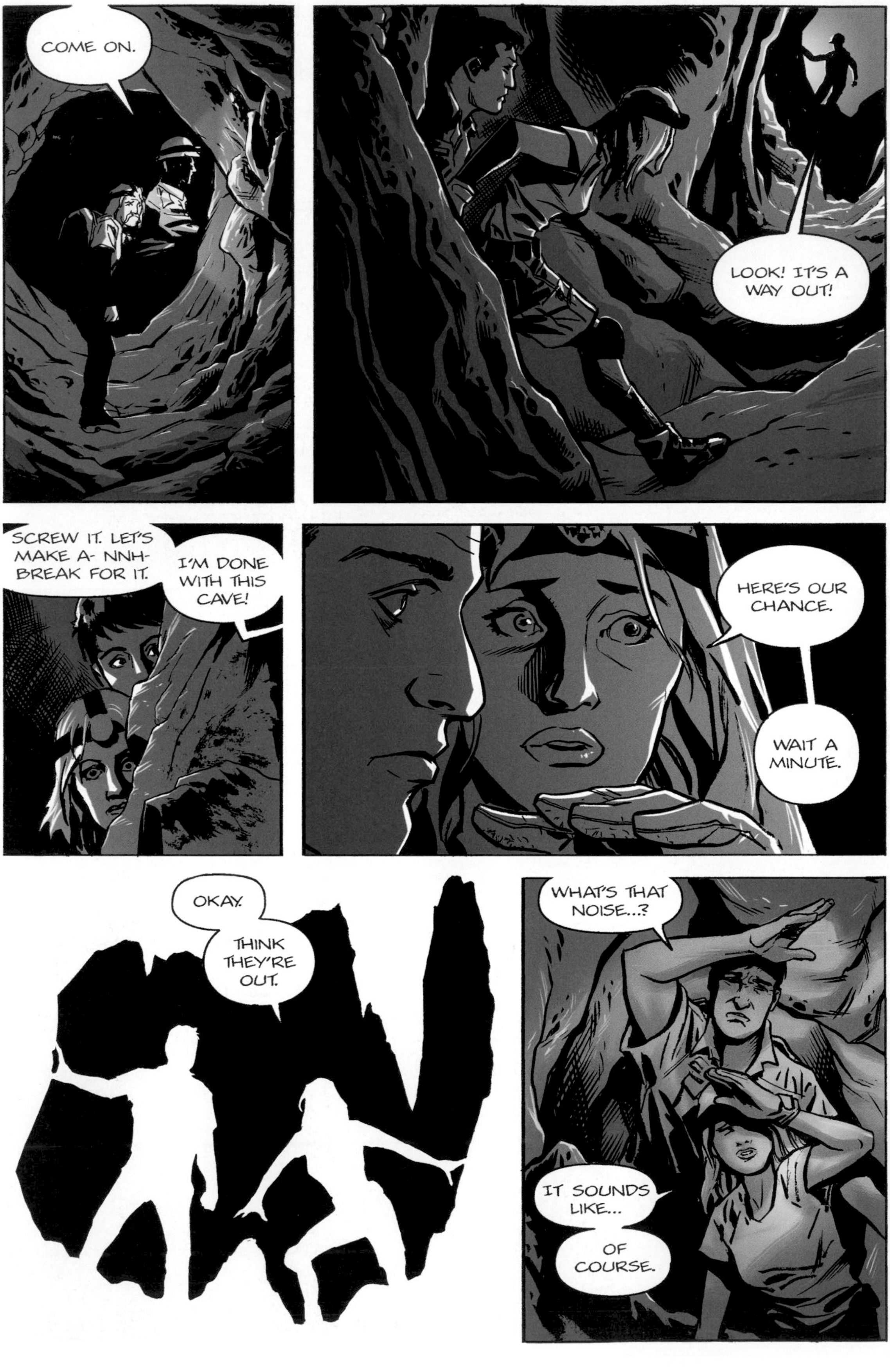
COME ON.
LOOK! IT'S A WAY OUT!
SCREW IT. LET'S MAKE A- NNH- BREAK FOR IT.
I'M DONE WITH THIS CAVE!
HERE'S OUR CHANCE.
WAIT A MINUTE.
OKAY.
THINK THEY'RE OUT.
WHAT'S THAT NOISE...?
IT SOUNDS LIKE...
OF COURSE.

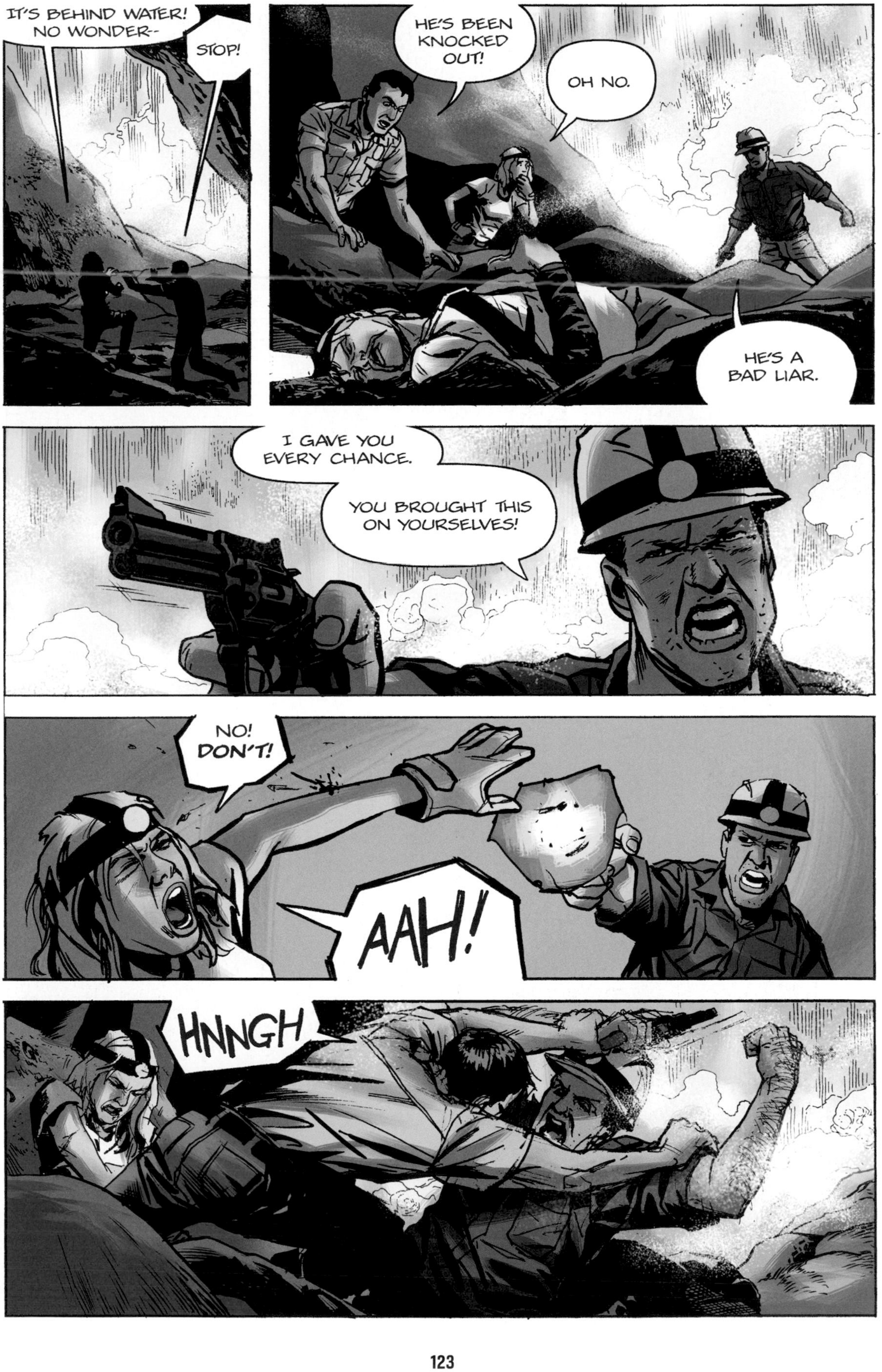
IT'S BEHIND WATER! NO WONDER--
STOP!
HE'S BEEN KNOCKED OUT!
OH NO.
HE'S A BAD LIAR.
I GAVE YOU EVERY CHANCE.
YOU BROUGHT THIS ON YOURSELVES!
NO! DON'T!
AAH!
HNNGH

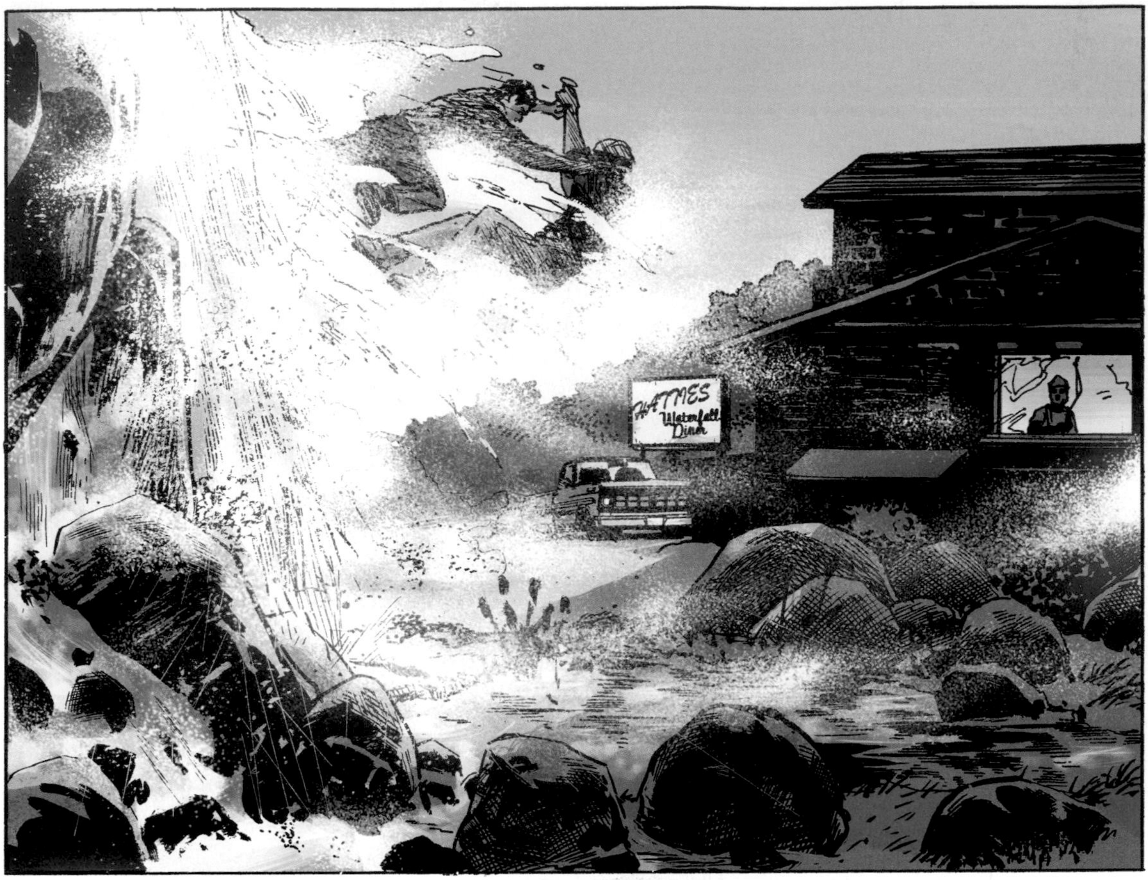
HATTIES
Waterfall
Diner

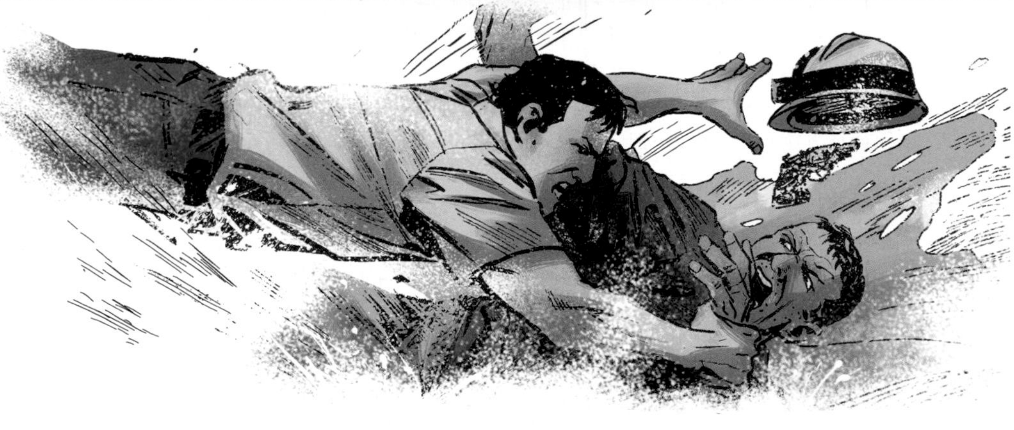

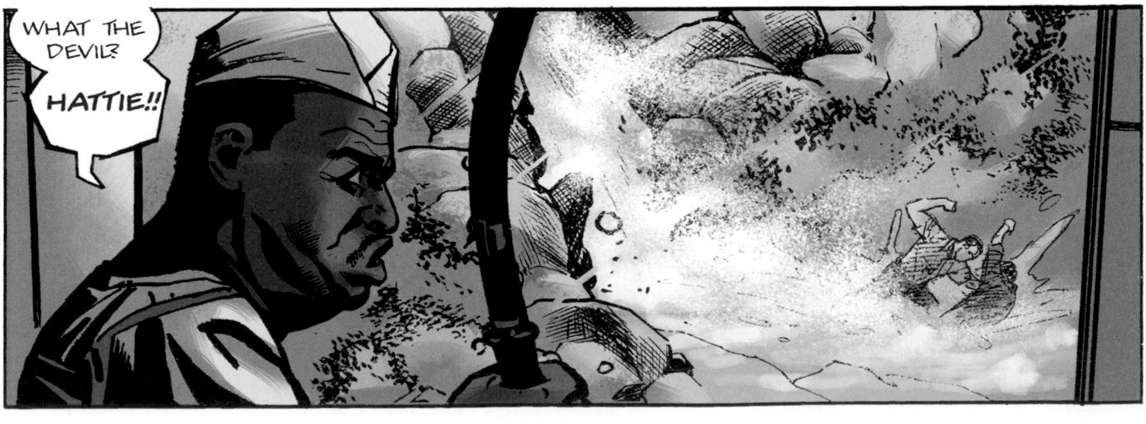
WHAT THE DEVIL?
HATTIE!!

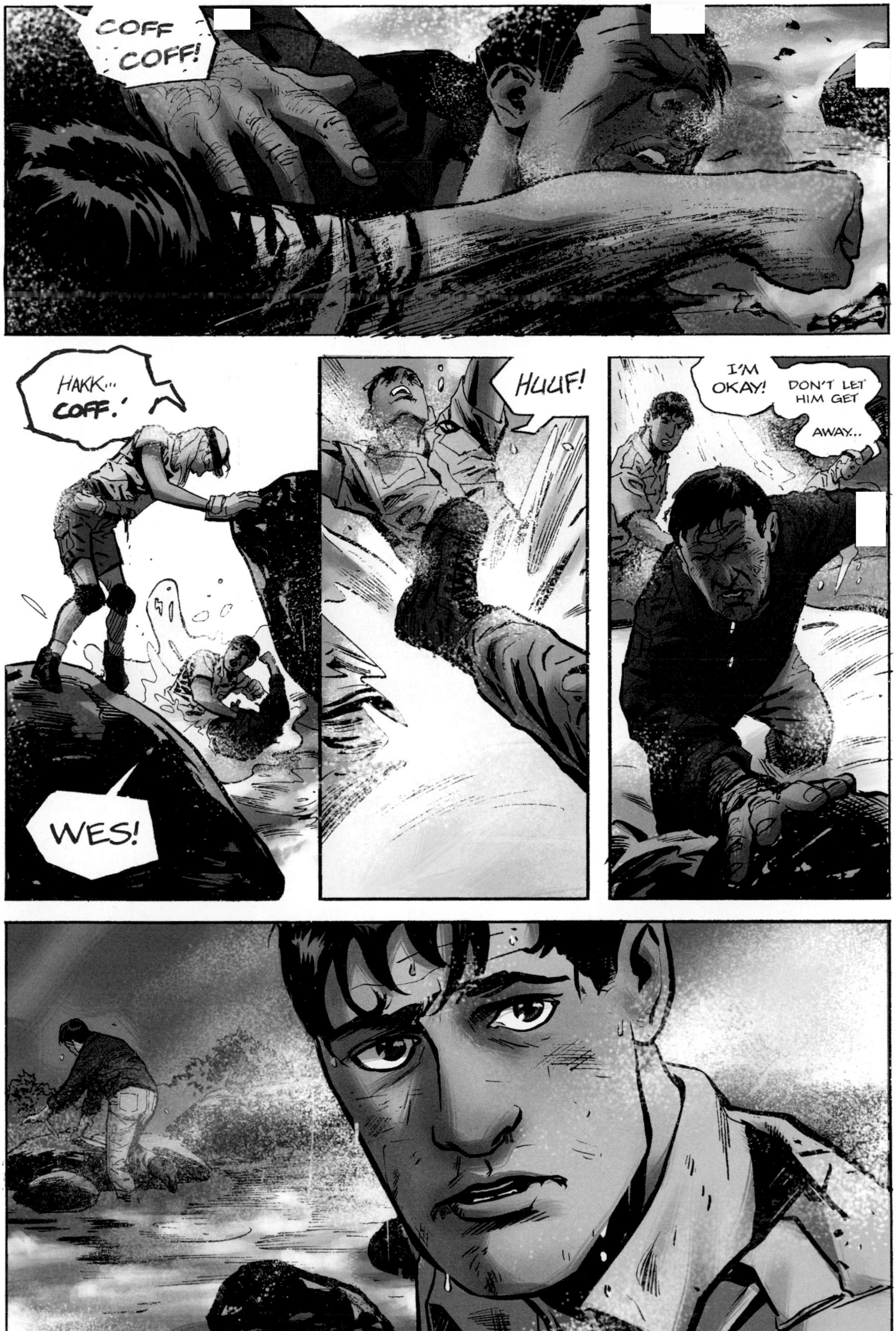
COFF COFF!
HAKK... COFF.
WES!
HUUF!
I'M OKAY!
DON'T LET HIM GET AWAY...

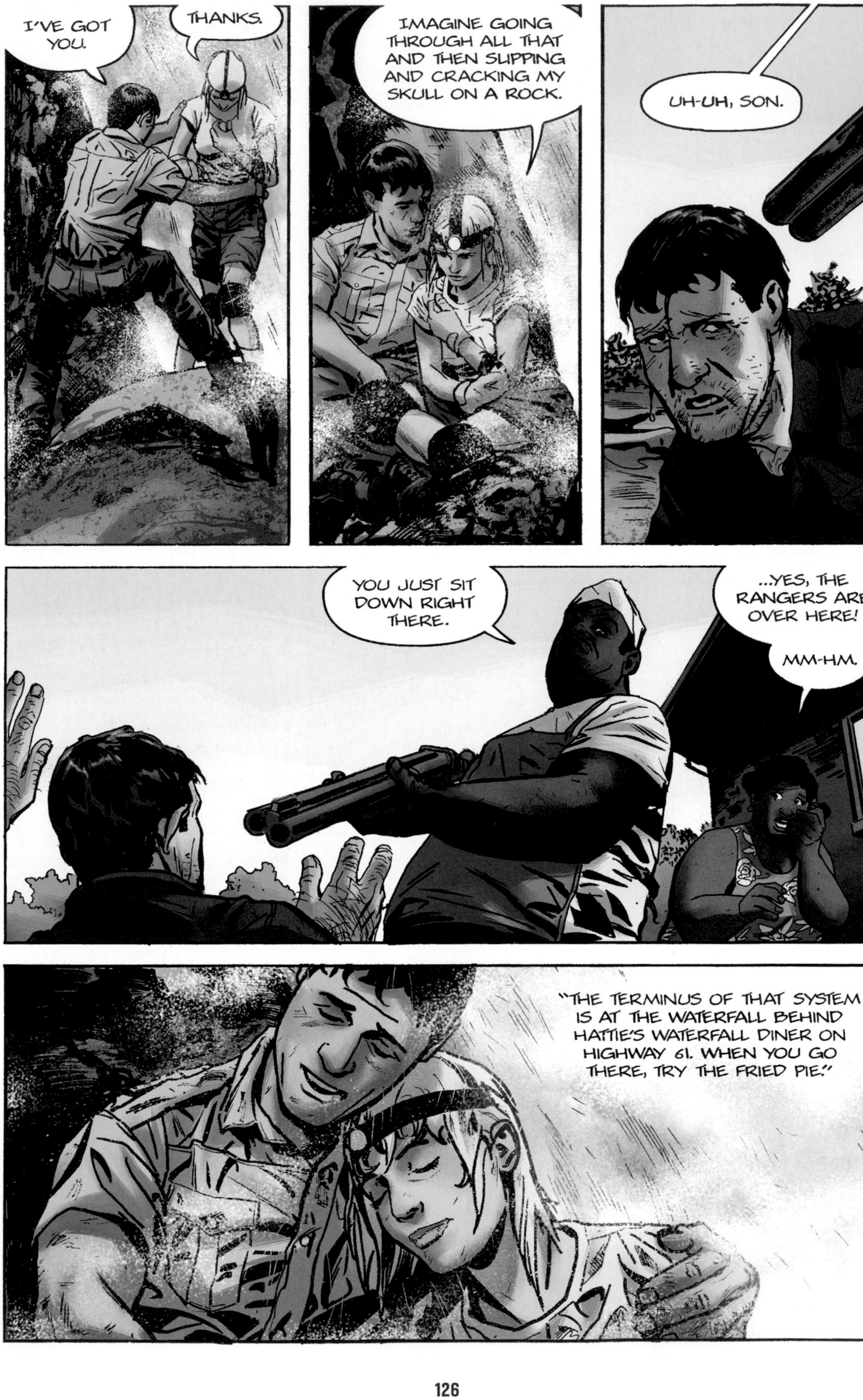
I'VE GOT YOU.
THANKS.
IMAGINE GOING THROUGH ALL THAT AND THEN SLIPPING AND CRACKING MY SKULL ON A ROCK.
UH-UH, SON.
YOU JUST SIT DOWN RIGHT THERE.
...YES, THE RANGERS ARE OVER HERE!
MM-HM.
"THE TERMINUS OF THAT SYSTEM IS AT THE WATERFALL BEHIND HATTIE'S WATERFALL DINER ON HIGHWAY 61. WHEN YOU GO THERE, TRY THE FRIED PIE."

Stillwater Cave
Two Years Later
Reporter Nora Cochran revisits Marion, Kentucky

On the second anniversary of that day, I found a town transformed.

"The damage had been done," said Dupree. "This was a chance to take control and preserve the rest."

"This was the site of the Bat Guano explosion..."

-Stillwater Tour Guide Jackson Baker

The development of Stillwater Cave into a show cave was supervised by Wesley Fischer, who was at first uneasy about the video presentation that detailed events of that day, but recognized the historical value.

The pathway now extends beyond "The Ballroom" with plans to have it reach all the way to "The Drop" next year.

In addition to calling shots about how the system is presented, Fischer has been able to explore more, mapping a tunnel that leads out to the gorge stream.

Visitors often snap photos of other women rangers hoping to see her, but Fischer is as elusive as she was on the day of the chase.

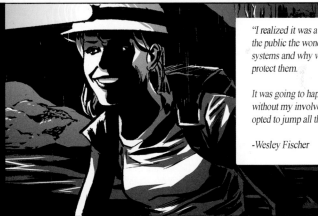

"I realized it was a chance to show the public the wonders of cave systems and why we need to protect them.

It was going to happen with or without my involvement, so I opted to jump all the way in."

-Wesley Fischer

Less interested in caving and also wanting to avoid glamorizing a day on which three people died, Seth Ridge opened a whitewater rafting tour company.

"I know people come here after visiting the cave- and I can tell they want to talk to me about it... but most of them are pretty cool and just have fun in the raft."

-Seth Ridge

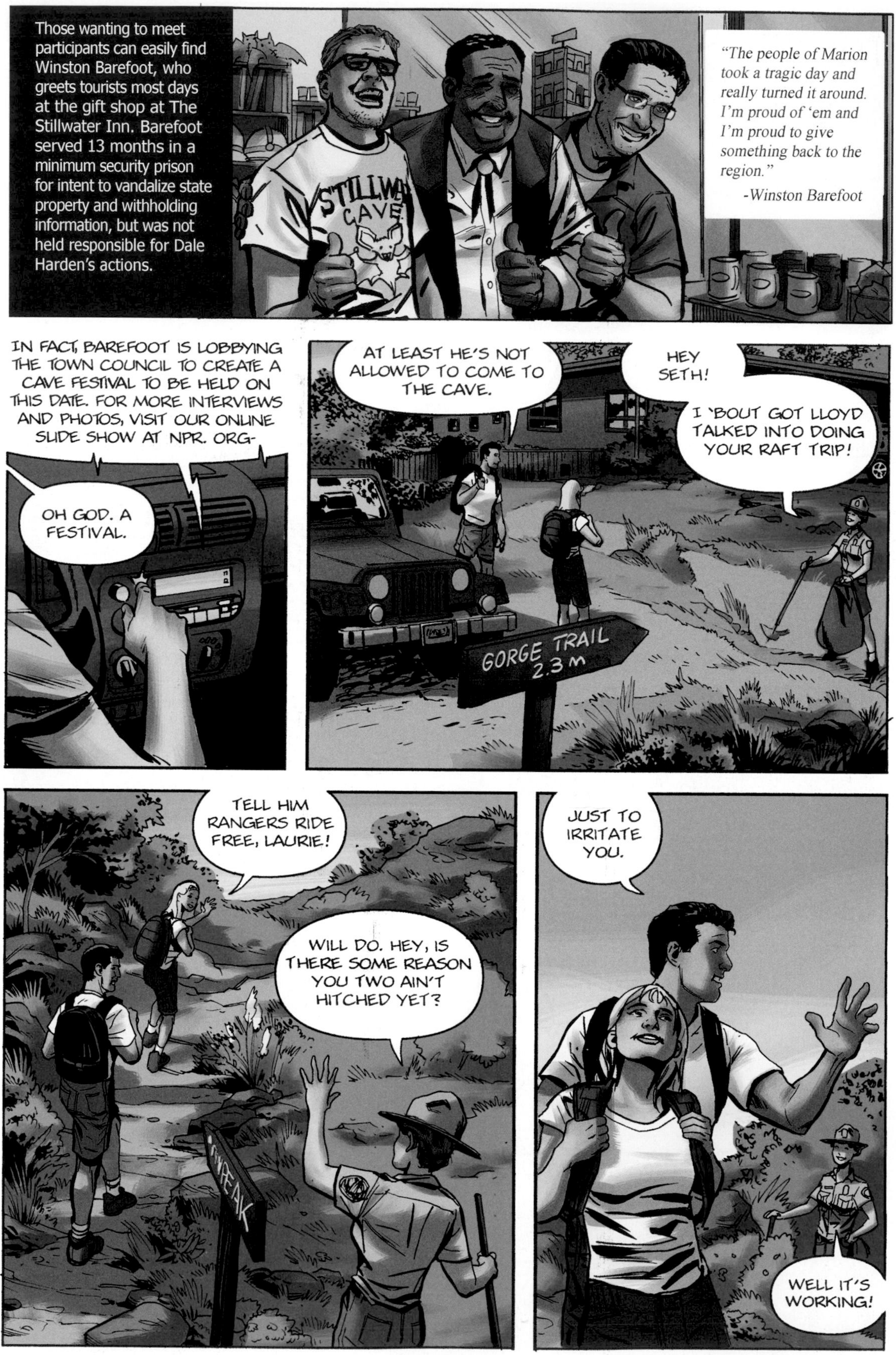
Those wanting to meet participants can easily find Winston Barefoot, who greets tourists most days at the gift shop at The Stillwater Inn. Barefoot served 13 months in a minimum security prison for intent to vandalize state property and withholding information, but was not held responsible for Dale Harden's actions.
"The people of Marion took a tragic day and really turned it around. I'm proud of 'em and I'm proud to give something back to the region."
-Winston Barefoot
IN FACT, BAREFOOT IS LOBBYING THE TOWN COUNCIL TO CREATE A CAVE FESTIVAL TO BE HELD ON THIS DATE. FOR MORE INTERVIEWS AND PHOTOS, VISIT OUR ONLINE SLIDE SHOW AT NPR. ORG-
OH GOD. A FESTIVAL.
AT LEAST HE'S NOT ALLOWED TO COME TO THE CAVE.
HEY SETH!
I 'BOUT GOT LLOYD TALKED INTO DOING YOUR RAFT TRIP!
GORGE TRAIL
2.3 M
TELL HIM RANGERS RIDE FREE, LAURIE!
WILL DO. HEY, IS THERE SOME REASON YOU TWO AIN'T HITCHED YET?
JUST TO IRRITATE YOU.
WELL IT'S WORKING!

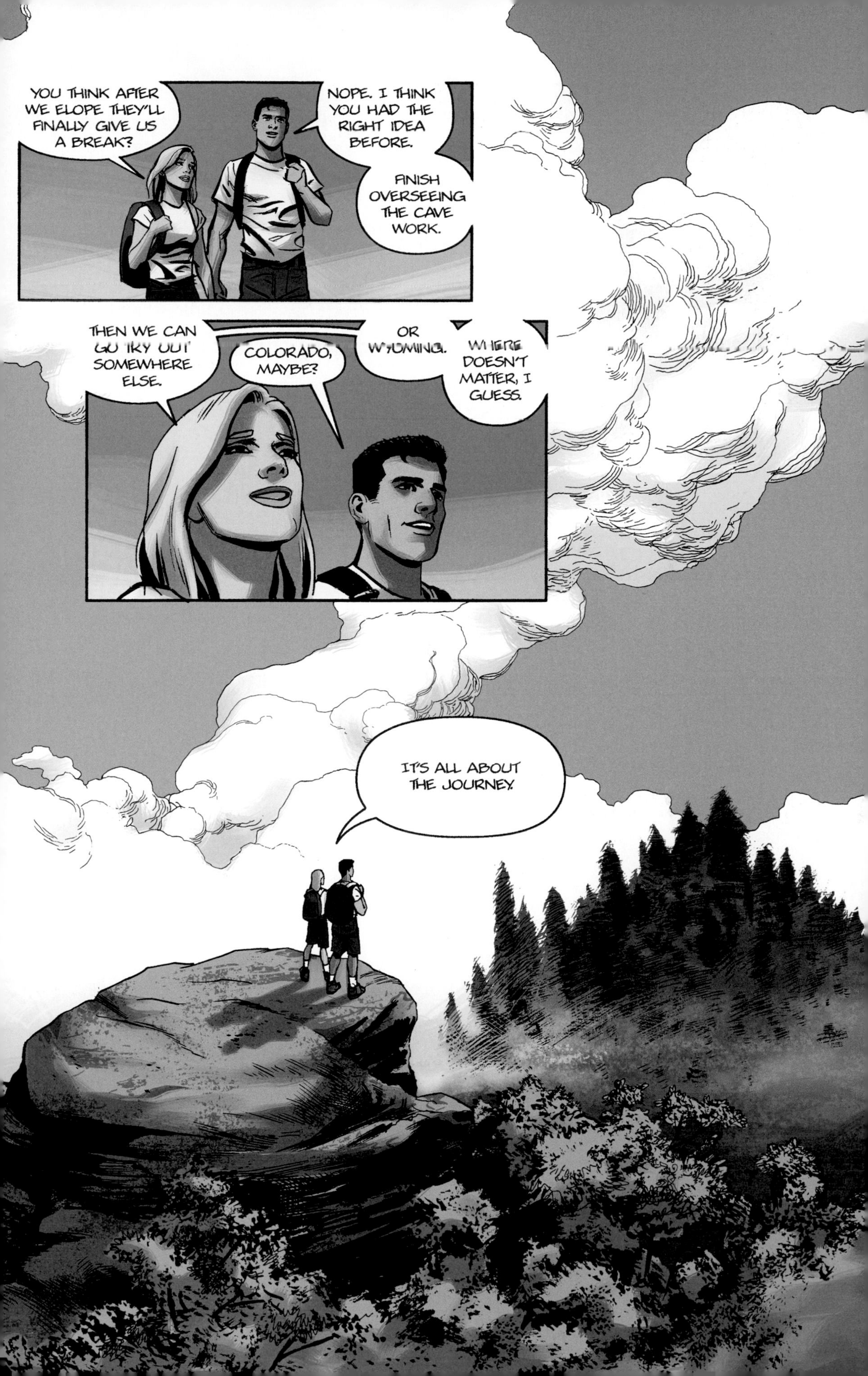
YOU THINK AFTER WE ELOPE THEY'LL FINALLY GIVE US A BREAK?
NOPE. I THINK YOU HAD THE RIGHT IDEA BEFORE.
FINISH OVERSEEING THE CAVE WORK.
THEN WE CAN GO TRY OUT SOMEWHERE ELSE.
COLORADO, MAYBE?
OR WYOMING.
WHERE DOESN'T MATTER, I GUESS.
IT'S ALL ABOUT THE JOURNEY.

UNDER GROUND: fell

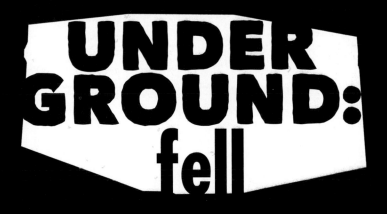

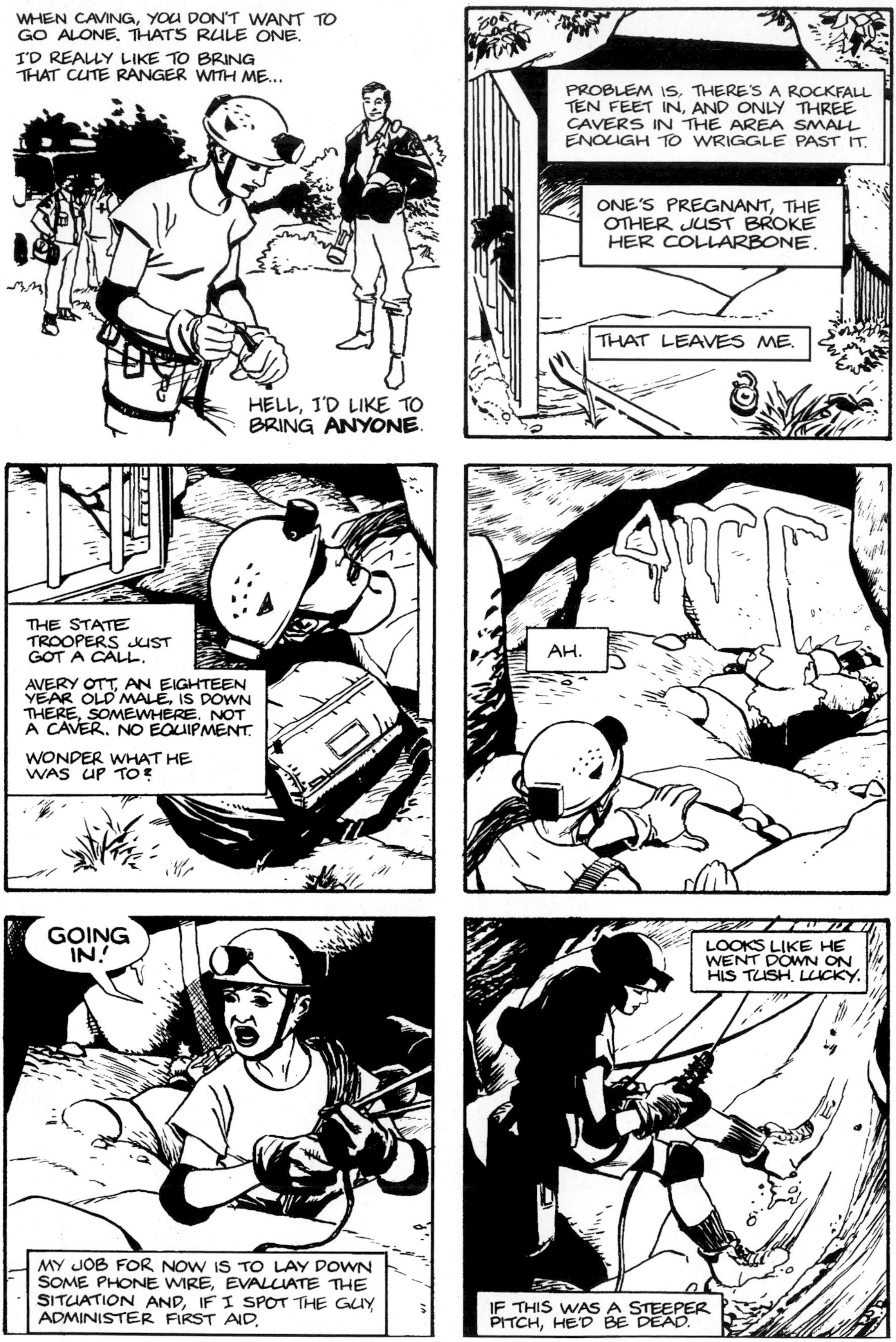
WHEN CAVING, YOU DON'T WANT TO GO ALONE. THAT'S RULE ONE.
I'D REALLY LIKE TO BRING THAT CUTE RANGER WITH ME...
HELL, I'D LIKE TO BRING **ANYONE**.
PROBLEM IS, THERE'S A ROCKFALL TEN FEET IN, AND ONLY THREE CAVERS IN THE AREA SMALL ENOUGH TO WRIGGLE PAST IT.
ONE'S PREGNANT, THE OTHER JUST BROKE HER COLLARBONE.
THAT LEAVES ME.
THE STATE TROOPERS JUST GOT A CALL.
AVERY OTT, AN EIGHTEEN YEAR OLD MALE, IS DOWN THERE, SOMEWHERE. NOT A CAVER. NO EQUIPMENT.
WONDER WHAT HE WAS UP TO?
AH.
GOING IN!
MY JOB FOR NOW IS TO LAY DOWN SOME PHONE WIRE, EVALUATE THE SITUATION AND, IF I SPOT THE GUY, ADMINISTER FIRST AID.
LOOKS LIKE HE WENT DOWN ON HIS TUSH. LUCKY.
IF THIS WAS A STEEPER PITCH, HE'D BE DEAD.

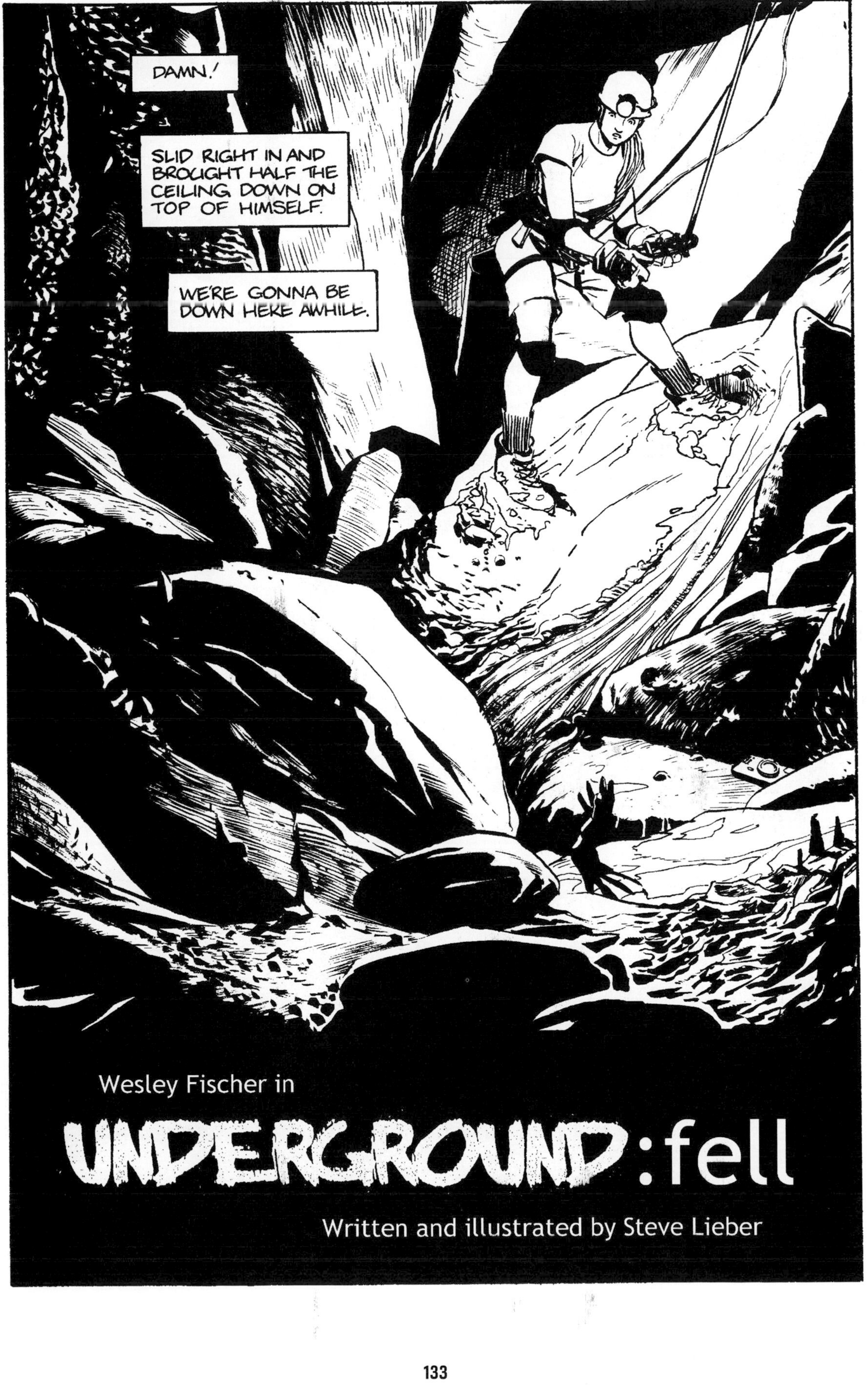
DAMN!
SLID RIGHT IN AND BROUGHT HALF THE CEILING DOWN ON TOP OF HIMSELF.
WE'RE GONNA BE DOWN HERE AWHILE.
Wesley Fischer in
UNDERGROUND:fell
Written and illustrated by Steve Lieber

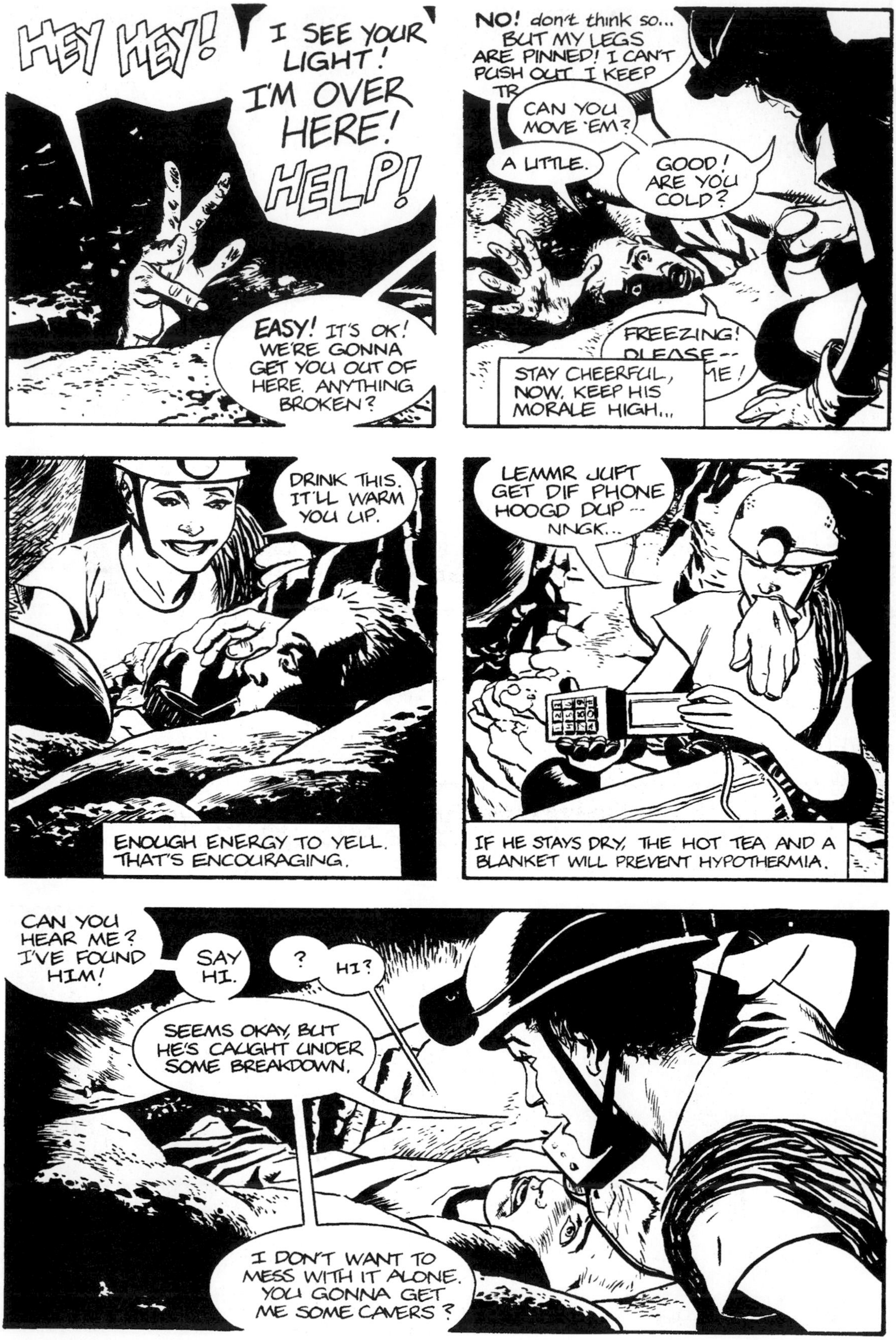
HEY HEY!
I SEE YOUR LIGHT! I'M OVER HERE! HELP!
EASY! IT'S OK! WE'RE GONNA GET YOU OUT OF HERE. ANYTHING BROKEN?
NO! don't think so... BUT MY LEGS ARE PINNED! I CAN'T PUSH OUT I KEEP TR
CAN YOU MOVE 'EM?
A LITTLE.
GOOD! ARE YOU COLD?
FREEZING! PLEASE--
STAY CHEERFUL, NOW. KEEP HIS MORALE HIGH...
DRINK THIS. IT'LL WARM YOU UP.
ENOUGH ENERGY TO YELL. THAT'S ENCOURAGING.
LEMMR JUFT GET DIF PHONE HOOGD DUP-- NNGK...
IF HE STAYS DRY, THE HOT TEA AND A BLANKET WILL PREVENT HYPOTHERMIA.
CAN YOU HEAR ME? I'VE FOUND HIM!
SAY HI.
?
HI?
SEEMS OKAY, BUT HE'S CAUGHT UNDER SOME BREAKDOWN.
I DON'T WANT TO MESS WITH IT ALONE. YOU GONNA GET ME SOME CAVERS?

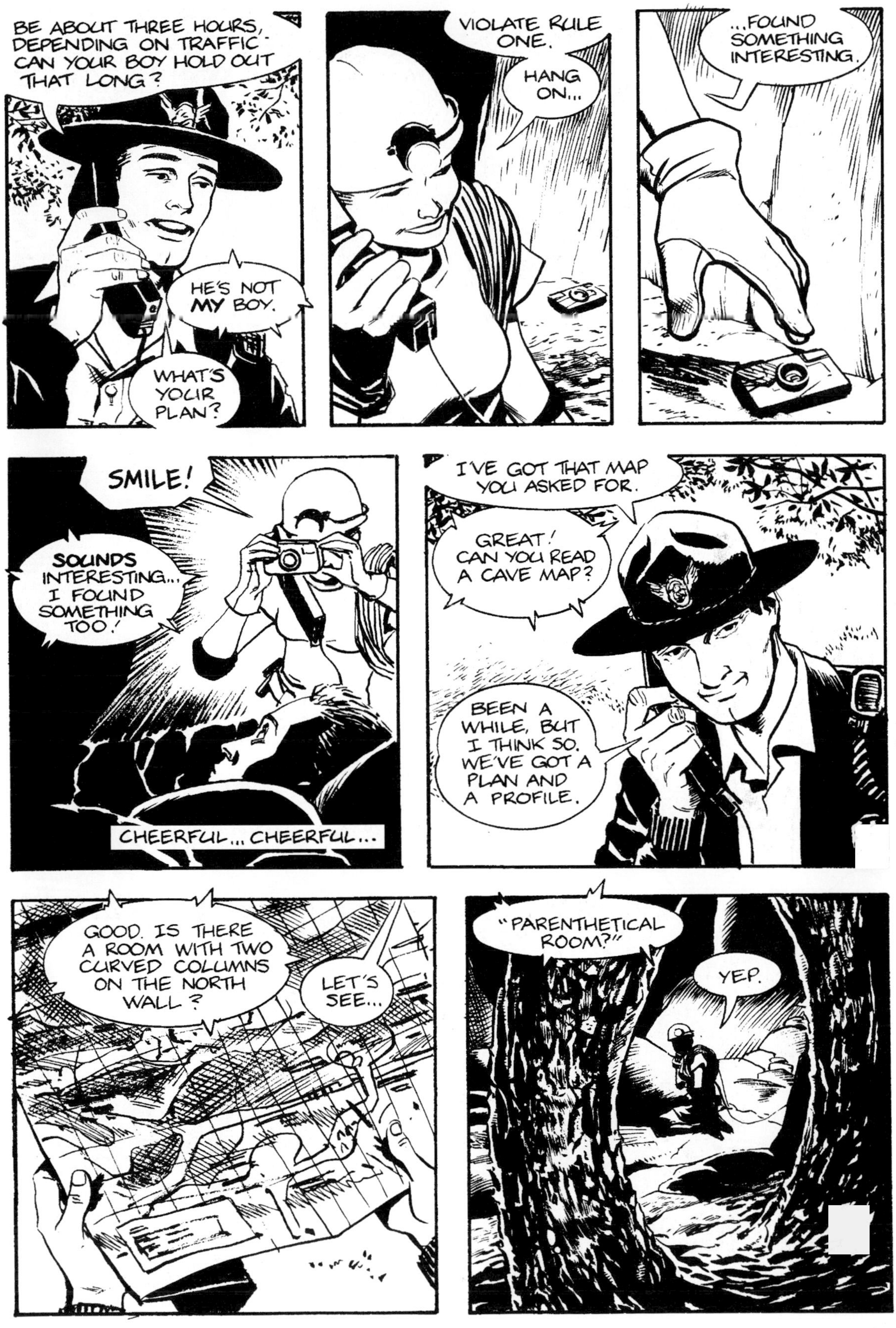
BE ABOUT THREE HOURS, DEPENDING ON TRAFFIC · CAN YOUR BOY HOLD OUT THAT LONG?
HE'S NOT MY BOY.
WHAT'S YOUR PLAN?
VIOLATE RULE ONE.
HANG ON...
...FOUND SOMETHING INTERESTING.
SMILE!
SOUNDS INTERESTING... I FOUND SOMETHING TOO!
CHEERFUL... CHEERFUL...
I'VE GOT THAT MAP YOU ASKED FOR.
GREAT! CAN YOU READ A CAVE MAP?
BEEN A WHILE, BUT I THINK SO. WE'VE GOT A PLAN AND A PROFILE.
GOOD. IS THERE A ROOM WITH TWO CURVED COLUMNS ON THE NORTH WALL?
LET'S SEE...
"PARENTHETICAL ROOM?"
YEP.

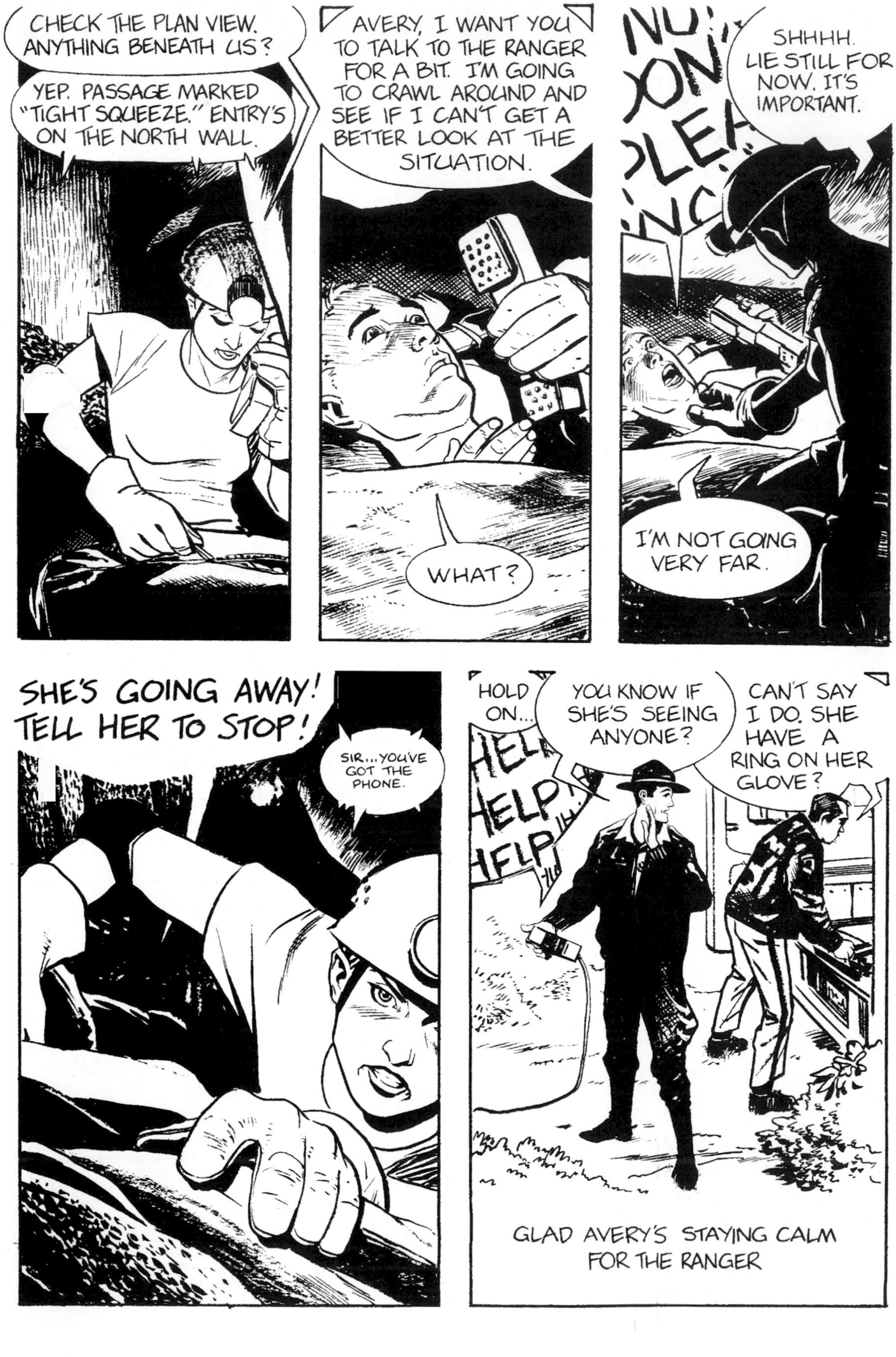
CHECK THE PLAN VIEW. ANYTHING BENEATH US?
YEP. PASSAGE MARKED "TIGHT SQUEEZE." ENTRY'S ON THE NORTH WALL.
AVERY, I WANT YOU TO TALK TO THE RANGER FOR A BIT. I'M GOING TO CRAWL AROUND AND SEE IF I CAN'T GET A BETTER LOOK AT THE SITUATION.
WHAT?
SHHHH. LIE STILL FOR NOW. IT'S IMPORTANT.
I'M NOT GOING VERY FAR.
SHE'S GOING AWAY! TELL HER TO STOP!
SIR...YOU'VE GOT THE PHONE.
HOLD ON...
HELP! HELP! HELP!
YOU KNOW IF SHE'S SEEING ANYONE?
CAN'T SAY I DO. SHE HAVE A RING ON HER GLOVE?
GLAD AVERY'S STAYING CALM FOR THE RANGER

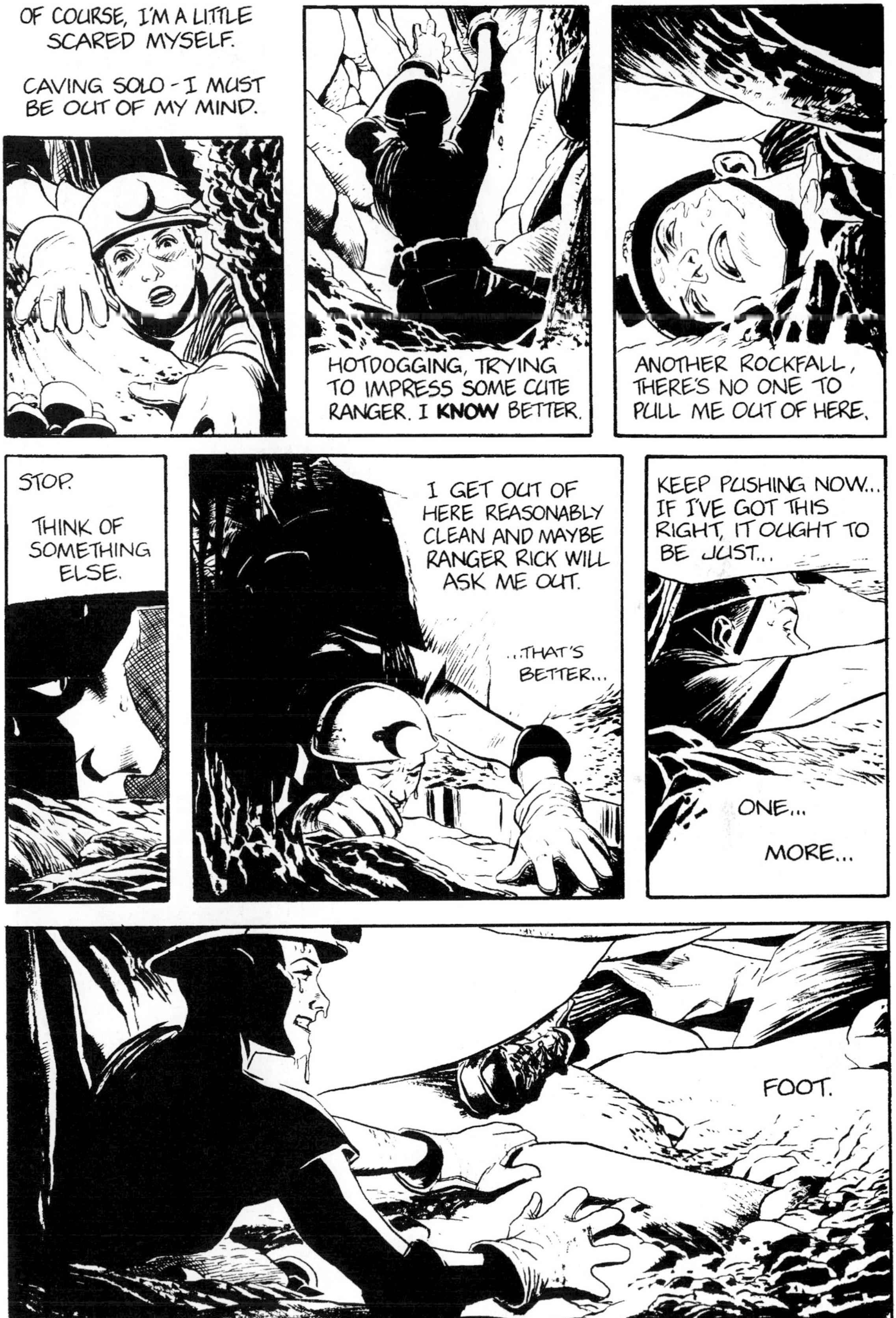

OF COURSE, I'M A LITTLE SCARED MYSELF.
CAVING SOLO - I MUST BE OUT OF MY MIND.
HOTDOGGING, TRYING TO IMPRESS SOME CUTE RANGER. I **KNOW** BETTER.
ANOTHER ROCKFALL, THERE'S NO ONE TO PULL ME OUT OF HERE.
STOP.
THINK OF SOMETHING ELSE.
I GET OUT OF HERE REASONABLY CLEAN AND MAYBE RANGER RICK WILL ASK ME OUT.
...THAT'S BETTER...
KEEP PUSHING NOW... IF I'VE GOT THIS RIGHT, IT OUGHT TO BE JUST...
ONE...
MORE...
FOOT.
6

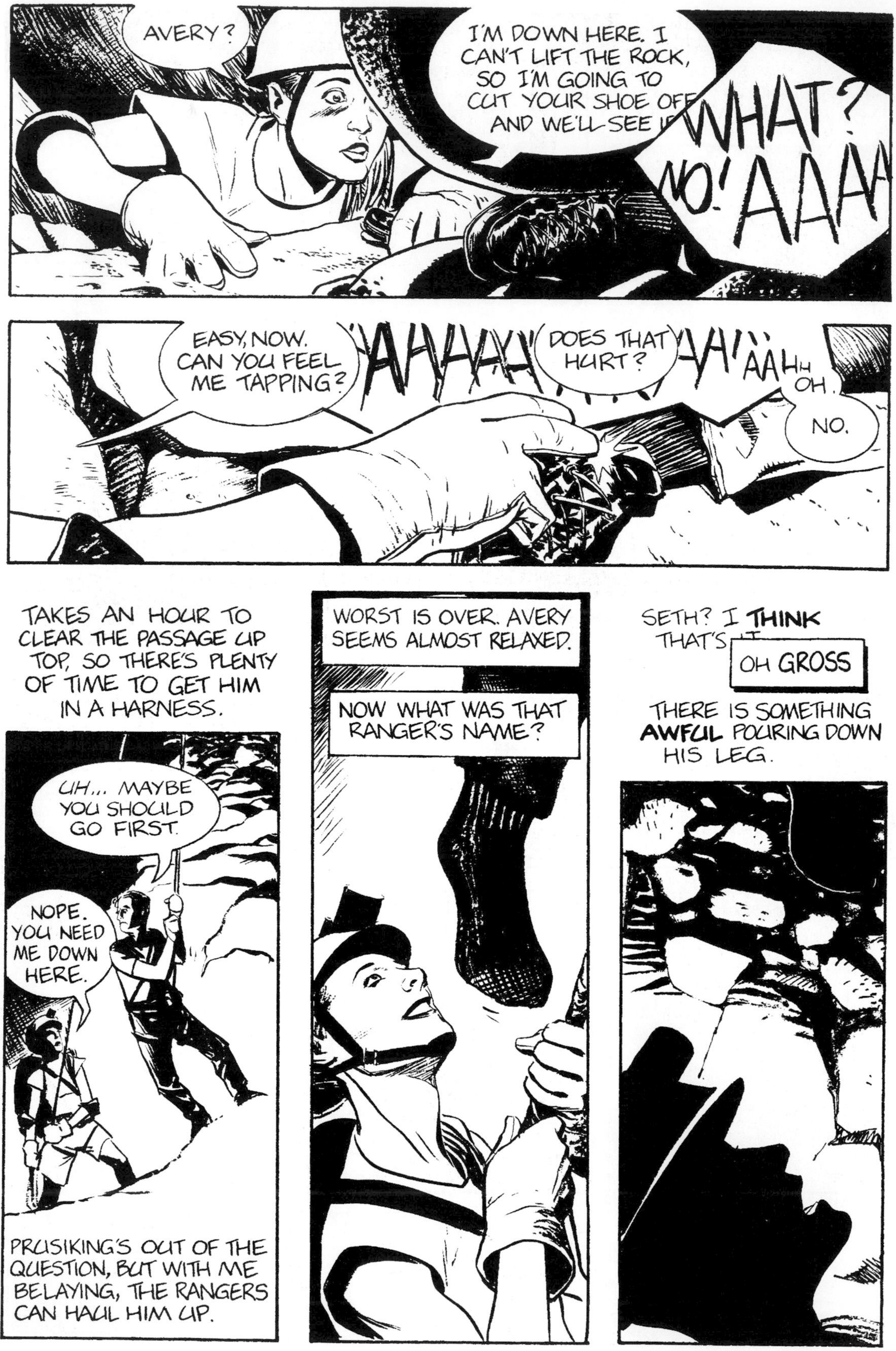
AVERY?
I'M DOWN HERE. I CAN'T LIFT THE ROCK, SO I'M GOING TO CUT YOUR SHOE OFF AND WE'LL SEE
WHAT? NO! AAAA
EASY, NOW. CAN YOU FEEL ME TAPPING?
AAAAAH
DOES THAT HURT?
AH'... AAHH
OH.
NO.
TAKES AN HOUR TO CLEAR THE PASSAGE UP TOP, SO THERE'S PLENTY OF TIME TO GET HIM IN A HARNESS.
UH... MAYBE YOU SHOULD GO FIRST.
NOPE. YOU NEED ME DOWN HERE.
PRUSIKING'S OUT OF THE QUESTION, BUT WITH ME BELAYING, THE RANGERS CAN HAUL HIM UP.
WORST IS OVER. AVERY SEEMS ALMOST RELAXED.
NOW WHAT WAS THAT RANGER'S NAME?
SETH? I **THINK** THAT'S
OH GROSS
THERE IS SOMETHING **AWFUL** POURING DOWN HIS LEG.

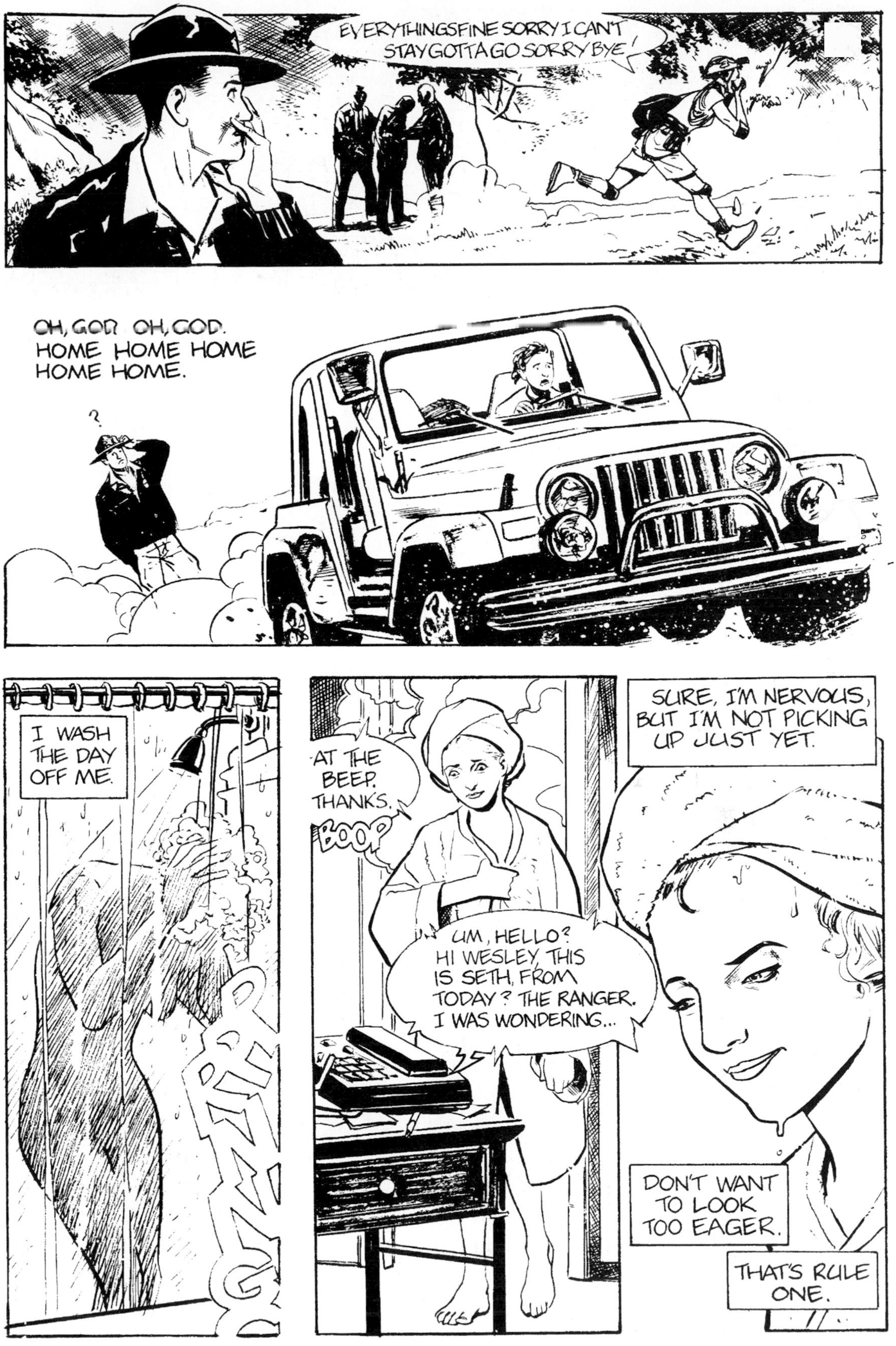
EVERYTHINGSFINE SORRY I CAN'T STAY GOTTA GO SORRY BYE!
OH, GOD. OH, GOD. HOME HOME HOME HOME HOME.
?
I WASH THE DAY OFF ME.
AT THE BEEP. THANKS.
BOOP
UM, HELLO? HI WESLEY, THIS IS SETH, FROM TODAY? THE RANGER. I WAS WONDERING...
SURE, I'M NERVOUS, BUT I'M NOT PICKING UP JUST YET.
DON'T WANT TO LOOK TOO EAGER.
THAT'S RULE ONE.

COVER GALLERY

UNDER
GROUND
JEFF PARKER
STEVE LIEBER

ISSUE #1

UNDER
GROUND
JEFF PARKER
STEVE LIEBER

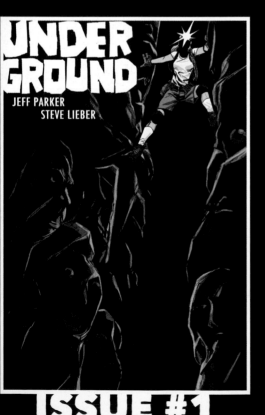

ISSUE #2

ISSUE #3

ISSUE #4

TUNNEL VISION

Steve Lieber and I met at a comics show in Philadelphia, 1993, both eager young artists tr[redacted] to get our work noticed. I don't think either of us landed any jobs that weeken[redacted]t our work was noticed–by each other. Not that we were brilliant, we weren't [redacted]), but we were almost the only new cartoonists in the building going for naturalism in a period that was all about hyper-stylization. Now the industry has broadened and has room for most approaches, but then? Not so much.

Steve was into the same artists I idolized: Alex Toth, Doug Wildey, Alex Raymond, Milt Caniff, Hal Foster. They drew some fantastic tales of course, but they mostly focused on real life-scale adventure with fallible, human characters. Steve and I kept in touch, faxing each other whatever pages we were working on (Yes, fax. Like savages!). Eventually we started helping each other on projects. When I was racing to finish my first graphic novel *The Interman*, Lieber came to the rescue by drawing the Wyoming countryside. Later we both ended up in a studio space full of monstrously talented creators, but we'd never created a new story together...

...Until Steve decided he wanted to do a thriller set in a cave system. He wrote a short story [redacted]ou see here, "Fell," for the Image anthology *Four Letter Worlds* and felt the[redacted]se was rich for exploring. Here's the insidious part; as I worked [redacted]eet away, Lieber kept sharing all the research he'd done on spe-[redacted]ki[redacted]verns and so on–until I knew the same facts he did. So when he floated [redacted] me writing the longer work, I had *cave opinions*. So we started breaking the story of Wesley Fischer.

Steve had many story goals that we never deviated from. No one is a true villain. The conflict snowballs because of the hazardous environment. Embrace the chaos of the way things really happen–too fast for anyone to get a solid grasp or make an informed decision. Hard-won knowledge makes the difference for survival, not muscle or weapons. And our hero is someone who has the advantage in the caverns: a small, smart woman.

Our studio was a huge help with *Underground*. Anyone who left their seat for a minute got roped into posing for reference. Phenomenal artist Ron Chan offered to color; go back and marvel at how inspired his treatment of the cave is. This is one of the few books I've done where we acted out scenes like you might do in blocking live-action film–it helped us nail the more harrowing parts like the water traversal[redacted]and I also went to the Ape Cave in Washington. Though it's a lava tube and[redacted]imestone system like Stillwater, it helped us with the dynamics of th[redacted]as what one could actually hear, or see with only headlamps. We [redacted]ude how much you trip on the cave floor or the whole book would have [redacted]acters stumbling.

We emerged from this project–*as if from a cave*–transformed, better creators. It's one of the works we're both extremely proud of and happy that it can reach a new audience with this edition. Thank you for coming along with us.

How We Make a Page of Underground

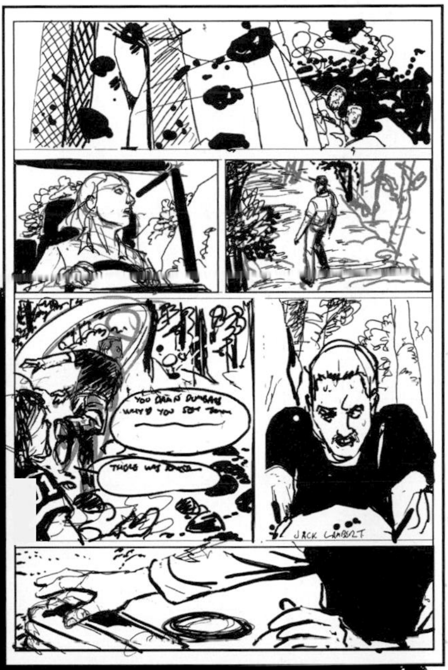

First I scribble out a doodly layout directly on my Cintiq. Laying out this comic has been easy because Parker, a former artist, writes very artist-friendly scripts.

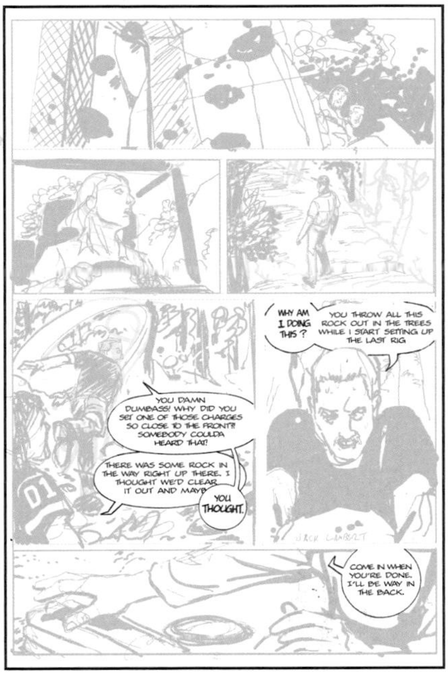

WHY AM I DOING THIS?
YOU THROW ALL THIS ROCK OUT IN THE TREES WHILE I START SETTING UP THE LAST RIG
YOU DAMN DUMBASS! WHY DID YOU SET ONE OF THOSE CHARGES SO CLOSE TO THE FRONT?! SOMEBODY COULDA HEARD THAT!
THERE WAS SOME ROCK IN THE WAY RIGHT UP THERE. I THOUGHT WE'D CLEAR IT OUT AND MAYB
YOU THOUGHT.
COME IN WHEN YOU'RE DONE. I'LL BE WAY IN THE BACK.

Then I turn it blue in Photoshop and add the lettering. The font I use in *Underground* was designed by Tom Orzechowski, based on my lettering from *Whiteout*.

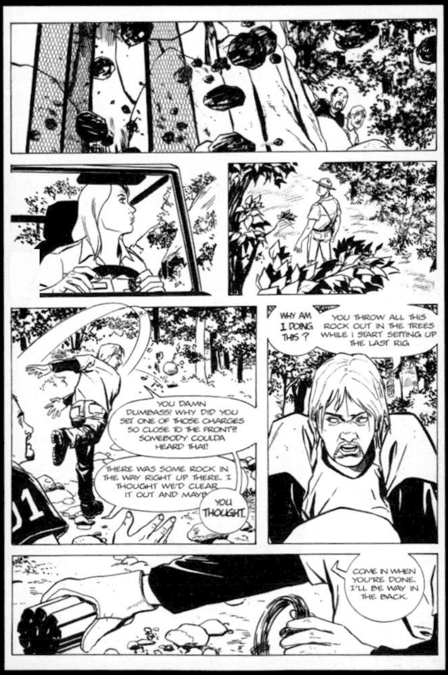

WHY AM I DOING THIS?
YOU THROW ALL THIS ROCK OUT IN THE TREES WHILE I START SETTING UP THE LAST RIG
YOU DAMN DUMBASS! WHY DID YOU SET ONE OF THOSE CHARGES SO CLOSE TO THE FRONT?! SOMEBODY COULDA HEARD THAT!
THERE WAS SOME ROCK IN THE WAY RIGHT UP THERE. I THOUGHT WE'D CLEAR IT OUT AND MAYB
YOU THOUGHT.
COME IN WHEN YOU'RE DONE. I'LL BE WAY IN THE BACK.

I print this out onto bristol board and start drawing with brush and ink. There's a look I want that I can't get digitally.

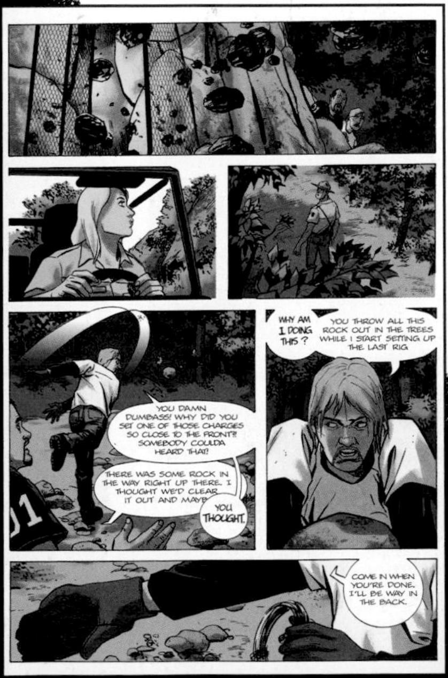

WHY AM I DOING THIS?
YOU THROW ALL THIS ROCK OUT IN THE TREES WHILE I START SETTING UP THE LAST RIG
YOU DAMN DUMBASS! WHY DID YOU SET ONE OF THOSE CHARGES SO CLOSE TO THE FRONT?! SOMEBODY COULDA HEARD THAT!
THERE WAS SOME ROCK IN THE WAY RIGHT UP THERE. I THOUGHT WE'D CLEAR IT OUT AND MAYB
YOU THOUGHT.
COME IN WHEN YOU'RE DONE. I'LL BE WAY IN THE BACK.

Finally, Ron Chan colors the art in Photoshop, using a full palette for the overground scenes, monochromatic in the cave.

More from ONI-LION FORGE

WHITEOUT
by Greg Rucka
and Steve Lieber

ROGUE PLANET
by Cullen Bunn,
Andy MacDonald, and
Nick Filardi

BACKTRACK VOL. 1
by Brian Joines,
Jake Elphick, and
Doug Garbark

THE VAIN VOL. 1
by Eliot Rahal,
Emily Pearson, and
Fred C. Stresing

METEOR MEN
by Jeff Parker
and Sandy Jarell

DRYAD VOL. 1
by Kurtis Wiebe,
Justin Barcelo, and
Francesco Segala

For more information on these and other fine Oni Press comic books
and graphic novels, visit www.onipress.com.